Educating Citizens
for a Pluralistic Society

EDITED BY

ROSA BRUNO-JOFRÉ

NATALIA APONIUK

2001 Canadian Ethnic Studies
Calgary

Canadian Cataloguing in Publication Data

Main entry under title:

EDUCATING CITIZENS FOR A PLURALISTIC SOCIETY

Papers resulting from a research project
by the same name
Research and publication funded by a grant
from Canadian Heritage/Patrimoine canadien

Includes bibliographic references.

ISBN 0-9683327-1-4

1.   Education
2.   Citizenship - Canada
3.   Pluralism

Edited by Rosa Bruno-Jofré and Natalia Aponiuk

Legal Deposit - National Library of Canada

Canadian Ethnic Studies Journal
c/o Department of History
University of Calgary
2500 University Drive NW
Calgary, Alberta, Canada   T2N 1N4

Cover by Artichoke Design
Typeset by Jo-Ann Cleaver
Printed by McAra Printing Ltd.

Contents

Acknowledgements

We gratefully acknowledge the support of Canadian Heritage/Patrimoine canadien which made possible this publication. We would like to thank all the participants in the research project which resulted in the articles included in this volume. It was an interesting, challenging, and pleasant experience working with them. We would also like to thank all the reviewers for their helpful comments on the articles. We are most grateful to our editorial assistant, Carol Fournier Dicks, and to the editorial assistant at Canadian Ethnic Studies, Jo-Ann Cleaver, who spent countless hours working with us on this project.

Rosa Bruno-Jofré
Natalia Aponiuk

Contributors / Collaborateurs

SHEILA ANDRICH is a reference librarian at the Elizabeth Dafoe Library of the University of Manitoba. She is assistant to the Director of the History of Education in Manitoba Project and published a bibliography on the project in *Manitoba History*.

NATALIA APONIUK is the founding Director of the Centre for Ukrainian Canadian Studies and Associate Professor of Slavic Studies at the University of Manitoba. She has published on Ukrainian Canadian literature, on the depiction of Ukrainians in English-language Canadian literature, and on Ukrainian-area studies in books and journals, including the *University of Toronto Quarterly*, the *Journal of Ukrainian Studies*, and *Canadian Ethnic Studies/Études ethniques au Canada*. She edited a special issue of *Canadian Ethnic Studies/Études ethniques au Canada* entitled *Ethnic Themes in Canadian Literature*.

BEVERLEY BAILEY is Associate Professor at Brandon University. She teaches Counselling and Educational Psychology in the Faculty of Education and has also taught in the First Nations and Aboriginal counselling degree program. Her research interests are currently focussed on change in both schools and faculties of education.

HELEN BOCHONKO is the coordinator of the computer laboratories in the Faculty of Education, University of Manitoba. She teaches computer applications courses, and is the producer of the *TimeLinks Image Archive* and *TimeLinks Reference*.

ROSA BRUNO-JOFRÉ is Professor and Dean, Faculty of Education, Queen's University. She is the author and editor of books and articles on the history of education in Latin America and in Manitoba and on gender and higher education. Her most recent articles have been published in *Historical Studies in Education*, *Manitoba History*, *Canadian Journal of Higher Education*, and *Canadian and International Education*. She is the co-editor of the recently published monograph *Encounters in Education*.

CHRIS DOOLEY is an independent scholar specializing in early twentieth-century Western Canadian history. He was the editor of the *TimeLinks Image Archive* and the *TimeLinks Reference*, and he is currently preparing a monograph on housing development in early Winnipeg.

ROBERT J. GRAHAM is Professor and Chair of the Department of Curriculum and Instruction at the University of Victoria. His areas of interest are in teacher education curriculum, multicultural teacher education, autobiography and narrative approaches to research and teaching, aesthetic approaches to curriculum inquiry, and theories of rhetoric and composition. With Jon Young, he has been engaged in a three-year action research project tracking pre-service teachers' identity formations as they negotiate personal and professional roles.

DICK HENLEY is Associate Professor of Education at Brandon University. He has worked for over fifteen years in the Brandon University Northern Teacher Education Program, which has established nine teaching centers in northern Manitoba. He has published extensively in the areas of cross-cultural education and the history of education in Manitoba and Nova Scotia, particularly on compulsory schooling.

BERYLE MAE JONES has lectured as an Assistant Professor in the Department of English and the Bachelor of Education Program, University of Winnipeg, and as a Sessional Instructor, University of Manitoba. She has done research and taught courses in the areas of language and literacy in schools; ESL/multicultural education; multicultural/anti-racist education; multicultural/citizenship education; and teacher education, including the supervision of pre-service teachers, after many years of teaching in the Manitoba public school system.

JOHN LONG is Professor in the Department of Educational Administration, Foundations, and Psychology at the University of Manitoba. His area of special interest and publication is educational law, policy, and politics. His contribution in this volume extends an area of scholarship which he and Romulo Magsino first published in the *Education and Law Journal* (1993) and in the book *Teaching, Schools, and Society* (1990), ed. Orteza y Miranda and Romulo Magsino. It also reflects the results of recent funded research, "Canadian Pluralism, the Charter, and Citizenship Education," with his colleagues Raymond Théberge and Romulo Magsino.

JAMIE-LYNN MAGNUSSON is Associate Professor in the Higher Education Group, Department of Theory and Policy, OISE/University of Toronto. Her current work examining issues of equity in higher education is published in higher education and feminist journals. She is one of the core organizers of a network of scholars and scientists committed to advancing science and social science practices consistent with principles of equity and environmental sustainability. She was a member of the editorial team for the *Canadian Journal of Higher Education* from 1997-1999.

ROMULO F. MAGSINO is Professor and Dean of the Faculty of Education at the University of Manitoba. He specializes in educational policy studies, has authored and edited several books and monographs, and has been published in Canadian and American books and journals. Among his most recent publications is *Teachers in Trouble: An Exploration of the Normative Character of Teaching*, of which he is co-author. He is past president of the Canadian Philosophy of Education Society.

KEN OSBORNE is Professor Emeritus in the Faculty of Education at the University of Manitoba. He is the author of numerous articles and over a dozen monographs, among the more recent of which are *Teaching for Democratic Citizenship: In Defence of History: Teaching the Past and the Meaning of Democratic Citizenship;* and *Education: A Guide to the Canadian School Debate, or, Who Wants What and Why?* In 2000 OISE/University of Toronto awarded him the Distinguished Educator Award for his contributions to education.

ERIC STOCKDEN teaches history in the International Baccalaureate and the Alberta Social Studies Curriculum for the Calgary Board of Education. He is a recipient of an Alberta government "Excellence in Teaching Award," and has a long-time interest in moral and civic education and liberal education.

ANTONIO (TONY) J. TAVARES is a consultant with the Program Implementation Branch of Manitoba Education and Training. His responsibilities include multicultural/anti-racism education, English as a Second Language, and international/heritage languages. In 1989-94 he co-facilitated a series of summer institutes on anti-racism education at the University of Manitoba. Several years ago he co-authored and instructed a course on the Dynamics of Racism for the Intercultural Trainers Certificate at Red River College. More recently, he has been a sessional instructor on cross-cultural education in the Faculty of Education at the University of Manitoba.

RAYMOND G. THÉBERGE holds a doctorate in Linguistics from McGill University. He is currently Dean of Education at Collège universitaire de Saint-Boniface and Director of a research centre which specializes in minority language issues. His publications have focused on the numerous factors affecting the development of Francophone communities in Western Canada.

JON YOUNG is Professor and Head of the Department of Educational Administration, Foundations and Psychology in the Faculty of Education at the University of Manitoba. He is the author of a number of educational books and articles, including *Understanding Canadian Schools: An Introduction to Educational Administration* (with Ben Levin); *Breaking the Mosaic: Ethnic Identity and Canadian Schools* (editor); and "Intercultural Education in Canada" (with John Mallea) in *The World Yearbook of Education, 1997: Intercultural Education.*

Educating Citizens
for a Pluralistic Society

1 Introduction: Educating Citizens for a Pluralistic Society

ROSA BRUNO-JOFRÉ AND NATALIA APONIUK

This collection of articles is the result of a research project entitled "Educating Citizens for a Pluralistic Society," which was funded by a grant from Canadian Heritage/Patrimoine canadien awarded to Rosa Bruno-Jofré, then Associate Dean of Education at the University of Manitoba. The research team she assembled included members from the Faculties of Education at the Universities of Manitoba and Brandon and Collège universitaire de Saint-Boniface, the Division of Education at the University of Winnipeg, the Ontario Institute for Studies in Education/University of Toronto, the Faculty of Arts at the University of Manitoba, the Manitoba Department of Education and Training, and a Calgary public school.

The research project, in turn, resulted from a number of concerns centering on schooling and education — the way the market economy has penetrated this, like every other aspect of life; the need to deal with the dynamics of inclusion and exclusion in light of the new wave of international migration; and the impact on the understanding of space and time generated by information technology. Diversity also involved the national question in Canada because the presence of Quebec and the Aboriginal First Nations adds special parameters to being Canadian. The articles are written from a national perspective, mainly using Manitoba as a point of reference. Quebec issues are interwoven into the analysis, but are not discussed in any depth.

The collection divides naturally into four thematic parts: historical and philosophical perspectives on the impact of globalization on citizenship education; group rights and schooling; multicultural and anti-racist education; and decoding cultural images in the classroom.

The first thematic grouping — historical and philosophical perspectives on the impact of globalization on citizenship education — comprises articles by Ken Osborne, Rosa Bruno-Jofré and Dick Henley, Eric W. Stockden, and Jamie-Lynn Magnusson.

Ken Osborne's paper, "Public Schooling and Citizenship Education in Canada," provides a historical overview and identifies the paradigmatic shifts in the understanding of the functions of citizenship in the school setting. Osborne argues that, historically, schools were expected to fulfill cultural, social, and vocational functions. Policy makers today neglect the first two and concentrate on the third, thus converting education into career preparation. Citizenship then becomes an obstacle to the imperative of the global marketplace when raising questions of identity, loyalty, tradition, heritage, and community that go beyond economic rationality. Osborne uses as an example a personal exchange with a former Manitoba Minister of Education, while lobbying against the proposal to remove Canadian history from the Grade XI curriculum in Manitoba schools. The Minister wanted "pure literacy," which apparently meant the ability to understand instructions, read and write reports, and to explain oneself clearly — with no great concern for content or context. In Osborne's view, education is being sacrificed for training, knowledge is seen as disposable, and values are being displaced by skills.

Osborne discusses the historical character of national citizenship and the problems which national citizenship presents. In his view, the theory and practice of citizenship education exist in a dialectical relationship with the exercise of hegemony, thereby creating a tension between control and emancipation, socialization and education, and emphasizing one or the other at different times. Osborne's article, with its commonsensical educational reflections, enriched by a historical reading of schooling and pedagogical practices, opens a door for the discussion of what he refers to as the false dualisms permeating the current educational debate. His conception of citizenship in relation to the classroom is something of a manifesto for a critical approach to citizenship education.

Osborne's understanding of citizenship within the context of hegemony might be transported from the national to the international setting in relation to the rhetoric on globalization. The debate over the character of citizenship has been moved to the international arena, and international economic and financial institutions, multinational corporations, and new political configurations set the tone for the discussion of the global citizen.

Rosa Bruno-Jofré and Dick Henley's article, "Public Schooling in English Canada: Addressing Difference in the Context of Globalization," addresses Canadian polity formation in relation to the national question and to the impact of economic globalization. Multiculturalism acknowledges diversity as a key element of Canadian identity. However, multicultural education did not address, or did so in a fragmentary manner, issues regarding the national question in relation to the nationalist aspirations of Aboriginal peoples and the Québécois. Multicultural education has had a culturalist tone. The anti-racist education movement, with its oppositional character, addressed issues related to the structures sustaining racism and the differential distribution of power. Bruno-Jofré and Henley argue, however, that there is a danger of addressing issues of difference while leaving the common ground to be eclectically defined by the market (corporate power). They urge that multicultural/anti-racist educators pay more attention in the classroom and beyond to the new layer of meaning generated by globalization.

Bruno-Jofré and Henley organize their article around a conception of Canadian polity formation that encourages teachers to distinguish concepts of democracy and concomitant values and explore the notion of public good in relation to the students' lived experience. The understanding of the Canadian polity is placed at the core of multicultural/anti-racist education and, therefore, of citizenship and its articulation in educational discourse and practice. Bruno-Jofré and Henley, who rely on Kymlicka's interpretation of Canada as a multinational and poly-ethnic state, move the pedagogical debate beyond the attributes of citizenship toward an understanding of Canada and its place in the world.

The issue of economic globalization and the increasing influence of corporatism, particularly corporate capitalism, on determining the scope of citizenship is discussed from a philosophical perspective by Eric W. Stockden in "Pluralism, Corporatism, and Educating for Citizenship." To an important extent the article goes back to the "basics" when the author explores the understanding of citizenship within corporatism and poses fundamental questions that illustrate the ambiguities of democracy. For example, democracy is defined as a form of government in which the people rule, but Stockden poses such questions as "Who are to be considered 'the people'?"; "What kind of role is imagined for them?"; "What conditions are assumed to be beneficial to participation?"; and "What is the appropriate field of democratic activity?"

Stockden proposes an argument to critique how the values of corporate capitalism are influencing schooling — schools are perceived in terms of preparing the young to assume their prospective economic roles and to ensure the country's corporations success in the global economy. One of the results of this approach has been the introduction of outcome-based curricula, which Stockden criticizes for its negative impact on the development of the characteristics required for full participation in a democratic society. Stockden is concerned about the increasing possibility that developing moral autonomy and independent thought diminishes in importance and that oligarchic tendencies in both public and private organizations become reinforced through the schools. Stockden links this core issue with the need to support the arts and humanities since they foster the abilities central to political life in a pluralistic society, including the ability to imagine the experiences of others and to "participate" in their sufferings. Stockden urges a liberal education, which is understood as an education in the public interest. His argument rests on the belief that formal education may be seen as a deliberative enterprise for the realization of democratic ideals. The elucidation of the country's basic democratic ideals becomes an imperative for building a foundation for the education of citizens. Stockden is not optimistic that what he believes to be important will come to pass.

Jamie-Lynn Magnusson's article, "Examining Higher Education and Citizenship in a Global Context of Neoliberal Restructuring," is an interesting contribution to the discussion on the entrepreneurial university and how to strengthen the relationship between the university and the socio-economic environment. Magnusson explores the discursive formation of the Canadian university in relation to the development of the Canadian capitalist welfare state and the impact of the shift toward a neoliberal economic agenda. The article pays particular attention to Ontario where Premier Mike Harris has expounded the most explicit neoliberal economic ideology and motivated a quite radical restructuring of universities. This process of change was generated by indirect policies like the ones favouring the introduction of alternative providers in Ontario or by direct policies such as deregulation of fees in some professional faculties and the conditions for accessing the Challenge Fund. Magnusson argues that the reshaping of Canadian universities cannot be denied. The impact of these changes has been described by various authors. However, Magnusson directs the reader toward the social function of universities in relation to Canadian civic life. This is not a new concern, as the author herself indicates, especially in view of the apparent threat to the liberal arts, the continuing deterioration of the collegial system, as well as the subordination of the democratic system to market imperatives. However, Magnusson takes the argument further to explore the possibilities of generating spaces of contestation in the post-secondary system and not limiting this role to the universities, which are only one component of that system. The article poses important questions in relation to the unsettling and unfinished process of changing structures in post-secondary institutions and, particularly, in universities.

The second thematic grouping — group rights and schooling — includes articles by Romulo F. Magsino, John C. Long, and Raymond G. Thebérge, Beryle Mae Jones, and Beverley Bailey.

In the first article, "Canadian Pluralism, the Charter, and Citizenship Education," Magsino, Long, and Thebérge look at the legal parameters of citizenship in light of the Charter of Rights and Freedoms and its impact on schooling, not only at the individual but at the cultural group level. The authors examine recent Charter litigation on Francophone linguistic educational rights, on the rights of minority religious groups, and on the rights of ethnocultural groups. The conclusions drawn by Magsino, Long, and Thebérge may be provocative, especially for those with strong secular views on public education. For example, the authors argue that the judicial results of Charter-inspired litigation are proving disappointing for minority groups, and that the emergent Charter doctrine does not necessarily reflect an unambiguous embrace of multiculturalism or pluralism in public schooling arrangements or structures. At the center of the argument is the contention that the judiciary's definition of state neutrality has become a challenge, in particular to the educational aspirations of religious groups. The article deals with the Canadian concept of multiculturalism and with Charter litigation on ethnic rights positively, concluding that multiculturalism, as espoused in policies and legislation and entrenched in the Charter, has been of great benefit to ethnocultural communities. Magsino, Long, and Thebérge propose an inclusive curriculum that is in line with multiculturalism, and recommend the accommodation of religious minorities as being just.

Beryle Mae Jones addresses multiculturalism and multicultural education from the perspective of visible minorities in the article "Multiculturalism and Citizenship: The Status of 'Visible Minorities' in Canada." Jones, utilizing experiences as a grassroots leader in the Black community and in immigrant women's organizations, embraces the understanding that Canada's concept of multiculturalism is rooted in the notion of ethnicity, although the concept goes beyond ethnicity to include broader human rights. It did not surprise her that the Multiculturalism Directorate, which was part of the machinery responsible for implementing multiculturalism, decided to include immigrant women in the priority list of groups receiving assistance.

Jones refers to visible minorities as the "other" ethnic groups vis-à-vis Aboriginal peoples and French-Canadians, as well as non-visible groups. These "other" ethnic groups do not pose a threat to national unity and so, in her view, are likely to receive less attention. Jones builds an argument to generate a link between multiculturalism, citizenship, and curriculum from the ethnocultural minority perspective, and advocates the need to move from multiculturalism for all to a framework capable of bridging the gap between "we" and "they." She is guided by the need to create opportunities for all to participate in public life. Jones then identifies building blocks relevant for the construction of a regime of citizenship education: a) the identification of sources of unity within the multicultural state; b) the approach to citizenship from a multi-disciplinary educational perspective transcending civics; c) the development of an international component; and d) the relevance of having voiced representation of ethnocultural minorities in the process of designing and delivering citizenship education. Jones also deals with what she refers to as the paradoxes in multiculturalism and citizenship education, and consequent tensions such as those emerging from the articulation of group differentiated rights or the lack of mechanisms to evaluate foreign credentials. This article, written from the standpoint of visible minorities in relation to the practice of multicultural and citizenship education, contains challenging views and propounds developing multiculturalism as a foundation for a model of citizenship education which would include all members of society.

In her article, "A White Paper on Aboriginal Education in Universities," Beverley Bailey relates her concerns about cultural genocide from her position as a white, female, middle-aged university professor. Her argument in examining the university in relation to Aboriginal education is based on three concerns: a) how we frame our own racism; b) how we disadvantage Aboriginal students; and c) how teacher educators can begin to model ways of becoming culturally sensitive. Bailey narrates her reflective journey as a teacher educator witnessing the clash of cultures and the dilemmas she confronts. Her examples deal with the need to understand the core beliefs of others, coming together with our stories, and, the most difficult, changing the institution. In her view, the idiosyncratic direction that any institution would take would be based on the needs of the institution working within the context of its community. Part of the difficulty rests in the complexity of the lived experiences of Aboriginal peoples over time and their history of oppression, resistance, and contestation.

The third part of the collection – multicultural and anti-racist education – includes articles by Jon Young and Robert J. Graham and Antonio J. Tavares.

"School and Curriculum Reform: Manitoba Frameworks and Multicultural Teacher Education," by Jon Young and Robert J. Graham, focuses on the school reform that has been occurring in Manitoba. As in other parts of Canada and elsewhere, the reform in Manitoba has been government-directed and based on a political analysis that claims that reform is needed to break with dominant practices. Young and Graham examine how the discourse on race, culture, and diversity has been articulated in public policy statements and in their implementation within the public school system. The analysis centers on curricular reform in the English language arts, and explores how curricular reform has influenced the experience of pre-service teacher candidates.

The public policy documents contain statements that incorporate issues of diversity, including the acknowledgement of Aboriginal perspectives, within an infusion model of curriculum development. However, Young and Graham state that the impact of these statements is mediated by the curriculum framework documents, standards tests, and curriculum implementation documents. Based on their own research, Young and Graham analyze the experiences of pre-service teacher candidates as they try to implement the curriculum while paying attention to anti-racist education goals. The authors conclude that the implementation of the policies deflected the attention of the prospective teachers away from anti-racist education, shifted the responsibility for anti-racist education to individual teachers, and legitimized a technical orientation to teaching.

Antonio J. Tavares' article, "From Heritage to International Languages: Globalism and Western Canadian Trends in Heritage Language Education," discusses a specific dimension of reform. Tavares provides a historical overview of the development of heritage language programs throughout the late 1970s and 1980s. He notes the shift in terminology from "heritage languages" to "international languages," which reflects the impact of both globalism and economic globalization on education in Canada, as well as significant shifts in multicultural policies. Tavares argues that there are tensions, on one side, between the impact of economic globalization and the resistance it has generated and, on the other, the benign understanding of globalism as an ideology encouraging the notion of an equitable and sustainable world. Based on Tavares' analysis, the Western Canadian Protocol for Collaboration in Basic Education could be construed as an example of Osborne's understanding of the citizenship education process as existing in a dialectical relationship with the exercise of hegemony.

The final section — decoding cultural images in the classroom — consists of an article which describes a unique educational tool for teaching about ethnic relations.

Helen Bochonko and Chris Dooley's article, "The *TimeLinks Image Archive*: A Case Study in Using Photographic Images in Teaching about Ethnic Relations," introduces the reader to a virtual archive with two thousand visual representations of life in Manitoba in the second decade of the twentieth century. *TimeLinks* began as a project of River East Collegiate in Winnipeg in early 1996, and was loosely modelled on *Village Prologue*, an Internet site developed in Quebec that provides the opportunity to visit a village in Lower Canada in 1853. This kind of program gives students the opportunity to correspond via e-mail with fictional townspeople played by teachers, archivists, historians, and others.

An analysis of the visual representation in *TimeLinks* enables students to explore the tensions between the Anglo-Canadian majority culture and the challenges set by the emergence of culturally and linguistically different communities. *TimeLinks* provides a creative avenue for the teaching of identity issues, Canadianism, colonization, citizenship formation, and life on the prairies, among other topics.

The project that generated this collection motivated inter-faculty and inter-institutional collaborations that resulted in many hours of discussion and scholarly research. The articles are of differing character, and, on occasion, they have an unconventional tone that challenges the often overregulated academic world. The reader who is not familiar with the uniqueness of education will be engaged in a journey that will reveal the challenges that educators encounter today and the efforts displayed by the authors to move beyond what is construed as obvious and inevitable. All the articles try to generate questions and answers that embody the transformative power of the teaching and learning process.

2 Public Schooling and Citizenship Education in Canada

KEN OSBORNE

A B S T R A C T / R É S U M É

This article examines the role of public schools in Canada as agents of citizenship education. The historical development of citizenship education in Canada is outlined and the current neglect of citizenship education in favour of economic and vocational priorities is examined. The article describes seven elements of citizenship education and illustrates the ambiguities and contradictions of the concept of citizenship in a school setting. The article also presents some suggestions for the reinvigoration of citizenship education in the schools, in terms both of curriculum and pedagogy.

Cet article examine le rôle de l'instruction publique canadienne dans le cadre de l'éducation pour la citoyenneté. L'auteur offre un sommaire de l'histoire de l'éducation pour la citoyenneté au Canada et examine le fait que cette éducation soit negligée pendant les années récentes, car les écoles portent leur attention surtout à la préparation les jeunes pour le monde du travail. L'article décrit sept composantes de l'éducation pour la citoyenneté et examine les ambiguités et les contradictions de ce concept dans le contexte scolaire. L'article propose aussi quelques suggestions à propos du renouvellement de l'éducation pour la citoyenneté dans l'optique non seulement du curriculum, mais aussi de la pédagogie.

Introduction

From their very beginnings public schools in Canada, as in other countries, were expected to prepare the young for citizenship. That, in fact, was the very reason why the state compelled parents to send their children to school in the first place since in school they would be subject to an officially approved curriculum, taught by officially trained and certificated teachers, using officially authorized curricula and textbooks, and subject to officially appointed inspectors and officially organized examinations — all designed with the goal of producing citizens. It is true that, for pragmatic and political reasons, governments often had to make some allowance for private schooling, but they did so reluctantly and did their best to bring it under some degree of state control and supervision. Hence, for example, the sporadic quarrels between church and state over the years, in Canada and elsewhere, concerning the content and organization of schooling. Althusser oversimplified a complex reality and grossly underestimated the autonomy of schools when he described them as part of what he called the "ideological state apparatus," but he had a point notwithstanding, for public schools are intended to teach those things that the state desires to be taught.[1] Normal schools, for example, were so called because they were supposed to establish the officially approved norms that governed what and how teachers were required to teach.

By the end of the nineteenth century the combined pressures of industrialism, nationalism, and liberalism (in the sense of elected legislatures with more or less power depending on a given political regime) had made the idea of public schooling virtually irresistible in the industrialized world. Boys and girls were no longer to be left to their own devices or to do as their parents chose. They had to be turned into national citizens. As the historian Eugen Weber stated, "peasants" had to be turned into "Frenchmen"[2]— and Frenchwomen, presumably. In the well-known remark of an Italian nationalist after the unification of Italy in 1870, "We have made Italy; now we must make Italians."[3] In the world of the nation-state, children had to speak the national language, read the national literature, learn the national history and geography, and internalize the national values. And, if they were of working class or peasant background, as inevitably the majority were, they had to learn to know and keep their place in the social order. In Gramscian terms, schooling was designed as an instrument of ideological and cultural hegemony by which those in positions of power endeavoured, with more or less success, to shape the thinking of society at large.

This process of creating national citizens was and is subject to many different, and often conflicting, interpretations, and schooling has always been more than the imposition of ruling class hegemony. In *The Communist Manifesto*, Marx and Engels claimed free, compulsory schooling as a right, and it was a constant demand of socialists and trades unionists from the early nineteenth century onwards. On the political left, schooling was seen, at least potentially, as an instrument of emancipation, not of oppression. As a British Columbia socialist Angus McInnis wrote in 1924, "Education, even present-day education, with all its defects tends to stimulate the imagination and sharpen the perceptions of those who receive it; and under adverse circumstances they begin to question the fitness of things." McInnis went on: "The laborer or artisan when he has finished his day's work should find pleasure in taking down from his shelf his Keats, Byron or Shakespeare, his Macaulay, Scott, Dickens, and spending an evening with them as that the banker, lawyer, doctor or professor should have access to and be able to appreciate them." Knowledge, he concluded, was "essential for universal progress, but fatal to class privilege."[4] As this example illustrates, schooling was never a simple, top-down imposition of social control. Schooling was resisted, sabotaged, manipulated, and diverted as those who were supposed to be its object sought to blunt its impact or turn it to their own advantage. As has been often observed, hegemony is as much a process of negotiation as it is of imposition.

Moreover, even those people who hoped to impose their hegemony on others did not always agree on just what it was that they wanted to do. Most people, though not all, found it easy to agree on the importance of educating the young for citizenship, but they often disagreed fundamentally on just what citizenship was and how it should be taught and learned. Nonetheless, both their agreements and their disagreements ensured that, for much of the twentieth century, educationists paid conspicuous and continuing attention to the role of schooling in producing citizens.

The Decline of Citizenship Education

Beginning in the mid-1980s, however, Canadian policy-makers, like their counterparts in Western Europe and the United States, more or less abandoned citizenship, however defined, as a goal of general education in their haste to turn schools into training grounds for the new global economy. At the level of the individual school, teachers often engage students in activities that have implications for citizenship, notably environmental campaigns, intercultural awareness, human rights, social justice, and the like, but at the policy-making level the talk is increasingly of international competitiveness and entrepreneurialism. To the extent that citizenship continues to be discussed, it is largely confined to social studies and related subjects, though there are some recent signs that it is beginning to attract more general attention.[5] In practice, however, citizenship education is now largely seen as the special territory of social studies and history teachers and tends to be equated with civics. It has become the province of enthusiasts and specialists, but not of the policy makers at large. Such, at least, is the conclusion to be drawn from the evidence collected by Sears and Hughes.[6]

In his 1987 report on Ontario drop-outs, George Radwanski described education, not as the training ground of citizens, but as "the paramount ingredient for success in the competitive world economy" and as essential to "our very survival as an economically competitive society."[7] In 1991 the Manitoba Department of Education and Training explained its new policy direction in these words: "The workforce will demand highly skilled and adaptable workers who have the ability to upgrade existing skills and develop new skills, who can help and participate in a climate that encourages entrepreneurship, innovation and economic growth, and who can understand the complex dynamics of a competitive global environment."[8]

These two examples reflect the sentiments of every department and ministry of education in Canada, regardless of political party, and now largely shape public debate over schooling.[9] They are the visible tip of an agenda which seeks to convert education into career preparation, to turn schools into vocational training centres, to define students and parents as customers and clients. It is an agenda which says nothing about citizenship, and, in fact, seems to see citizenship as an obstacle to its plans and priorities for citizenship gets in the way of the imperatives of the global marketplace. Citizenship, after all, prizes imperatives other than those of economic rationality. Citizenship raises questions of identity, loyalty, tradition, heritage, and community that run counter to the corporate forces that are seeking to reshape the global economy. Canadian citizenship could well be dysfunctional in the north-south world of the North American Free Trade Agreement, in the global arena of the World Trade Organization, in a world where national governments find their sovereignty shrinking, or in a political climate where Canada's provincial governments will accept Quebec's distinctiveness only on condition that they receive whatever special powers might be needed by Quebec.

Historically, in Canada as elsewhere, schools have been expected to serve a triple function: to help students make the most of their lives and develop their individual talents, to prepare students for citizenship, and to train them for the world of work. Traditionally, the three were often described as the cultural, social, and vocational functions of schooling.

Today, however, policy-makers seem to be neglecting the first two in order to concentrate on the third. This is why we see moves around the country to reduce the time devoted to such subjects as art, music, history, social studies, and even physical education, in order to create more space for computers, career preparation, so-called life skills, cooperative education, and job training. In 1995, for example, I was part of a small delegation lobbying the then Manitoba Minister of Education to reconsider a decision to remove Canadian history from the provincial Grade 11 program. In the course of the discussion the Minister told us that he saw literacy as all-important. Our delegation agreed, and what better subject, we asked, to promote literacy than history with its heavy emphasis on reading, writing, and discussion? The Minister, however, told us that we had misunderstood him. What he wanted was what he called "pure literacy," which, as far as I could gather, meant the ability to read and write reports, understand instructions, explain oneself clearly, and so forth — all laudable objectives but, if stripped of context, opening up a world where it does not matter what one reads provided that one reads something. It is a world where education is sacrificed for training, where knowledge is seen as disposable, and where values are displaced by skills.

There was a time when things were very different. In 1916, when introducing compulsory school attendance, a decision which was not popular in all parts of the province, Manitoba's Minister of Education could not have been clearer. "Boys and girls," he said, "the citizens of the future must be qualified to discharge the duties of citizenship."[10] In 1925 in British Columbia, an influential Royal Commission on education voiced similar sentiments: "The development of a united and intelligent citizenship should be accepted without question as the fundamental aim of our schools."[11] At about the same time, the American historian Carl Becker, a man of progressive and liberal views, said much the same thing, noting that "it is and must remain a fundamental assumption that the chief purpose of free education in a democratic society is to make good citizens, rather than good scholars."[12] It would be easy to find many other similar quotations, all making the point that the primary purpose of public education was the development of citizenship. Just about every subject in the curriculum was defended in terms of its contribution to citizenship, not only in the case of such obvious subjects as history, language, and literature, but also gardening, art, music, nature study, physical education, health, science, and on and on. Here are two typical examples: first, a statement from 1907: "The moral influence of a properly conducted school garden cannot be estimated too highly."[13] Again, this time from 1920: "music is going to do more for the nationalization of the country than any other single agency."[14]

The Debate over Citizenship

Citizenship, though much used, is a deceptive word. Philosophers describe it as a concept that is "essentially contested," that is to say, one whose meaning can never be once and for all decisively fixed, but which will always be the subject of debate and disagreement.[15]

Conservatives define citizenship largely in terms of loyalty, duty, respect, tradition, and of accepting change slowly, even grudgingly, and only when absolutely necessary. They put social stability and order ahead of individual rights, or, rather, believe that these rights can only be properly secured when the social order is given priority. Liberals, on the other hand, define citizenship above all in terms of civil liberties and individual rights. For them, to be a citizen is to be the bearer of rights, of freedom of belief and expression, of freedom from arbitrary arrest, and so on, and no one or no thing is to be allowed to abridge or infringe upon these rights except for the most compelling reasons and sometimes not even then. Socialists, for their part, following Marx's dictum that the workers have no country, generally rejected citizenship entirely as a propaganda smokescreen behind which those in power cloak their real interests. More recently, socialists have begun to define citizenship in terms of social justice, equity, community, the redistribution of wealth and power, and they are, or were, perfectly prepared to accept, indeed to welcome, whatever social reforms are needed to achieve them. And beyond and around these three major divisions circle assorted feminists, communitarians, libertarians, anarchists, Marxists, neo-conservatives, neo-liberals, and others, all of whom have their own ideas about just what constitutes citizenship.

In the real world these distinctions are blurred. Few people are pure conservatives, liberals, socialists, or whatever. We combine, or try to, elements of each position in our definition of the social good and what has to be done to achieve it. And, no matter how pure our principles, when we come to deal with concrete problems in the real world, we find ourselves forced to come to terms with the messy reality of everyday life in which compromise and second-best are often unavoidable. I used to teach my high school history students what I called Osborne's first law of politics. It ran as follows: to any political problems there are two solutions — one is bad, the other is worse. My point was simple enough: if a problem can be solved easily, it is unlikely to be a political problem. It will be administrative or technical or managerial, but it will not involve fundamental divisions of beliefs and values, which is the very essence of politics and which makes citizenship so important if we are to manage political problems reasonably.

In other words, citizenship is not only an essentially contested concept, it is also fundamentally political in the broad sense of being inextricably connected with questions of governance and social living, of identity, of equity and justice, especially in any society which aspires to be democratic, where citizens have a voice in deciding the shape of their society and how they are governed, where, ideally, they govern themselves. As Aristotle wrote over two thousand years ago, to be a citizen is to know both how to be ruled and how to rule — and how to do both in ways that are respectful and tolerant of all other citizens, even those with whom we fundamentally disagree.

The Evolution of Citizenship Education

This, in part, is why, when compulsory public education was instituted in Canada roughly a hundred years ago, citizenship was seen as so important. In a country where most men, and eventually women, had the vote, the very least that needed to be done was to ensure that they would vote intelligently, as the popular phrase went, especially when many of them were immigrants who were often ignorant of the values and traditions of the society to which they had moved. This required, for example, that voters could read and think well enough to understand the issues they faced, were independent enough not to allow their votes to be bought, were interested enough in public affairs to follow politics between elections and perhaps even become involved in political life themselves, and to live with political disagreement, conflict, and ambiguity. A Harvard professor of government stated in 1924, in words that commanded assent in Canada as much as in the United States:

> No sound system of government can be founded on illiteracy. What we spend for public education is in large measure an expenditure for the preservation of individual liberty. There is only one way in which the world can be made safe for democracy, and that is by making it unsafe for ignorance. Until men and women are able to read their ballots and understand what they are voting for, until they have at least a minimum of education, it is dangerous to place the suffrage in their hands. It is putting democracy in peril. The more political freedom you give a people, the greater is their opportunity for abusing it.[16]

At one level, these remarks are uncontentious, even platitudinous, but it is not difficult to see in them the fear of the so-called respectable classes – the property-owners, the native-born, the middle-classes broadly defined – that their social inferiors – the workers, the immigrants, the property-less – might too easily be tempted by radical or subversive ideas. The theory and practice of citizenship education exist in a dialectical relationship with the exercise of hegemony. They pursue a double mission of control and emancipation, of socialization and education, sometimes emphasizing the one and sometimes the other. According to radical critics, citizenship education pays rhetorical lip-service to the one, speaking glowingly of autonomy, liberation, participation, and the like, while, in fact, devoting all its efforts to enforcing conformity, subordination, and acquiescence.[17]

Since voting does not take place in a geographical vacuum, but in the defined territorial space of the nation-state, voters were, and are, expected to identify with their country, to see themselves not as citizens in the abstract or as citizens of the world, but as citizens of the state in which they live, willing and able to cast their votes and form their opinions in terms of what is best for their country, with more or less regard for the rights and interests of other countries and of the world as a whole. At the extreme, they have to be willing to lay down their lives for their country. In the words of the French historian and educationist Ernest Lavisse in 1912:

> If the schoolboy does not carry within himself the living memory of our national glories; if he does not know that his ancestors have fought on a thousand battlefields for noble causes; if he has not learned how much it cost in blood and toil to forge our country's unity and to draw out of the chaos of our outmoded institutions the laws that have made us free; if he has not become a citizen who is conscious of his duty and a soldier who loves his rifle, then the teacher will have wasted his time.[18]

Not all educationists were this belligerent, though a significant number were in pre-World War I Europe and have been in various parts of the world ever since. Thus, one can see why H.G. Wells held schools generally, and history teachers in particular, responsible for creating the climate of opinion that made the First World War possible.[19] It was in their history classes, said Wells, that young men learned the false lessons of nationalism and militarism, of the glory of war and the heroism of sacrifice. Even those who did not go as far as Lavisse and his counterparts in other countries agreed that students needed to have a sense of national identity and, better yet, of patriotism, which meant knowing something of their country's history and heritage, of visualizing its geography, of cherishing its culture.

In the years before and immediately after the First World War, citizenship was often seen in harsh and coercive terms and contained more than its share of racist, sexist, and social class motivations and assumptions. It was in the name of Canadian citizenship, for example, that First Nations children were sent to residential schools where the use of their native languages was forbidden and their indigenous cultures were brought under attack, for only in this way, it was argued, could they be turned into good Canadian citizens.[20] Linguistic and religious minorities similarly found the school being used against them in the name of citizenship, as in the case of Mennonites, Hutterites, Doukhobors, Roman Catholics, Black Canadians in eastern Canada, Francophones, and most immigrant groups.[21] For them, citizenship meant assimilation into the dominant culture which was defined largely in Anglo-Canadian terms, centering upon command of the English language, loyalty to Canada as a nation of British heritage, commitment to Canada's British traditions, and pride in Canada's membership in the British Empire.

Paradoxically, while policy-makers lauded the school as the great agent of Canadianization and citizenship, they simultaneously starved it of the resources it needed to do its job. Outside the big city school systems, with their reasonably adequate tax base and their growing professionalism, teachers were minimally trained and worse paid, faced with the task of teaching an overcrowded curriculum with minimal resources, and often hindered by the suspicions of small, rural communities which were not convinced that anything beyond the most basic schooling was all that useful anyway. A 1923 report on history teaching in Canada noted the "hopeless task" facing many teachers. It quoted the 1921 report of the Superintendent of Education for Prince Edward Island to the effect that "many schools are actually vacant, attendance is irregular, teachers are poorly qualified and immature girls in most cases, and that the public is apathetic to these conditions," and concluded: "These conditions are not confined to any one province; in fact, it is only by means of the most heroic efforts that they are kept from invading all."[22] In the circumstances, it is easy to sympathize with the comment of a Manitoba observer who noted in 1923 that "the only wonder is that the young teacher in the little lonely school on the prairie does as well as she does."[23] Citizenship, it seems, like so much else in education, was more honoured in the breach than in the observance.

Despite all the talk of educating for Canadian citizenship, no province was willing to cede its control of education to the national government. In the 1890s, for example, there was considerable talk to the effect that Canada needed a national history curriculum. As Ontario's Minister of Education stated in 1892:

> I have perused with great care the various histories in use
> in all the provinces of the Dominion, and I have found them

merely to be provincial histories, without reference to our common country. ... Can't we agree upon certain broad features common to the whole of this Dominion with which we can indoctrinate our pupils, so that when a child takes up the history of Canada, he feels that he is not simply taking up the history of Canada, such as the old Canada was, but that he is taking up the history of a great country?[24]

In this spirit, the Dominion Education Association sponsored a competition to produce a truly national history textbook, but, even though a winner was declared, only half of the provinces adopted it. No matter how much they wanted a national citizenship, the provinces were not prepared to give up their control of education. Their solution was to pass the burden on to the teachers. As Manitoba's Minister of Education stated in 1920: "A teacher should be a teacher, not for one province only but for all Canada. Our schools should not be Manitoba schools, but Canadian schools located in Manitoba."[25]

A large part of the problem was deciding just what a national citizenship entailed. Most English-speaking educationists were convinced that Canada was one nation, or was well on the way to becoming one, and what made it such were its British heritage and English language. Citizenship, therefore, consisted of the imposition of what some historians describe, perhaps oversimply, as "Anglo-conformity." This meant riding roughshod over the sensibilities of Aboriginal peoples and other minorities. Equally important, this concept was, for obvious reasons, unacceptable to Quebec, which, with considerable justification, saw all the talk of citizenship in English-speaking Canada as a threat to its distinct identity. Quebec had entered Confederation on the understanding that its language, culture, and heritage would be respected, indeed that Confederation would protect them better than would any other political arrangement. It was not, therefore, prepared to agree to a vision of citizenship that seemed predicated on the absorption of Quebec into a British Canada. In the 1904 words of a leading Quebecer, who saw no necessary contradiction between Quebec nationalism and a certain kind of federalism, Henri Bourassa:

The fatherland, for us, is the whole of Canada, that is to say, a federation of distinct races and autonomous provinces. The nation that we wish to see developed is the Canadian nation, composed of French Canadians and English Canadians, that is to say, two elements separated by language and religion and by the legal arrangements necessary for the conservation of their respective traditions, but united in an attachment of brotherhood, in a common attachment to a common fatherland.[26]

This was not, however, a position that appealed to most English-speaking educationists, who saw Canada as a nation-state along conventional American and European lines, united by a common language and a common culture.

This question of the nature of Canadian nationalism and what it means for citizenship education in the schools remains unanswered. It is part of the distinctiveness of Canada that any attempt to arrive at a definitive answer would be far more divisive than unifying. This is, after all, why we have commonly thought of Canada as a mosaic and not a melting pot, why we have adopted the maxim of unity in diversity, and why since the 1970s we have made bilingualism and multiculturalism part of the official definition of Canada. In education, the debate has taken many twists and turns. We have spoken variously of appreciation of Canada, of patriotism, of the Canadian identity, of limited identities, of hyphenated Canadianism, of knowing ourselves, of pan-Canadian understanding, and, most recently, of something called the Canadian spirit. It is this lack of agreement that has made the teaching of Canadian history a matter of public debate in recent years, with calls for a return to the tradition of using history to foster a sense of national identity and unity in the young.[27]

Perhaps the most fruitful solution to the question of dealing with the Canadian identity in the classroom is not to try to fix on one particular definition of it or on one authorized version of national history, but to introduce students to the debates surrounding it, both past and present.[28] As citizens, they will, if they take any interest in public issues at all (and surely as citizens they should), constantly face questions such as these: What kind of country are we and do we want to be? Is government too big or too small? What should be the balance between the private and the public sector? What level of taxation is desirable? What should we do about medicare and the social services more generally? What should be done to correct the historical injustices inflicted upon the First Nations? What, if anything, should we do to change the constitution? Is the justice system too soft on crime? How do we reconcile multicultural diversity and provincial authority with national unity? Should we rethink our standard of living in order to protect the environment? These and a host of other questions confront Canadian citizens. The way they are answered defines the nature of Canada. They cannot be answered in the abstract, but only in the context of Canada's past and present reality. They are not susceptible to definitive solution, but are matters of continuing dialogue, and so require a process of considerate, tolerant, and open public debate. Dialogue and discussion are the essence of democracy and, if we are serious about educating citizens, this is what we must prepare students to engage in.

Historically, citizenship education in Canada has included, as it must, more than this.[29] From the 1890s through the 1920s, the dominant thrust of citizenship education was assimilation to a certain conception of Canada as a British nation, but after the First World War, and even more noticeably after the Second, this assimilative approach weakened. The First World War had demonstrated the consequences of unchecked nationalism, and by the late 1920s a certain anti-war sentiment had crept into Canadian education. The First War, after all, had been, in H.G. Wells's phrase, the war to end war, and Canadian educators began to include the fostering of an international spirit in their vision of citizenship. Between the Wars this took the form of explicit teaching about the League of Nations, a development which was officially endorsed by most provincial departments of education, and, for some years after 1945, about the United Nations, but more important than any particular institutions was the idea, now widely accepted, that any approach to Canadian citizenship had to see Canadians as citizens not only of their own country but of the world. As the Dean of Education at Queen's University stated in 1919, the goal should be "to secure through our schools a patriotism in which national pride is fostered and national arrogance is discouraged, a patriotism which finds its meaning and its justification in the place which our nation can take along with all other nations in the common work to which people of all races and languages and colours are called."[30]

Between the Wars citizenship education was also defined in terms of character and service, two words that were much used at the time. Men and women of good character, it was argued, would more or less automatically do the right thing, and the right thing was defined in terms of "mutual service." In the words of Manitoba's Minister of Education in 1920, "Citizenship means service that we must do for the community — something over and above what one does for oneself."[31]

In part, this emphasis on service and character arose from the War. It was based on the conviction that the enormous sacrifices of the War could be justified only by building a better society for those who survived. The War had also shown what was possible when people worked together in a common cause. In the words of the popular novelist Ralph Connor, who, as the Reverend Charles Gordon, had served as a military chaplain, "I believe that here lies the solution of many of our present problems, that we should try to insert into our common everyday affairs that marvellous thing that held our men together on the front line, that life-bond that made them one — comradeship."[32]

In part, also, this emphasis on service and character and comradeship was seen as ensuring social stability. The post-War years saw a good deal of social turmoil and protest in Canada, of which the 1919 Winnipeg General Strike and its associated sympathy strikes across the country were only the tip of the iceberg. Moreover, the Russian Revolution of 1917, followed by Mussolini's seizure of power in Italy in 1922, opened the prospect that foreign models might appeal to those who were dissatisfied with Canadian capitalism and parliamentary democracy. As a worried Canadian educationist stated in 1938, fearing that teachers would not be able to counter young people's "preference for a black or coloured shirt," "In many cities of Canada children hear practical discussions of imported political philosophies in their homes. They are aware of suppressed enthusiasm for some foreign government system."[33]

Some years earlier, the President of the University of Toronto Sir Robert Falconer told a national audience: "Extremists among the manual toilers have got a taste of the fascination of power and are pressing for drastic measures such as the dethronement of the rich employer and director, who, in their judgment, arrogantly use their influence for their own selfish interests." For Falconer and others like him, the solution was clear: "... to educate our people together into a community spirit beginning with the children, teaching them that they constitute one body and have reciprocal duties to one another."[34] As a Manitoba school trustee more candidly stated, "If Canada is a nation of intelligent and educated people, we need fear neither the Bolshevist nor the reactionary. Education is the best national insurance."[35] This became a regular theme in the inter-war years as Canadian educators, like their counterparts in the capitalist democracies generally, watched with increasing concern developments in the Soviet Union, Fascist Italy, and, after 1933, Nazi Germany. Here, to take another example, is the Putman-Weir report on education in British Columbia in 1925: "From the viewpoint of self-preservation alone, society recognizes that the best form of state insurance against anarchy and bolshevism is an efficient system of public education."[36]

Resistance to Citizenship Education

These last quotations reveal another aspect of citizenship education. Not only is citizenship education essentially contested and fundamentally political, as officially defined, it also tends to be conservative in nature. As a form of socialization to the status quo, it can hardly be otherwise. Citizenship is not designed to overthrow the existing order of things, but to preserve it. This is why, for example, citizenship education was subject to often fierce attack in the early decades of this century from critics on the left.[37] Feminists saw it as perpetuating the subordinate status of women for, if the ideal of the good citizen was active participation in public affairs, this automatically worked against women as long as conventional sex-roles confined them to the home and as long as the home was defined as part of private life and was thus safe from public regulation. In a very real sense, the political activity of men depended on the behind-the-scenes and unacknowledged activity of women. Men's contribution to public life was contingent upon women's confinement to the private sphere.[38] In their heyday, the farmers' movements, especially in Western Canada from the 1890s through the 1920s, were equally critical. Opposed to what they saw as the division of society into haves and have-nots and to the competitive principle of the capitalist marketplace, the farmers envisioned a society based on cooperation and equality. They called for the schools to emphasize the principle of cooperation, to show students the way the political system really worked as opposed to how it was supposed to work, to open their eyes to the evils of the world around them, for example, by teaching a more realistic version of history.[39] Socialists and trade unionists agreed. They repeatedly condemned what they saw as the class bias of the schools and called for education to contribute to the building of a new and more just social order.[40] Internationalists and pacifists, for their part, rejected what they saw as the militaristic tendencies of the schools. They called for the end of cadet training and the revision of curricula, especially in subjects such as history, literature, and music, to emphasize peace rather than war, or at the very least to de-romanticize war.[41]

All these were more than paper arguments. Critics of citizenship education, as conventionally defined, won election to school boards. They obtained jobs as teachers. They organized pressure groups. They were active in political parties. The historian Norman Penner tells a revealing story about his school days in North-End Winnipeg in the 1930s. The son of a Communist city councillor, Penner found himself picked on by a teacher for his political views and complained to the principal. When the principal asked him what the problem was, Penner explained that he was being victimized because he was a Communist. On hearing this, the principal closed his office door and said, "So am I."[42] The story might be apocryphal, but it is worth remembering that people like Agnes Macphail, Canada's first woman Member of Parliament and a left of centre activist; Dick Johns, one of the organizers of the 1919 Winnipeg General Strike and a militant socialist; M.J. Coldwell, the leader of the CCF after J.S. Woodsworth's death; William Aberhart, the Social Credit leader of Alberta; and others like them, were all teachers at one time or another. It seems unlikely that their political ideas did not in some way influence their teaching. W.L. Morton once noted that agrarian reform ideals were kept alive on the Prairies in the form of "the democratic dream that men might be free and independent," in part by "the young women who taught school in Ontario and the West," but we know next to nothing about them.[43]

All of which is to say that though citizenship education is essentially conservative by definition, it is not monolithically so. If, on the one hand, it prepares people for the status quo, on the other, it offers a promise of democracy and change. If it once threatened assimilation to a narrowly defined version of Canadian nationality, it also opened up the possibility of exploring alternative visions of what it meant to be Canadian. If, on the one hand, it taught conformity to conventional wisdom, on the other, it made it possible to question it. All the people who were excluded from the tent of citizenship at various times — Aboriginals, women, trade unionists, minorities of various sorts, political dissenters — have been able to use the language of citizenship to press their claims. Citizenship education has never totally been the stabilizing force that its more conservative advocates have hoped it would be. Like education itself, it was and is an arena in which competing beliefs and interests meet.

As historians remind us, the rights of citizenship have not just grown of their own volition, nor have they simply been handed down from on high. They are the result of struggle and conflict. What we now take for granted as our birthright as citizens had to be fought for in times past, sometimes literally. Indeed, the most important purpose citizenship education should serve is to introduce students to the questions that lie at the heart of Canadian citizenship, give students the knowledge to understand them, the skills to pursue them, and the values and dispositions to do so in ways that respect the processes and commitments of democracy.

The Elements of Citizenship Education

Whatever the disagreements over the nature and content of citizenship education, over the years it has come to consist in Canada of some seven elements. People can and do disagree over just what these elements contain and how they should be taught, but they generally agree that they comprise the program of citizenship education. They are: a sense of identity; an awareness of one's rights and respect for the rights of others; the fulfilment of duties; a critical acceptance of social values; political literacy; a broad general knowledge and command of basic academic skills; and the capacity to reflect on the implications of all these components and to act appropriately.

All of these elements of citizenship education are open to interpretation and debate. In the case of national identity, for example, just what vision of Canada should education promote? Can we define our national

identity in a way that would be acceptable to all citizens of Canada? Is
Canada one nation, or two, or three, or even more? Is John Ralston Saul
right when he says that we are not a nation-state in the conventional
sense?[44] Should we be content with the concept of "limited identities" in
the spirit suggested by Cook and Careless some years ago?[45] And is
identity enough, or should citizenship education be explicitly organized
to promote national unity and national pride, as Granatstein has recently
suggested? Moreover, should schools not also be teaching students to
identify not only with Canada, however defined, but with the whole
human race and the planet so that citizenship education comes to include
the promotion of a sense of global identity?[46]

The elements of citizenship rights and duties raise similar questions,
especially since the enactment of the Charter of Rights and Freedoms.
What are and should be our basic rights? Is health care a right? Or a job?
Are rights best protected by the state or by the marketplace? Where
should the balance be struck between individual and collective rights?
Are political theorists like Guy LaForest right to see the Charter as a
threat to the collective rights of Quebec?[47] Is Richard Gwyn correct when
he suggests that we have fallen victim to a "rights frenzy"?[48] Has our
pursuit of rights outweighed our concern for the fulfilment of duties?
And just what are and should be the duties of citizenship anyway? Are
communitarians like Amitai Etzioni correct when they argue that we
should think and act much more in terms of the good of the community
than of the interests and rights of the individual?[49]

The element of social values is no less controversial. In any country
citizenship is obviously an intensely value-laden concept, entailing not
just knowledge and skills, but behaviour and action based on values.
Such values will differ according to the political system in which they are
rooted. In Canada, the Charter of Rights and Freedoms might well come
to serve as the basis of a set of Canadian social values. Even without such
written documents, citizens come to accept, often without realizing it, a
set of values and beliefs that they see as characteristic of their society. In
his work with the Citizens' Commission, for example, which was set up
in connection with the Charlottetown Accord, Keith Spicer identified the
following as core Canadian values: equality and fairness; respect for
minorities; consultation and dialogue; accommodation and tolerance;
compassion and generosity; respect for Canada's natural beauty; and
respect for Canada's world image of peace, freedom and non-violent
change.[50]

Some political theorists speak explicitly of "democratic values" or
"virtues," and argue that they should be taught as part of citizenship
education. To take only one example, the political philosopher Carol

Gould has described the "democratic character," which she sees as consisting of reliance on reason; reciprocity in dealing with other people; receptivity to diverse opinions and viewpoints; respect for human rights; mutuality; flexibility and open-mindedness; commitment and responsibility; cooperativeness and a concern for community.[51]

The element of political literacy is these days defined in terms of participation in the political process, and is a relatively new arrival on the agenda of citizenship education.[52] It has always been accepted that good citizens should play their part in the public affairs of their community, but this was usually seen as little more than casting an informed vote at election time. There were always a few teachers who went beyond this and who taught their students that it was their right and duty as citizens to participate directly in the political process, but only in the last twenty or thirty years has it become orthodoxy to say that citizenship education should prepare the young to participate directly in the political process in ways other than voting. In the classroom this has taken the form of teaching students about the real world of politics and not only about the ideals of civics, about how decisions are really made, about who holds power and who does not, about how public opinion is shaped, and so on. Outside the classroom it takes the form of engaging students directly in the political process as students, even in the elementary grades, and not treating politics as something that is reserved for adults only. Thus, students work in environmental campaigns, in elections, and on social issues of various kinds.[53]

Any consideration of questions such as these, and many others like them, obviously demands both a good deal of general knowledge and the skills to use it. Thus, the sixth element of citizenship education consists precisely of knowledge and intellectual skills. To some extent, citizenship is a craft, like medicine, plumbing, carpentry, engineering, law, or any other such specialty, and, like them, it requires that its practitioners carry in their heads and at their fingertips a body of knowledge and skills ready for immediate use. There is a good deal of talk in education these days to the effect that knowledge as such is not particularly important, that what matters is knowing how to access and process knowledge, to find it when it is needed, and to assess and apply it once found. The economic agenda of much of today's schooling endorses this emphasis on content-free, generic skills which are seen as key ingredients of the flexibility and adaptability required of the modern workforce. In the words of one corporate executive:

> Memorized facts ... are of little use in the age in which information is doubling every two or three years. We have expert systems in computing and the Internet that can

provide the facts when we need them. Our workforce needs to utilize the facts to assist in developing solutions to problems. The worker needs to be able to utilize the systems that give him or her access to information when it's required in the problem-solving process.[54]

However true this is when applied to the labour force (and in this age of de-skilling and Mac-jobs there is good reason to doubt it), it most certainly does not apply to citizenship. One can see why employers might want workers with lots of skills but no knowledge, for their skills would help them follow instructions and their lack of knowledge would leave them with no basis on which to question what they were instructed to do. Such workers, like Adolf Eichmann, would make sure that the trains ran on time without ever caring that they were running to the extermination camps.

When confronted with questions of public policy and personal decision, citizens cannot forever be running to the nearest computer terminal or reference book, useful as these are. They must carry with them at least a basis of knowledge that helps them understand and assess the world in which they live. To function within their own societies they must possess what Hirsch has called "cultural literacy."[55] Indeed, as Hirsch points out, the very existence of a society depends upon its members sharing at least a minimum of common knowledge. This, for example, is why the teaching of history is so important in schools, not for creating a spirit of national unity or pride, but because, as Kymlicka writes, "it defines the shared context and framework within which we debate our differing values and priorities. ... It becomes the implicit background for our thinking, providing the symbols, precedents, and reference points by which we make sense of issues."[56]

Beyond this, citizens need that broad general knowledge that we have traditionally thought of as comprising a liberal education, for this, appropriately taught, serves as a source of those ideas which enable us to question, to challenge, to move beyond the conventional wisdom of our own times. We need in education a healthy dose of that belief in the emancipatory power of knowledge that was so strongly held by nineteenth century radicals like England's William Lovett:

> Education will cause every latent seed of the mind to germinate and spring up into useful life, which otherwise might have lain buried in ignorance, and died in the corruptions of its own nature; thousands of our countrymen, endowed with all the capabilities for becoming the guides and lights of society, from want of this glorious blessing, are doomed to grovel in vice and ignorance, to pine in

obscurity and want. Give to a man knowledge, and you give him a light to perceive and enjoy beauty, variety, surpassing ingenuity, and majestic grandeur, which his mental darkness previously concealed from him — enrich his mind and strengthen his understanding, and you give him powers to render all art and nature subservient to his purposes — call forth his moral excellence in union with his intellect, and he will apply every power of thought and force of action to enlighten ignorance, alleviate misfortune, remove misery, and banish vice; and, as far as his abilities permit, to prepare a highway to the world's happiness.[57]

In the nineteenth century, Matthew Arnold famously declared that education should consist of "getting to know, on all the matters which most concern us, the best which has been thought and said in the world," not for reasons of false gentility or snobbish pride, but because this would help us turn "a stream of fresh and free thought upon our stock notions and habits, which we now follow staunchly but mechanically, vainly imagining that there is a virtue in following them staunchly which makes up for the mischief of following them mechanically."[58] As the political philosopher Alan Ryan recently said, "What liberal education does is to offer its beneficiaries the chance to take an interest in everything that humanity has cared about over the past several millennia."[59] There are obvious connections here with citizenship education, and, indeed, Ryan elsewhere persuasively connects liberal education with education for citizenship.[60]

It is true that history, literature, science, and the other staples of liberal education can be badly taught. It is also true that they have often been used as ideological weapons to enforce a particular sort of cultural and ideological hegemony.[61] There is no need to repeat here the by now well-known arguments over the "canon" of the "dead, white European males" of Western Civilization. Indeed, the very concept of Western Civilization, at least in its curricular form, was in large part originally created as an ideological weapon.[62] Nonetheless, these problems are not inherent in the concept of liberal education, which, in practice as in theory, as Martha Nussbaum and others have shown, is open to continuous and continual revision. And as Gerald Graff has suggested, the arguments over the curriculum can themselves form an invaluable basis for education.[63] Even if one adopts the post-modernist position that all is discourse, that there is nothing outside the text, that all knowledge is partial and suspect, the fact remains that the practice of citizenship nonetheless depends on familiarity with the discourse that characterizes and defines it. Not to teach this discourse to students, therefore, deprives them of the chance to become citizens in any real sense of the word.

There have been various attempts over the years to outline the knowledge that citizens need if they are to act as citizens. Suffice it to say here that citizens need to possess not just skills, but actual knowledge, and that school is the best place to begin to teach what citizens need to know. It is a depressing commentary on the state of educational discussion today that this even needs to be said, but in recent years it seems that acquiring knowledge had been displaced as a goal of education. In opposition to the policy-makers' insistence on the economic priorities of schooling, educationists turn to a rhetoric of needs, growth, development. They contrast so-called product-based learning with process-based learning to the disadvantage of the former, all the while ignoring that they are really two aspects of the same thing. They contrast child-centred education with subject-centred education, all the while ignoring that teaching involves doing both at the same time. Educational debate is full of such false dualisms, and in pursuing them we too easily lose sight of the importance of knowledge for citizenship. It is true that any attempt to define curricular knowledge can itself be controversial, as demonstrated most recently in the debate over the National History Standards in the United States, but debate and dissent are at the heart of democratic citizenship, and, if citizenship education is to prosper, it is better to argue over what knowledge schools should teach than to dismiss the whole idea of useful knowledge as unimportant.[64]

All the elements of citizenship education described in this paper are, in fact, open to debate. They present not simple verities, but contestable propositions, especially when they have to be applied to concrete cases. Thus, the seventh element of citizenship education consists of the capacity to reflect upon the other six and to act appropriately. In other words, an essential component of citizenship is dialogue, a willingness and an ability to enter into discussion with fellow citizens on matters of common concern no matter how divisive they might be. Theoretically, this ought not to present a problem for schools since it draws on abilities and skills that have long been central to educational theory if not always honoured in educational practice. The most obvious are critical and reflective thinking; problem solving; working cooperatively with others; discussion; empathy with other people. To the extent that schools are able to teach such skills, and they obviously can, they make an important contribution to citizenship.

Citizenship, Curricula, and Pedagogy

Occasionally it has been suggested that citizenship itself be explicitly taught as a subject, a suggestion which has recently been revived in the United Kingdom, but apart from occasional lessons here and there or special events such as Empire Day or Remembrance Day, this has rarely been done in Canada, though it is now being revived in Ontario and Quebec.[65] For the most part, however, educators have seen citizenship as something that was best taught through the conventional subjects of the curriculum, not as something that needed its own slot on the timetable. The advantage of this, of course, was that it made no extra demands on an already overcrowded timetable or on hard-pressed teachers. The drawback was that it was all too easy for citizenship to fall through the cracks, especially when it was not subject to examination.

By the 1970s, a variety of subjects dealt with topics that were relevant to the education of citizens. For example, history, long a staple of citizenship education, was increasingly abandoned for courses organized around contemporary problems, all intended to rouse students' interest in the issues of the day. In a similar spirit, units of study or whole courses were introduced in human rights, native studies, law-related education, holocaust studies, environmental problems, media literacy, and other citizenship-oriented topics. Science courses also departed from a pure science approach to take on more of what was called a science-in-society orientation. Home economics curricula grew to include discussions of the environment, resources, and social justice generally. Literature was oriented to contemporary concerns of obvious citizenship application, among them questions of racism, sexism, war and peace, and the like. From the 1970s onwards, schools have paid increasing attention to Canadian content and approached all subjects in a multicultural framework that has obvious implications for some aspects of citizenship.

In Canada, as elsewhere, these developments have attracted some criticism both from those who see them as not going nearly far enough and from those who think they have already gone too far. Among the former are some Aboriginal Canadians who see the schools as still too assimilationist and too neglectful of Aboriginal culture and tradition. Some Afro-Canadians have voiced similar concerns and have also accused the schools of failing to take systemic racism seriously. Some advocates of multiculturalism have further criticized the schools for taking only a song-and-dance approach to ethnic and cultural diversity and thereby failing to address more fundamental issues. On the other side are those who regret what they see as the lowering of academic standards as schools move from academic to social priorities; who level charges of so-called "political correctness" against the schools; who are uncomfortable with the abandonment of familiar traditions such as the observance of specifically Christian festivals; who criticize multiculturalism for what they see as its divisiveness; and who, most recently, want to see the schools take a much more active stance in the promotion of national unity.

Thus, the curriculum has become, perhaps more than ever before, the subject of considerable debate. For the most part, however, this debate has not involved any serious discussion of citizenship except in the most indirect way. The debate has been about whether the curriculum is adequately inclusive, whether it is sufficiently rigorous, whether it is ideologically partisan, whether it properly prepares students for the high-tech global economy, but rarely about whether it effectively prepares young Canadians for citizenship.

No matter what the curriculum includes, how it is taught cannot be ignored. Students learn important lessons from how teachers teach as well as from what they teach. Teachers' choice of teaching strategies and their general approach to students play some part in the kinds of citizens that students become.

Some theorists maintain that a one-to-one relationship exists between democratic citizenship and democratic classroom methods, with the latter being defined in terms of student-centred teaching, activity-based learning, student participation in classroom life, and so on. There is obviously something to this. Students who in the classroom are taught to be critical, to use their minds, to ask questions, to think for themselves, to expect a voice in decisions, and so forth, are likely to carry these attitudes outside the classroom. However, the argument can be pressed too far. Process alone is inadequate. To take an obvious example: whether an activity-based project fosters democratic citizenship or not depends upon the nature of the project and the way it is organized. Students can learn more about democracy from a careful reading of the classic texts than from any amount of apparently democratic classroom discussion. We need to remember that the most powerful democratic theorists, John Stuart Mill, John Dewey, T.H. Green, and the rest, all had decidedly non-democratic educations in terms of process. What they did have was a deep acquaintance with history, philosophy, and literature, and the capacity to pursue the ideas they gained from their knowledge. As Emberley and Newell and others have argued, a good liberal education still has much to offer in terms of a preparation for citizenship.

At the same time, teaching strategies do matter. They have an impact on students and on how they interact with the world. Students can learn that they know nothing and that their task is to remember and repeat what their teacher tells them, Gradgrind fashion. Or they can learn that they have ideas of their own, that they know how to ask intelligent questions, to think for themselves.

It needs to be added that this kind of question-raising, critical, open-ended teaching is good for all students. All too often there are unacceptable differences in the teaching given to middle-class students compared to that given to their working-class counterparts. Middle-class students are taught to question, to inquire, to participate, and in the process they learn that they can control, or at least influence, their world. Working-class students, on the other hand, especially if they are also poor, receive a less demanding level of teaching. Rather than learning how to question, they learn to fill in the blanks. They learn that the world is an arbitrary place over which they have little control. Thus, they do the rational thing and withdraw from it. In effect two different kinds of citizenship education are in operation: middle-class students are taught to be active, to participate, to take charge; working-class students are taught to follow instructions.[66]

Some researchers are now suggesting that teaching methods also affect boys and girls differently. There is plenty of evidence that boys generally dominate classroom life. They get more than their share of their teachers' attention. They are usually more aggressively competitive than girls. They demand more of their teachers' time. We also know that there can be an unacceptably high level of sexual harassment in schools. Some researchers are suggesting that many girls have a different learning style than do boys, but that this learning style is undervalued and under-utilized in many classrooms. Thus, for example, recent years have seen a small but noticeable trend to all-girls classes in some schools, and some researchers are suggesting that single-sex schools might be better for many girls. Thus, there is a gender dimension to teaching strategies which affects boys and girls differently and might go some way to explaining why men have been so heavily overrepresented in politics. Boys, especially middle-class boys, are taught to become active citizens; girls, at least until recently, for the most part are not.[67]

The classroom is not the only place where learning occurs in school. Indeed, it might be argued that some of the most important school learning takes place outside the classroom, not in it. This, after all, is why schools have long organized extra-curricular programs and special events for students. From the early days of compulsory schooling in Canada, educationists have been well aware of the power of this kind of learning for citizenship education. In the early 1900s, for example, Prairie school inspectors promoted the value of school gardens, school fairs, field days, and school outings for promoting a sense of citizenship in children. Across the country schools organized special events with an explicit citizenship purpose. Empire Day was one such. Others were Arbor Day, Goodwill Day, Remembrance Day, special occasions such as the sixtieth anniversary in 1897 of Queen Victoria's accession to the throne, or the fiftieth, sixtieth and one hundredth anniversaries of Confederation in 1917, 1927, and 1967. School sports, music programs, and student clubs of all types have also long been seen as important contributors to citizenship. This is where students learn both to compete

and cooperate, to deal graciously with both victory and defeat, to set and
surpass personal goals, to put aside personal gain for a common cause
— all valuable citizenship lessons. Other forms of extra-curricular
activity are aimed specifically at involving students in the world outside
school and thus teaching lessons in citizenship. Such was the motivation
between the Wars, for example, for the Junior Red Cross, the 4-H
movement, the Canadian Girls in Training, and today of countless
environmental clubs, international development projects, peace groups,
and the like, all of which are designed to show students that they can
indeed make a difference in the world.

Finally, citizenship education has, from its beginnings, been seen as
carried out through the whole corporate life of the school. As the school
superintendent of Brandon, Manitoba stated in 1918:

> Through such subjects as history, civics, literature, hygiene,
> opportunities will occur to teach the principles underlying
> democracy. It is folly to imagine, however, that we can
> transform a people merely by talking or teaching I
> would like to say with all the conviction that I am capable
> of expressing, that the spirit of democracy can only be
> made a part of the lives of our children when it becomes the
> prevailing spirit of the school itself, and I might also add,
> of the home and the church.[68]

Schools usually see themselves as communities and do what they can
to teach their students to act as responsible community members,
however defined. Hence the emphasis on school spirit, on school
traditions, on standards of behaviour, from dress codes to students' bills
of rights.

Over the years, however, there has often been a gap between the
rhetoric of citizenship and the practice of the schools. Citizenship has
been emphasized in statements of aims, in curricular preambles, in
official pronouncements, but it has been absent from the actual courses
of study. Often the citizenship impulse has been diverted or diluted or
simply overtaken by other, allegedly more practical, purposes, most
often passing examinations, preparing for jobs, or simply covering the
course of study. Even when citizenship was more than a matter of
rhetoric, the lessons that students actually learned often differed from
what schools thought they were teaching, in part because the concept of
citizenship was itself left too vague and undefined. Often schools
depoliticized the concept, equating the good citizen with the good
person. There is, however, more to being a citizen than this. Ever since
the Greeks, the essence of citizenship has been seen as involvement in the
public life and affairs of one's society. As Pericles famously said in the
Funeral Oration:

Here each individual is interested not only in his own affairs but in the affairs of the state as well; even those who are mostly occupied with their own business are extremely well-informed on general politics — this is a peculiarity of ours: we do not say that a man who takes no interest in politics is a man who minds his own business; we say that he has no business here at all.[69]

This political dimension of citizenship has too often been submerged in a concern with the shaping of personality and character. Here, for example, are the categories used on a 1936 school report card, which were described as constituting the "habits and attitudes desirable for good citizenship": obedience, courtesy, thrift, promptness, initiative, reliability, self-control, good sportsmanship, service, industry and workmanship, cleanliness, good judgement.[70] Each of these qualities is admirable in its own right but what is most obvious about this list is what is omitted. With the possible exception of "initiative" — which is further described as "Ambition to know and ability to do the right thing without being told. Leadership."— it says nothing about the qualities that fit citizens for participation in public life in a democracy. Indeed, despite their individual merits, taken collectively this list of qualities presents a very passive view of citizenship. It is not, however, untypical of the way schools have seen citizenship education over the years.

Consider, for example, the case of "assertive discipline" which enjoyed a certain popularity in some school systems a few years ago. Its rules ran as follows:

1. Students will follow the directions of all teachers and superiors the first time.
2. Students shall be on time for class.
3. Students shall have all equipment and supplies at all times.
4. Students will keep their hands, feet, and other objects to themselves.
5. Students will practise good citizenship and courtesy to all students and to each other.

In schools that adopted assertive discipline programs these rules were posted prominently in classrooms and around the school generally, leading one to wonder what impression was created on students who were thus told, right from the first, that they were not to be trusted, that their job was to do as they were told, no questions asked, and that "citizenship" was above all a matter of obeying orders and following procedures.

The problem does not lie so much in any of the rules in themselves. Students should certainly be on time for class, respect others, have their equipment with them (though at appropriate, not at "all" times), and so on. But what is striking is the overwhelmingly negative tone of the rules. Why not, for example, display rules such as these in classrooms?

1. Students will think for themselves whenever possible.
2. Students will be as creative as possible at all times.
3. Students must always read more than their textbook.
4. Students will ask original and provocative questions.

And so on. Moreover, once these rules are posted, they must be enforced. One can imagine a worried principal phoning parents to complain that their son or daughter has not had an original idea or asked an interesting question all week and telling them that they had better come to the school for a meeting to discuss what disciplinary measures might be taken. It presumably says something about our views of schooling that whenever I have floated this idea past audiences of parents and teachers it has always been treated as a joke and never as a serious possibility.

What is most striking about assertive discipline, however, is that few people saw it as anything more than a method of keeping order in the classroom. It was only ever discussed in restricted terms: Was it worth the time and effort involved? How did students respond to it? Did parents like it? Above all, did it work? No one apparently saw its implications for citizenship education.

A Conception of Citizenship Education

What we need is a conception of citizenship which is rich enough to include its many dimensions, but also simple enough to be of practical service to teachers, so that they can easily judge the extent to which their everyday activities are consistent with the kind of citizenship we need. Just as when we drive we know more or less automatically that there are certain things we must do, such as staying on the proper side of the road and obeying traffic signals, without consciously thinking about them, so teachers need to govern their teaching by an internalized conception of citizenship. Elsewhere I have suggested that such a conception might best be thought of as the "twelve C's" (with the C's being used purely for mnemonic purposes, to serve as a rough and ready checklist), as follows:

The first C is **Canadian** and it asks whether their schooling teaches students enough about Canada — its history, geography, artistic, scientific, and other achievements, and its current problems — to help them understand and to participate in the continuing debate that is so quintessentially Canadian: what kind of country are we and what kind of country do we want to be?

The second C stands for **cosmopolitan**, in the traditional sense of the world. It asks whether their schooling teaches students that they are citizens not only of Canada, but of the world. Do they think not only of their own country or their own group, but also of the world as a whole?

The third C stands for **communication**, and asks whether schooling gives sufficient emphasis to teaching students to communicate effectively, in all the different forms that communication can take: speech, writing, numeracy, graphics, and so on.

Since the ability to communicate cannot be separated from the content to be communicated, the fourth C stands for **coherence** or **content**. Does schooling give students adequate command of a broad body of subject matter, representing the spectrum of human endeavour, the humanities and social sciences, mathematics and science, the expressive arts, and so on?

This leads to the fifth C which stands for **critical**. It asks whether schooling teaches students to think critically and whether teachers approach knowledge, not as sacred dogma but as invitation to inquiry and reflection, since acquiring knowledge but never using it is of little benefit since it does not lead one to think and to improve one's reasoning powers.

Criticism, however, can be little more than a reactive process and education should involve more than simply responding to the ideas of others. Thus, the sixth C represents **creativity**, which is something that all people possess in one form or another, and it draws attention to the extent to which schooling actively seeks to foster creativity in students, not only in the arts but in all subjects.

Creativity goes hand in hand with **curiosity** which is the seventh C, representing the willingness and the capacity to ask questions and to continue learning.

Creativity and curiosity do not exist in a vacuum. They draw upon, while also going beyond and sometimes reacting against, the work of others. They draw their inspiration from what Robert Hutchins has called the "great conversation," the continuing dialogue that has existed for centuries in all civilizations concerning the meaning and nature of life. Thus, the eighth C stands for **civilizations**. It asks whether schooling seeks to convey to students an adequate understanding of the heritage of civilizations (in the plural) of which they are both the heirs and the trustees for the future.

Civilization is a collective, cooperative enterprise and this leads to the ninth C, **community**. It raises the question of whether and to what extent schooling seeks to prepare students to become informed, participating, and involved members in their various communities — local, regional, national, and global.

This in turn leads to the tenth C which stands for **concern**, and asks whether and how schooling creates in students a sense of concern and a readiness to act on that concern, both for other people and for the environment which makes life possible.

The eleventh C is **character**. The development of character used to be described as one of the key goals of education, but we do not use the word much these days. It stands for the commitment to do what is right, to follow one's conscience, and to balance one's own interests and concerns against the rights and welfare of others.

Finally, the twelfth C is the sum total of the previous eleven, and stands for **competence**. It asks how effective schooling is in playing its part in preparing students to be effective and competent citizens, workers and human beings.

All this may seem overly ambitious, but not when it is spread out over twelve years of schooling. The list is not intended to be applied to one particular lesson but to the whole range of a school's activities. In their schematic way, the twelve C's represent the whole of schooling. If attained, they will equip any student for citizenship. Equally important, they will contribute to the shaping of the kind of community in which individual success derives from and contributes to social purposes. More specifically they can help us focus on just what it is that we expect from our schools. In the words of the 1992 Newfoundland Royal Commission on education, school effectiveness depends on everyone involved pursuing a "common vision."[71] Such a vision is best provided by a conception of citizenship.

Such a conception has recently been offered by an international project in citizenship education which describes it as "multidimensional" citizenship. The argument here is that citizenship is best thought of as comprising four dimensions: the personal, the social, the temporal, and the spatial. The personal dimension is described as the "personal capacity for and commitment to a civic ethic characterized by individually and socially responsible habits of mind, heart and action." Such personal qualities, however, while important, are not enough in themselves. Citizens are social beings not hermits. They must be able to interact with other people in a variety of settings, to engage in public debate, to participate in public life, and to contribute to the many forms of civil society that underlie effective democracy in the public sphere. This kind of involvement takes place within, and is conditioned by, a tradition of beliefs and assumptions so that citizenship also contains a temporal dimension, requiring that citizens, while being understandably concerned with the problems they face in the present, never lose sight of the connections that the present has with both the past and future. Citizens need a rich knowledge of history and an awareness that their present actions will have an impact on the future and then act accordingly. Finally, the spatial dimension of citizenship recognizes that citizenship is not one single locus of identity, but that citizens are members of various overlapping communities — local, regional, national, and global.[72]

This level of abstraction might seem to be a long way removed from the daily realities of the classroom, but it can readily be translated into terms that even young children can handle, as shown by this example. A class of Grade 7 students was studying world geography, and the particular lesson that I observed was devoted to the Brazilian rain forests. The students had already learned something of the value of rain forests as climatic regulators and as homes of all types of flora and fauna. They were also learning that rain forests were being destroyed at a rapid rate and, with the certainty of thirteen-year-olds, quickly concluded that the people responsible were either stupid or thoughtless or both. What they did not take into account was that people were cutting down the rain forests because they had little choice in the situation they faced. Poverty, the need for land, patterns of international trade and economic pressures of various kinds shaped the attack on the rain forests, not silliness or ignorance. The students were led to consider that Canada had destroyed much of its forest cover since the beginning of European settlement and was continuing to do so. They were also asked to put themselves in the position of Brazilian peasants facing a range of equally difficult choices. It was suggested to them that, if the rain forests were indeed important to the world as a whole, and if one of the problems Brazilian peasants faced was that patterns of international trade worked to their disadvantage, then perhaps people in rich countries such as Canada should be prepared to pay a small surcharge, say a penny or so on every cup of coffee, which would be used to protect the rain forests. The idea is not far-fetched, being only an extension of the fair trade and fair price practices that some social justice agencies now sponsor. And what was central to the lesson was not the financial or economic practicalities of the proposal but, rather, the idea that rich consumers should be expected to help poor producers whose products they were consuming.

In this particular case, the students were not especially enthused about the proposal, but the point of the exercise was not to convert them to some political position but to lead them to think in ways they would otherwise have ignored. In the process, they were beginning to learn a lesson in multidimensional citizenship. They were led to think about the present in the context of past and future; to see how their personal lives connected with a broader problem, to note how Canada was involved with other parts of world, and to consider a wide range of alternatives and viewpoints. Obviously, one lesson by itself will achieve little, but if the kind of teaching described here were to be undertaken across the curriculum and throughout a student's stay at school, the cumulative effect could be considerable. And this kind of teaching can be easily accommodated within the most conventional curriculum. It is neither especially innovative nor unorthodox, though perhaps more unusual than it ought to be, and the pedagogical literature offers plenty of suggestions.[73] It embodies the problem-posing, critical thinking, reflective, open-ended approach to teaching which has always been taken to characterize true education. It also provides valuable citizenship education.

The Renewal of Citizenship Education

Today, however, to return to where this paper began, citizenship seems to have vanished from the educational agenda. Since about the mid-1980s, schools have directed their energies largely to economic ends. Policy makers have demanded that schools focus on the basics, meaning not only the traditional three R's but such contemporary additions as computer literacy, competitiveness, entrepreneurialism, and skills. In curriculum terms, the emphasis is placed on mathematics, science, literacy, and computer science.

As we enter the twenty-first century, perhaps the most urgent task facing us is to restore citizenship to its place in educational debate, not obviously in any narrowly national or restrictive sense, and not in the hegemonic and exclusionary sense that was common years ago, but in the sense of a participative, critical, and democratic involvement in public life. In 1932, in the heart of the depression, the principal of the Manitoba Normal School, W.A. McIntyre, wrote: "The only hope for curing the ills of the world is that young people may picture a better one and strive to realize it. To frame this picture and to cultivate this ambition is the greatest duty of the school."[74] A few years later, in 1937, the principal of McGill University said much the same thing, telling an audience of teachers: "The path to a better community lies before us, open but not clear. As I see it, the task of education is to give us the wisdom to see that path, hope to believe in our goal, and will to pursue it."[75] It is a vision of education, and of citizenship, that is far more attractive and worthwhile than our present preoccupation with training workers who can adapt to the imperatives of the global economy.

NOTES

1. Louis Althusser, *Lenin and Philosophy and Other Essays,* trans. Ben Brewster (New York: Monthly Review Press, 1970).

2. Eugen Weber, *Peasants into Frenchmen: The Modernization of Rural France, 1870-1914* (Stanford: Stanford University Press, 1976), 303-308.

3. Eric Hobsbawm, "Mass-Producing Traditions: Europe, 1870-1914," in *The Invention of Tradition,* ed. Eric Hobsbawm and Terence Ranger (Cambridge: Cambridge University Press, 1983), 263-307.

4. Jean Barman, "Knowledge Is Essential for Universal Progress but Fatal to Class Privilege: Working People and the Schools in Vancouver during the 1920s," *Labour/Le travail* 22 (1988): 20.

5. See, for example, Senate, Standing Committee on Employment, Education and Training, *Active Citizenship Revisited* (Canberra, Australia, 1991); Senate, Standing Committee on Social Affairs, Science and Technology, *Canadian Citizenship: Sharing the Responsibility* ([Ottawa]: The Committee, 1993); Qualifications and Curriculum Authority, Advisory Group on Citizenship, *Education for Citizenship and the Teaching of Democracy in Schools* (London, 1998).

6. Alan Sears and Andrew S. Hughes, "Citizenship Education and Current Educational Reform," *Canadian Journal of Education* 21, no. 2 (1996): 123-142.

7. George Radwanski, *Study of the Relevance of Education and the Issue of Dropouts* (Toronto: Ontario Ministry of Education, 1987), 2.

8. Manitoba Education and Training, "Building a Solid Foundation for Our Future: A Strategy Plan 1991-1996" (Winnipeg: Manitoba Education and Training, 1991), 1.

9. Ken Osborne, "The Emerging Agenda for Canadian High Schools," *Journal of Curriculum Studies* 24, no. 4 (1992): 371-379.

10. Richard Henley and John Pampallis, "The Campaign for Compulsory Education in Manitoba," *Canadian Journal of Education* 7, no. 1 (1982): 81.

11. J.H. Putman and G.M. Weir, *Survey of the School System* (Victoria: King's Printer, 1925), 38.

12. Carl Becker, *Our Great Experiment in Democracy: A History of the United States* (New York: Harper and Brothers, 1920), 274-275.

13. David C. Jones, "The Zeitgeist of Western Settlement: Education and the Myth of the Land," in *Schooling and Society in Twentieth Century British Columbia,* ed. J. Donald Wilson and David C. Jones (Calgary: Detselig, 1980), 75.

14. *Western School Journal* 15 (1920): 177.

15. The classic discussion of citizenship is T. H. Marshall, *Citizenship and Social Class, and Other Essays* (Cambridge: Cambridge University Press,

1950). See also Geoff Andrews, ed., *Citizenship* (London: Lawrence and Wishart, 1991); J.M. Barbalet, *Citizenship: Rights, Struggle, and Class Inequality* (Minneapolis: University of Minnesota Press, 1988); Ronald Beiner, ed., *Theorizing Citizenship* (Albany: State University of New York Press, 1993); Derek B. Heater, *Citizenship: The Civic Ideal in World History, Politics, and Education* (London: Longman, 1990); and Bryan S. Turner, *Citizenship and Capitalism* (London: Allen and Unwin, 1986).

16. William B. Munro, *Current Problems in Citizenship* (New York: Macmillan, 1924), 426.

17. See, for example, Ted Tapper and Brian Salter, *Education and the Political Order: Changing Patterns of Class Control* (London: Macmillan, 1978), esp. 68-87.

18. François Dosse, *New History in France: The Triumph of the Annales*, trans. Peter V. Conroy, Jr. (Urbana: University of Illinois Press, 1990), 23. For a slightly different translation of the same passage, see Pierre Nora, "Lavisse: The Nation's Teacher," in *Traditions*, vol. 2 of *Realms of Memory: The Construction of the French Past*, ed. Pierre Nora (New York: Columbia University Press), 181.

19. For Wells' criticisms of what he described as "the poison called history," see his *Travels of a Republican Radical in Search of Hot Water* (Harmondsworth: Penguin Books, 1939). See also Ken Osborne, "H.G. Wells: Education or Catastrophe?," *Journal of Educational Administration and Foundations* 6, no. 2 (1991): 117-38.

20. See John S. Milloy, *A National Crime: The Canadian Government and the Residential School System, 1879 to 1986* (Winnipeg: University of Manitoba Press, 1999); and J.R. Miller, *Shingwauk's Vision: A History of Native Residential Schools* (Toronto: University of Toronto Press, 1996).

21. See Adolf Ens, *Subjects or Citizens? The Mennonite Experience in Canada, 1870-1925* (Ottawa: University of Ottawa Press, 1994); Paul Axelrod, *The Promise of Schooling: Education in Canada, 1800-1914* (Toronto: University of Toronto Press, 1997), 69-87; Ronald A. Manzer, *Public Schools and Political Ideas: Canadian Educational Policy in Historical Perspective* (Toronto: University of Toronto Press, 1994), 51-67; and John McLaren, "Creating 'Slaves of Satan' or 'New Canadians'? The Law, Education, and the Socialization of Doukhobor Children, 1911-1935," in *British Columbia and the Yukon*, vol. 6 of *Essays in the History of Canadian Law*, ed. Hamar Foster and John McLaren (Toronto: Osgoode Society, 1995), 352-385.

22. National Council of Education, *Observations on the Teaching of History and Civics in Primary and Secondary Schools of Canada* (Winnipeg: Office of the General Secretary, National Council of Education, 1923), 14.

23. *Bulletin of the Manitoba Teachers' Federation* 28 (15 December 1923): 495.

24. Alf Chaiton and Neil McDonald, *Canadian Schools and Canadian Identity* (Toronto: Gage Educational Publishing, 1977), 14-15.

25. George S. Tomkins, *A Common Countenance: Stability and Change in the Canadian Curriculum* (Scarborough: Prentice-Hall, 1986), 147.

26. Ramsay Cook, *Canada and the French-Canadian Question* (Toronto: Macmillan, 1966), 117.

27. See, for example, Michael Bliss, "Privatizing the Mind: The Sundering of Canadian History, The Sundering of Canada," *Journal of Canadian Studies* 26, no. 4 (1991-1992): 5-17; J.L. Granatstein, *Who Killed Canadian History?* (Toronto: Harper Collins, 1998). For a rebuttal of Granatstein's criticisms of social history, see A.B. McKillop, "Who Killed Canadian History? A View from the Trenches," *Canadian Historical Review* 80 (June 1999): 269-299.

28. Bob Davis, *Whatever Happened to High School History? Burying the Political Memory of Youth, Ontario, 1945-1995* (Toronto: Lorimer/Our Schools Ourselves, 1995); and Ken Osborne, *In Defence of History: Teaching the Past and the Meaning of Democratic Citizenship* (Toronto: Our Schools/Ourselves Education Foundation, 1995). For a review that compares these books with Granatstein's *Who Killed Canadian History*, see Leon Fink, "Losing the Hearts and Minds, or How Clio Disappeared from Canadian Public Schools," *Labour/Le travail* 43 (Spring 1999): 211-215.

29. Alan Sears, "Social Studies as Citizenship Education in English Canada: A Review of Research," *Theory and Research in Social Education* 22 (1994): 6-43; and Ken Osborne, "'Education Is the Best National Insurance': Citizenship Education in Canadian Schools, Past and Present," *Canadian and International Education* 25, no. 2 (1996): 31-58.

30. H.T.J. Coleman, "Teaching for the New Citizenship," *Queen's Quarterly* 27 (1919): 21.

31. Quoted in *Western School Journal* 15 (1920): 177.

32. *Report of the Proceedings of the National Conference on Character Education in Relation to Canadian Citizenship, Convention Hall, Board of Trade Building, Winnipeg, October 20-22, 1919* ([Winnipeg?: s.n., 1919]), 6.

33. O.E. Nault, "Education for Peace," *Western School Journal* 33 (1938): 68.

34. *Report of the Proceedings of the National Conference on Character Education in Relation to Canadian Citizenship*, 21-22.

35. S.N. Forrest, "Annual Address," *Western School Journal* 15 (1920): 162.

36. Putman and Weir, *Survey of the School System*, 57.

37. For a description of the radical assault on citizenship education in one province in these years, see Ken Osborne, "One Hundred Years of History Teaching in Manitoba Schools, Part 1: 1897-1927," *Manitoba History* 36 (1998-99): esp. 19-22.

38. See Nellie L. McClung, *In Times Like These* (1915; reprint, Toronto: University of Toronto Press, 1972); Catherine L. Cleverdon, *The Woman Suffrage Movement in Canada* (Toronto: University of Toronto Press, 1950/1974); and Carol Lee Baachi, *Liberation Deferred: The Ideas of the English-Canadian Suffragists, 1877-1918* (Toronto: University of Toronto Press, 1983). For contemporary feminist reservations about the concept of citizenship, see Jean Bethke Elshtain, *Public Man, Private Woman: Women in Social and Political Thought* (Princeton: Princeton University Press, 1981); Susan M. Okin, "Women, Equality, and Citizenship," *Queen's Quarterly* 99 (1992): 56-71; Anne Phillips, *Engendering Democracy* (University Park, PA: Pennsylvania State University Press, 1991); and Anne Phillips, *Democracy and Difference* (University Park, PA: Pennsylvania State University Press, 1993).

39. Jeffrey M. Taylor, *Fashioning Farmers: Ideology, Agricultural Knowledge, and the Manitoba Farm Movement, 1890-1925* (Regina: Canadian Plains Research Center, 1994); and Louis A. Wood, *A History of Farmers' Movements in Canada* (1924; reprint, Toronto: University of Toronto Press, 1975).

40. Philip V. Curoe, *Educational Policies and Attitudes of Organized Labor* (New York: Columbia University Teachers College Bureau of Publications, 1926); and Bill Maciejko, "Public Schools and the Workers' Struggle, Winnipeg 1914-1921," in *Schools in the West: Essays in Canadian Educational History*, ed. Nancy Sheehan, J. Donald Wilson, and David Jones (Calgary: Detselig, 1986), 213-237.

41. Beverley Boutilier, "Educating for Peace and Cooperation: The Women's International League for Peace and Freedom in Canada," (master's thesis, Carleton University, 1986); Terry Crowley, *Agnes MacPhail and the Politics of Equality* (Toronto: Lorimer, 1990); Ruth Roach Pierson, ed., *Women and Peace: Theoretical, Historical, and Practical Perspectives* (London: Croom Helm, 1987); Barbara Roberts, *A Reconstructed World: A Feminist Biography of Gertrude Richardson* (Montreal: McGill-Queen's University Press, 1997); Thomas P. Socknat, *Witness against War: Pacifism in Canada, 1900-1945* (Toronto: University of Toronto Press, 1987); and Thomas P. Socknat, "For Peace and Freedom: Canadian Feminists and the Interwar Peace Campaign," in *Up and Doing: Canadian Women and Peace*, ed. Janice Williamson and Deborah Gorham (Toronto: Women's Press, 1989), 68-88.

42. Norman Penner, "The Making of a Radical: Winnipeg in the 1930s," in *The Canadian Worker in the Twentieth Century*, ed. Irving Abella and David Millar (Toronto: Oxford University Press, 1978), 146-150.

43. William L. Morton, "A Century of Plain and Parkland," in *A Region of the Mind: Interpreting the Western Canadian Plains*, ed. Richard Allan (Regina: Canadian Plains Research Center, 1973), 174.

44. John Ralston Saul, *Reflections of a Siamese Twin: Canada at the End of the Twentieth Century* (Toronto: Viking, 1997).

45 J.M.S. Careless, "Limited Identities in Canada," *Canadian Historical Review* 50, no. 1 (1969): 1-10; J.M.S. Careless, "Limited Identities Ten Years Later," *Manitoba History* 1 (1980): 3-9; and Ramsay Cook, "Canadian Centennial Celebrations," *International Journal* 22, no. 4 (1967): 659-663.

46. Martha C. Nussbaum and respondents, *For Love of Country: Debating the Limits of Patriotism* (Boston: Beacon Press, 1996).

47. Guy LaForest, *Trudeau and the End of a Canadian Dream*, trans. Paul Leduc Browne and Michelle Weinroth (Montreal: McGill-Queen's University Press, 1995).

48. Richard Gwyn, *Nationalism without Walls: The Unbearable Lightness of Being Canadian* (Toronto: McClelland and Stewart, 1995).

49. Amitai Etzioni, *The Spirit of Community: Rights, Responsibilities, and the Communitarian Agenda* (New York: Crown, 1993); and Amitai Etzioni, ed. *New Communitarian Thinking: Persons, Virtues, Institutions, and Communities* (Charlottesville: University Press of Virginia, 1995).

50. Keith Spicer, "Values in Search of a Nation," in *Identities in North America: The Search for Community*, ed. Robert L. Earle and John D. Wirth (Stanford: Stanford University Press, 1995), 13-28.

51. Carol C. Gould, *Rethinking Democracy: Freedom and Social Cooperation in Politics, Economy, and Society* (Cambridge: Cambridge University Press, 1988), 283-9; William Galston, *Liberal Virtues: Gods, Diversity, and Values in the Liberal State* (Cambridge: Cambridge University Press, 1991), 220-7; and Richard Dagger, *Civic Virtues: Rights, Citizenship, and Republican Liberalism* (New York: Oxford University Press, 1997).

52. Bernard R. Crick and Alex Porter, eds., *Political Education and Political Literacy: The Report and Papers of, and the Evidence Submitted to, the Working Party of the Hansard Society's Programme for Political Education* (London: Longman, 1978).

53. For discussion of political education and the teaching of politics, see Tom Brennan, *Political Education and Democracy* (Cambridge: Cambridge University Press, 1981); Shirley H. Engle and Anna S. Ochoa, eds., *Education for Democratic Citizenship: Decision Making in the Social Studies* (New York: Teachers College Press, 1988); Carole E. Hahn, *Becoming Political: Comparative Perspectives on Citizenship Education* (Albany: State University of New York Press, 1998); Derek Heater and Judith A. Gillespie, eds., *Political Education in Flux* (London: Sage, 1981); Cathie Holden and Nick Clough, eds., *Children as Citizens: Education for Participation* (London: Kingsley, 1998); Orit Ichilov, ed., *Political Socialization, Citizenship Education, and Democracy* (New York: Teachers College Press, 1990); Orit Ichilov, ed., *Citizenship and Citizenship Education in a Changing World* (London: Woburn Press, 1998); Jon Pammett and Jean-Luc Pépin, eds., *Political Education in Canada* (Halifax: Institute for Research in Public Policy, 1988); and Ken Osborne, *The Teaching of Politics: Some Suggestions for Teachers* (Toronto: Canada Studies Foundation, 1982).

54. Robert W. Galvin and Edward W. Bales, forward to *Teaching the New Basic Skills: Principles for Educating Children to Thrive in a Changing Economy*, ed. Richard J. Murnane and Frank Levy (New York: Free Press, 1996), xvii.

55. Edward D. Hirsch, *Cultural Literacy: What Every American Needs to Know* (Boston: Houghton Mifflin, 1987).

56. Will Kymlicka, *Finding Our Way: Rethinking Ethnocultural Relations in Canada* (Toronto: Oxford University Press, 1998), 174. See also Gail Cuthbert Brandt, "Canadian National Histories: Their Evolving Content and Uses," *History Teacher* 30 (1997): 137-144; and Robert Comeau and Bernard Dionne, ed., *À propos de l'histoire nationale* (Sillery: Septentrion, (1998).

57. Quoted in Brian Simon, ed., *The Search for Enlightenment: The Working Class and Adult Education in the Twentieth Century* (London: Lawrence and Wishart, 1990), 259. On working-class enthusiasm for education (of a certain kind), see also Stuart MacIntyre, *A Proletarian Science: Marxism in Britain 1917-1933* (Cambridge: Cambridge University Press, 1980); Jonathan Rée, *Proletarian Philosophers: Problems in Socialist Culture in Britain 1900-1940* (Oxford: Clarendon Press, 1984); and David Vincent, *Bread, Knowledge and Freedom: A Study of Nineteenth-Century Working Class Autobiography* (London: Methuen, 1982).

58. Matthew Arnold, *Culture and Anarchy* (1869; reprint, New Haven: Yale University Press, 1994), 5.

59. *The Times Higher Education Supplement* (20 August 1999): 17.

60. Alan Ryan, *Liberal Anxieties and Liberal Education* (New York: Hill and Wang, 1998). For another argument that liberal education provides the best preparation for citizenship, see Peter C. Emberley and Walter R. Newell, *Bankrupt Education: The Decline of Liberal Education in Canada* (Toronto: University of Toronto Press, 1994).

61. Michael W. Apple, *Ideology and Curriculum* (London: Routledge, 1979); Henry A. Giroux, *Ideology, Culture, and the Process of Schooling* (Philadelphia: Temple University Press, 1981); Geoff Whitty, *The Sociology of School Knowledge* (London: Methuen 1985); and Michael F.D. Young, ed., *Knowledge and Control: New Directions for the Sociology of Education* (London: Collier-Macmillan, 1971).

62. Gilbert Allardyce, "The Rise and Fall of the Western Civilization Course," *American Historical Review* 87 (1981): 695-725. For a different perspective, see David Gress, *From Plato to Nato: The Idea of the West and Its Opponents* (New York: Free Press, 1998).

63. Martha C. Nussbaum, *Cultivating Humanity: A Classical Defense of Liberal Education* (Cambridge: Harvard University Press, 1997); and Gerald Graff, *Beyond the Culture Wars: How Teaching the Conflicts Can Revitalize American Education* (New York: Norton, 1992).

64. For more on this point, see Ken Osborne, *Education: A Guide to the Canadian School Debate, or, Who Wants What and Why?* (Toronto: Penguin, 1999). For a description of the debate over the national history standards in the United States, see Gary B. Nash, Charlotte Crabtree, and Ross E. Dunn, *History on Trial: Culture Wars and the Teaching of the Past* (New York: Knopf, 1997).

65. Marie McAndrew and Caroline Tessier, "L'éducation à la citoyenneté en milieu scolaire québécois: situation actuelle et perspectives comparatives," *Canadian Ethnic Studies/Études ethniques au Canada* 29, no. 2 (1997): 58-81.

66. Jean Anyon, "Social Class and the Hidden Curriculum of Work," *Journal of Education* 162 (1980): 67-92; Jeannie Oakes, *Keeping Track: How Schools Structure Inequality* (New Haven: Yale University Press, 1985); Ray C. Rist, *The Urban School: Factory for Failure; A Study of Education in American Society* (Cambridge: MIT Press, 1973); and Paul E. Willis, *Learning to Labour: How Working Class Kids Get Working Class Jobs* (Farnborough: Saxon House, 1977).

67. Mary Field Belenky, Blythe McVicar Clinchy, Nancy Rule Goldberger, and Jill Mattuck Rule, *Women's Ways of Knowing: The Development of Self, Voice, and Mind* (New York: Basic Books, 1986); Lynn Mikel Brown and Carol Gilligan, *Meeting at the Crossroads: Women's Psychology and Girls' Development* (Cambridge: Harvard University Press, 1992); Carol Gilligan, Nona P. Lyons, and Trudy J. Hammer, *Making Connections: The Relational Worlds of Adolescent Girls at Emma Willard High School* (Cambridge: Harvard University Press, 1990); Nancy Goldberger, Jill Tarule, Blythe Clinchy, and Mary Belenky, *Knowledge, Difference, and Power: Essays Inspired by Women's Ways of Knowing* (New York: Basic Books, 1996). For sexism in education more generally, see Myra and David Sadker, *Failing at Fairness: How America's Schools Cheat Girls* (New York: Scribners, 1994); and Jane Gaskell, Arlene McLaren, and Myra Novogrodsky, *Claiming an Education: Feminism and Canadian Schools* (Toronto: Our Schools/Our Selves Education Foundation, 1989).

68. Alfred White, "Education for Democracy," *Western School Journal* 15 (1920): 174.

69. Thucydides, *History of the Peloponnesian War*, trans. Rex Warner (Harmondsworth: Penguin, 1954), 147.

70. Mildred B. McMurray, "Character Education and Social Problems," *Western School Journal* 31 (1936): 49-50.

71. Newfoundland and Labrador Department of Education, Royal Commission of Inquiry into the Delivery of Programs and Services in Primary, Elementary, and Secondary Education, *Our Children, Our Future* (St. John's: Royal Commission of Inquiry, 1992), 242-243.

72. John J. Cogan and Ray Derricott, eds., *Citizenship for the 21st Century: An International Perspective on Education* (London: Kogan Page, 1998), 115-134.

73. For example, see Maurianne Adams, Lee Anne Bell, and Pat Griffin, *Teaching for Diversity and Social Justice: A Sourcebook* (New York: Routledge, 1997); Patricia Bourne and John Eisenberg, *Social Issues in the Curriculum: Theory, Practise, and Evaluation* (Toronto: Ontario Institute for Studies in Education, 1979); Bob Davis, *What Our High Schools Could Be* (Toronto: Our Schools/Our Selves Education Foundation, 1990); and Ken Osborne, *Teaching for Democratic Citizenship* (Toronto: Our Schools/Our Selves Education Foundation, 1991).

74. William A. McIntyre, "The School Preparing for Life," *Western School Journal* 27 (1932): 44-45.

75. A.E. Morgan, "Education and Democracy," *Western School Journal* 32 (1937): 168.

3 Public Schooling in English Canada: Addressing Difference in the Context of Globalization

ROSA BRUNO-JOFRÉ AND DICK HENLEY

ABSTRACT/RÉSUMÉ

Our understanding of Canadian polity formation is based on a pluralistic moral democracy that recognizes a fluid concept of cultural retention, differentiated citizenship as explained by Kymlicka, and a social ethic of care. We argue that multicultural education has not addressed issues concerning the national question with respect to Aboriginal nationalist and Quebec demands, or has done so only in a fragmentary manner. Anti-racist education has developed a refreshing oppositional approach that deals with structures sustaining racism, sexism, and power issues. However, we contend that the dominance of globalization as an economic ideology and concomitant educational changes have generated conditions to deal with difference in terms of a democracy that has great faith in the power of the free market and lacks confidence in the possibility of conscious collective efforts to build a space to define and redefine a public good. There is no doubt that the economic agenda is influencing citizenship formation in our schools even as teachers and students mediate those influences. Relevant to the understanding of the building of a Canadian polity is the clarification of the concept of democracy in light of the market imperative which has permeated language and the construction of meanings.

Notre compréhension de la formation du régime canadien se base sur un modèle de la démocratie morale pluraliste qui reconnaît un concept fluide de la conservation culturelle, d'un humanisme décentralisé et d'une citoyenneté différenciée comme expliquée par Kymlicka et d'une éthique sociale de soin. On soutient que l'éducation multiculturelle n'a pas adressé les problèmes au sujet de la question nationale en ce qui concerne les revendications nationalistes des Autochtones ou des Québécois, ou l'a fait seulement d'une façon fragmentaire. L'éducation antiraciste a développé une approche oppositionnelle rafraîchissante qui traite des structures qui soutiennent le racisme, le sexisme et les questions du pouvoir. Cependant, on prétend que la prédominance de la globalisation comme idéologie économique et les changements éducatifs concomitants ont généré une nouvelle situation qui exige l'attention des éducateurs multiculturels/antiracistes critiques. Cependant, on prétend que la prédominance de la globalisation comme idéologie économique et les changements éducatifs concomitants ont généré des conditions pour traiter de la différence sur l'angle d'une démocratie qui a grande fois dans le pouvoir du marché libre mais qui manque de confiance dans la possibilité d'efforts collectifs conscients de construire un bien public. Il n'y a aucun doute que le programme économique est en train d'influer sur la formation des citoyens dans nos écoles au moment même où les professeurs et les étudiants servent d'intermédiare entre ces influences. Pertinente à la compréhension de la construction d'un régime canadien est la clarification du concept de la démocratie à la lumière de l'exigence du marché, qui a pénétré dans la langue et la construction des significations.

Introduction

In recent years Canadian scholars and political and social commentators have produced a spate of books which attempt to grapple with what many authors claim is a crisis of identity among Canadians.[1] Will Kymlicka argues that perhaps the most devastating cause of this malaise is that English Canada has lost confidence in its ability to define itself. Kymlicka worries that in their confusion over identity, English Canadians can never negotiate a satisfactory resolution to meet the constitutional demands of the two other groups (Aboriginal and Québécois) which claim national status within the structure of the Canadian federation.[2] Formerly the dominant force in brokering the cultural identity of Canada, English Canada, he contends, continues to harbour a traditional conception of the meaning of nationality which does not permit multiple nations to reside in a single state. Kymlicka, in our view, provides the best conceptual basis for the analysis of the contemporary version of the national question in Canada. The constitutional instability which has resulted has been further aggravated by what Charles Taylor calls a process of fragmentation in English-Canadian society, a phenomenon which may have been initiated by the threat of federal disruption, a situation made demonstrably worse by the impact of globalization on the democratic process.[3] The latter influence, he argues, has the potential to suppress citizenship participation, that is, developing an increasing sense of alienation from any expression of meaningful politics beyond the expression of voting privileges. The recent demonstrations on the streets of Seattle which interrupted the meetings of the World Trade Organization illustrate the growing frustration on the part of grassroots organizations with their inability to effect change through regular political channels. Concurring with the concerns identified by Kymlicka and Taylor, in this article we shall study the role schools in English Canada ought to play in the area of citizenship formation in Canada.

Public schooling in English-speaking Canada developed from the mid-nineteenth century as a key social institution in the creation of a Canadian polity which reflected a dominant, although not uncontested, British heritage. During the past thirty years, public schools have been the primary arena where multiculturalism has been implemented as the new conception of identity formation. This paper situates multiculturalism and multicultural education in an historical context and reviews its limitations as it has developed since 1971. The paper opens a discussion on the impact of globalization on the practice of multicultural education and the more recent anti-racist education and on contemporary educational reform movements. The highly vocational orientation of educational reform has the potential to cloud issues of democracy and difference. Citizenship education has not so much disappeared from the schools as its understanding has been increasingly related to a market democracy based on the promotion of self-interest with little emphasis on the promotion of the public good. The paper contends that this tendency must be questioned if schools are to play any role in the development of a national identity or, to cast an even bleaker outlook on the future, if there is to be a Canada at all.

Our understanding of Canadian polity formation in relation to citizenship education is grounded on a pluralistic moral democracy that recognizes cultural retention as a fluid process, differentiated citizenship, and a social ethic of care that gives students a common ground in terms of who they are. The notion of cultural retention as a fluid process is based on the understanding that identity is not fixed, that one's identity is never complete, but is historical, contextual, relational, and always in the making. It would facilitate what Kymlicka refers to as a process of integration on fair terms without imposed assimilation.[4] Canada is, as Kymlika states, a poly-ethnic and multinational state containing three national groups, English, French, and Aboriginal, which, in turn, are racially and ethnically mixed.[5] "Differentiated citizenship," a category developed by Iris Young and used by Kymlicka to interpret Canadian reality, allows for recognition and accommodation of ethnic and national differences. Kymlicka identifies three forms of group-differentiated citizenship in Canada, each trying to accommodate ethnic and national differences — self-government rights, poly-ethnic rights, and special representation rights.[6] It is our contention that a social ethic of care would cultivate a collective concern for each individual and promote individual responsibility for the collective well-being (the common good). It goes hand in hand with a tradition of social rights. We are thinking of democracy as a "mode of being" in which pluralism would move beyond the plurality of values and views and recognize that adjudication of competing values and views of the good, of justice, etc., may have to take place.[7] This approach would provide a frame of reference to the multicultural/anti-racist teacher in relation, for example, to issues of equity in different traditions. The democratic ideal of citizenship education does not aim at perfect harmony or at eliminating power, but is concerned with "how to constitute forms of power that are compatible with democratic values."[8]

Teaching and learning practices should also lead to a critical understanding of Canadian and global reality in the related processes of learning to be Canadian and learning to be democratic in the contemporary global world. Multicultural/anti-racist education cannot be developed in isolation from the larger institutional framework of Canadian economic, social, and political life. We have in mind Heather-Jane Robertson's observation that Canadians, where education is concerned, have become too complacent about a utilitarian worldview associated with global corporate power.[9] We propose pedagogical principles that aim at creating a "mode of being," understood as a democratic orientation in life that works across difference and cultivates a public culture characterized by a critical engagement with lived experience.

Multiculturalism as an Articulating Principle: Historical Background

Public schooling in Canada developed along with the modern state.[10] Its primary aim from the start, according to educational historians, was to build social cohesion on terms established by the elite members of nineteenth-century British North American society. Although schooling has been a provincial responsibility since 1867 (there are now thirteen provincial and territorial public school systems), it is possible to identify a general trend in English-speaking Canada where schooling promoted an Anglo-conformist worldview, one based on a Protestant Christian morality in a British parliamentary tradition. Civic accommodation of the Roman Catholic demands for a separate institutional structure was usually granted. In Quebec, Church-dominated French-language education reflected ultramontane Catholic ideals, while a Protestant system developed on its own. The near exclusive authority of the provinces over education allowed for variation in the meaning of Canadian identity, each variation having at its core the common assumption of a pan-Canadian Anglo-conformity, at least outside Quebec.

By the first decade of the twentieth century the nation-building role of schooling had become firmly attached to the liberalism which accompanied the growth of the industrial corporate state. School administrators in the burgeoning urban areas of the country were particularly enthusiastic about the part public education should play in shaping social harmony and economic progress in Canada. Duties and responsibilities were emphasized, while the state's obligations were minimal until World War II. The British connection was less vociferously emphasized in the aftermath of the Great War, but it was never entirely abandoned in the English-Canadian schools.

Even under strong assimilationist educational policies, however, the Canadian polity was created and recreated in the schools, and, from very early on, people from different parts of the world "became Canadians on their own terms deploying various identities following attachments and identifications."[11] There has also been a long-standing Canadian way of seeing Canada as a "mosaic" and comparing it to the "melting pot" of the United States. Even with assimilation, there was some room for difference. Indeed, a particular English-Canadian identity developed through lived experience. As Rosa Bruno-Jofré concluded in her analysis of schooling and citizenship in Manitoba between 1919 and 1945, "in the process of Canadianization the school became a public site where consciousness of collective identity, family values and identity, political standpoints, ways of talking, intersected with the official discourse of how to govern the soul and become a good citizen."[12] Oral narratives also indicate that in school districts where there was no collective action on the part of minorities, dissension from the norm could be threatening for school children. Kymlicka's notion of integration through cultural retention makes sense in light of oral histories of school experience.

The new international reality after World War II affected Canadians' view of themselves. The war had led to a questioning of racist and ethnocentric ideas, and theories of cultural relativism began to emerge. The decolonizing, liberating movements of the sixties increased this tendency. The civil rights movement in the United States and the women's movement, both in the United States and Canada, had an impact on society and on education. The Quebec/Canada issue began to show the potential for a crisis of citizenship and even of community when the language of education became a full fledged political issue and a breakup of Canada began to loom as a possibility. A movement toward political and cultural accommodation and change began to take place.[13] All of this was taking place in the 1950s and 1960s at the same time as the modern welfare state was being constructed in Canada, and there was a general mood of expansiveness in the country.

Multiculturalism, by and large, was developed as the practical articulating principle that offered an avenue to deal with issues of identity, allegiances, and with the place of Canada in the world. The Quiet Revolution in Quebec during the 1960s and the work of the Royal Commission on Bilingualism and Biculturalism (1963-70) set the stage for this development. The principle was also an attempt to reconcile the conflicting values of Québécois, English-Canadians, and those of non-Anglo and non-French descent. The principle was established by Pierre Trudeau's assertion in 1971 that Canada was a multicultural country within a bilingual context and that the federal government would take steps to give public recognition to ethnic diversity through the introduction of a policy of multiculturalism.[14]

In our view, multiculturalism and multicultural education acknowledged diversity as a key element of the Canadian identity and led to a redefinition of the common good as the development of a climate that would encourage social integration, while acknowledging difference, and facilitate a re-accommodation of French and Aboriginal issues within the Canadian federal state. Philosophically, Trudeau's multiculturalism was rooted in the liberal ideal of equalitarianism by encouraging cultural retention and integration within a framework of individual choice and the existence of a welfare state. The schools were expected to play a role in the construction of a multicultural Canada where cultural retention was encouraged, although there was little clarification of what cultural retention entailed and no indication of where the boundaries of demarcation, if any, should be.

Multicultural/Anti-Racist Education:
Social Integration and the National Question

In Canada, multiculturalism became the implicit core of the new educational discourse of citizenship. Since education is a provincial responsibility, multicultural education was implemented during the 1970s and 1980s at different times and with different emphases. Multicultural education policies and practices reflected the unique immigration history of Canadian provinces, thus acquiring regionalist overtones. For example, during the 1970s in British Columbia the efforts were directed toward ESL programs and the teaching of non-official languages, designated as heritage languages, particularly in the urban areas of the province. Elsewhere, for example, in Saskatchewan, Manitoba, Ontario, and Alberta, more extensive multicultural programs were developed. In those areas of the country such as New Brunswick and Nova Scotia, which lacked large communities of newcomers, it took longer for schools to embrace the new multicultural agenda, and, naturally enough, when it was introduced their provincial versions were steeped in their own historical heritage.[15] The Quebec government developed its own policy in relation to ethno-cultural groups, which it called "interculturalism." Quebec policy affirms the recognition of French as the language of public life, respect for liberal democratic values, and respect for pluralism.

The scholarly literature in multicultural education tended to be highly descriptive and locked in a cultural discourse that focussed on developments within Canada with some comparative references within the English-speaking developed world.[16] The understanding of colonization and post-colonization was not an integral part of multicultural education, however. Issues of global injustice and the global community were discussed not in the context of multicultural education, but under development education and international or global education, along with the work of non-governmental organizations such as OXFAM, Development and Peace, and centres for international work. Development education looked like an external version of multiculturalism aimed at making Canadians feel at home in a world of cultural diversity, but one that often developed strongly critical views on issues of global education and social justice.

In its early years of intellectual formulation, scholars writing about multicultural education mostly treated the multi-ethnic character of Canada as a discrete and self-contained social category which could be analysed without taking account of class and gender. John Porter's seminal work, *The Vertical Mosaic*, was always referenced, but his discussion of the mal-distribution of power in Canadian society was largely overlooked by multicultural educators. In a very influential theoretical article which appeared in 1979, for example, Jonathan Young disconnected the class question from his conception of a plural society by isolating his models of ethnic relations from what he termed the "social structure."[17] Young was not alone in making this crucial disengagement, which had the effect of implicitly casting an individualist liberal hue over the multicultural design in Canada. Accordingly, the good society was that which provided for diversity in the schools with minorities, if they chose to do so, exercising the freedom to retain their ethnic culture. The lack of consideration of socio-economic inequalities was pointed out by those committed to critical pedagogy and by those who understood multiculturalism beyond culture.[18]

Under multiculturalism, integration was conceived within the framework of cultural retention, thus bringing fairness to the process and, naturally, it was recognized that schools had an important role to play.[19] Multicultural educators, however, did not develop a framework to deal with possible limits to cultural retention in light of issues of gender equity, for example, or of the articulation of race and class. Nor, for that matter, did they develop pedagogical resources to equip students with the ability to deal with tensions between individual freedoms and demands from the specific communities, and to make their own decisions. In practice, liberal tolerance was the essential quality to be developed in this citizenship paradigm well into the eighties. By and large, a lack of conceptual clarification, abundance of tensions, and a failure to address pressing social and political issues characterized the writing and practice of multicultural education.[20]

From the start, multiculturalism as an ideology and multicultural education as a practice of citizenship formation did not develop an adequate response to contemporary nationalist demands on the part of French and Aboriginal Canadians, who perceived themselves as more than ethnic groups in the cultural and political fabric of the country. In 1976, the Parti Québécois won the November Quebec election, and on May 20, 1980 the first referendum on Quebec sovereignty took place. No less important, the Constitution Act of 1982 recognized Aboriginal Peoples as a unique entity within the Canadian state. It was almost as if those who were writing in the area of multicultural education in the 1970s and early 1980s refused to acknowledge the constitutional crisis that existed in the country. By the same token, issues related to Aboriginal education and issues of identity formation were not addressed in terms of the national question.

Perhaps the most significant shift from the dominant culturalist liberal approach, which emphasized the sensitization and celebration of difference, came in 1987 with the publication of two books. The first, *Breaking the Mosaic*, edited by Jon Young, was a collection of papers from a symposium, "Race, Ethnicity, and Education: Critical Perspectives," which had been held in Toronto in 1984.[21] It presented a powerful critique of the shortcomings of the existing theory and practice of multicultural education in Canada from the perspective of critical pedagogy. The contributors made an effort to theorize and understand exploitation and oppression in schooling and beyond.[22] The second important publication, *The Political Economy of Canadian Education*, was also a collection of articles, edited by Terry Wotherspoon of the University of Saskatchewan, with most of the contributors from Western Canada.[23] By the beginning of the 1990s, the analysis of systemic racial discrimination, the histories and practices that are integral parts of prejudice, the political structures sustaining racism and sexism, institutionalized racism in the classroom, and differential distribution of power became central issues in anti-racist education.[24] This oppositional approach is concerned with the realization of equality, justice, and emancipation in the school and in wider society. It is a refreshingly critical strand of analysis which also brought an epistemology that considered voice and representation and focussed on the learning environment and the lived experience of students and on identity politics. Moreover, as George Sefa Dei has written, "It [anti-racist education] is also about investigating and changing how schools deal with issues of White privilege and power-sharing."[25]

What about Globalization:
Democracy, Yes. But What Democracy?

Multicultural and anti-racist educators in Canada have not positioned their arguments in relation to school reform and globalization, the latter understood as an economic ideology as well as the development of world media spaces.[26] At the same time, the literature on school reform, while attending to issues of diversity, tends to neglect the analysis of the impact of globalization (in Canada, it takes the form of Americanization) on population changes and on multicultural/anti-racist practices in schools.[27] Indeed, the thrust of economic globalization, which aims at the penetration of the market into every aspect of life, resides in the pursuit of a homogeneous culture where the emphasis of citizenship is on consumerism and efficient production. As happened with multicultural education in the 1970s, by and large multicultural/anti-racist educators and school reform analysts refer to, but do not deeply examine, global educational issues.[28] Many education scholars, we suggest, are contributing with their timid political analysis to the surreptitious introduction of a school reform agenda which supports corporate economic interests.

Although in the 1990s, *Our Schools/Ourselves*, a journal for Canadian education activists, did provide a forum for discussing the corporate agenda and its relation to education politics, articles generally failed to consider the impact of globalization on national and provincial multicultural policies. There has also been an increasingly substantial body of literature that critically examines educational reform in Alberta and Ontario,[29] and well-known educationists such as Michael Apple, Peter McLaren, and David Livingston have addressed the socio-economic features of current educational restructuring under global capitalism in the United States and Canada in a comprehensive manner.[30] The latter writers explore how educational objectives reveal a new set of ideological commitments.[31] However, there is a need to critically examine the school reform movement in Canada and the process of internationalization in relation to multicultural/anti-racist education. School boards in Canada are marketing their schools overseas among the upper classes and changing the school population with the introduction of foreign students, most of them visible minorities whose parents are able to pay their way into Canadian schools.[32]

We acknowledge that there has been a marked improvement in the recognition of difference in current educational policy documents in Canada.[33] The political reality of the country (including the Charter of Rights) makes anti-racist and Aboriginal perspectives and the promotion of gender equality imperative. However, we think that a crucial problem exists in the constraining power of curriculum documents, standards tests, and much of the rest of the reform initiatives. In writing about student teachers' experiences in relation to school reform, Young and Graham have noted that a combination of circumstances, including the new emphasis on essential learning and a curriculum development process that does not stress social studies, deflects teachers' attention away from anti-racist education.[34] In our view, their study points out a serious practical matter, but we also think that there is room for an active mediation on the part of teachers, grounded on a politically reflective practice that relates the classroom to the larger community. Globalization, as a dominant economic ideology as well as a product of the information age, adds a new dimension to the treatment of diversity in the classroom, one that was not as evident in the 1970s and 1980s, and multicultural/ anti-racist educators need to broaden their analysis to take it into account.

The rhetoric related to the knowledge-based economy with its discourse of life-long learning, understood as the link between education/ training and economic strategy, has come to set parameters for important components of schooling. In this view, the individual becomes responsible for developing further skills and competencies, and schools are supposed to set the appropriate bases for that actualization to take place. By placing responsibility on individuals to upgrade themselves throughout their lives, the global knowledge-based economy privatizes the educational process. The responsibility is removed from employers and government agencies, thus abandoning an important area of public good.

Globalization generates conditions to deal with difference in terms of a democracy that has great faith in the power of the free market and lacks confidence in the possibility of conscious collective efforts to build and serve a public good. The current emphasis on private interest represents a shift between two historically competing traditions of democracy, from one related to the understanding of the democratic process as linked to the public good to another linked to the promotion of competing private interests.[35] The increasing dominance of a democracy thought of in terms of advancing the private interest takes on new characteristics in the context of the global market, the role of corporate power in civil society

– including schooling – and the impact of communication technology. This trend has little regard and/or room for dissenting views and even less for socially active interest groups. The free-market oriented Fraser Institute, for example, often attacks organized public concerns and the role of schooling when dealing with such issues as the environment and equity. In one of its publications, grade-school textbooks were condemned for teaching environmentalism: "Preaching the media-hyped misinformation known as environmentalism to grade-school children is no more a worthy use of our resources than preaching creationism, feminism, chauvinism, Lutheranism, or libertarianism."[36]

As a strong supporter of the globalization agenda, the Fraser Institute is not articulating an anti-democratic position, but, rather, a version of democracy which perceives private interests, individualism, and the market place as the proper mediators and generators of a common ground. It has no conception of a public good which, if it exists at all, is seen as the aggregation of private interests. In the public discourse expounded in the press and in some economic publications, the concepts of freedom and democracy are being increasingly associated with new corporate concepts, and it is not unusual to read phrases like "freedom of commercial speech," "freedom of choice in education," and "freedom in the labour market."[37] This new market language needs to be deconstructed to unveil vested interests in reproposing notions of freedom and democracy. Clarification of the concept of democracy and of the notion of the democratic citizen would provide educational meaning to commonly used concepts such as participation, active citizen, choice, responsible citizenship, social justice, global citizenship, anti-racist efforts, gender equity, etc. It would help to clarify the meaning(s) of many of the components of current educational reform.

There is also tension in current educational documents and at policy makers' meetings between a privatized market notion of democracy and an eclectic moral democracy as reflected in the language and in the issues on the agenda of continental meetings. At the conference held by the Canadian Foundation for the Americas (FOCAL) in Toronto on November 19-21, 1998, for example, educators from this hemisphere tried to build a common agenda for educational reform. Chile and Argentina addressed the reforms taking place in their countries through processes of decentralization, privatization, extension of the school day, and the use of assessment and evaluation procedures. At the same time, there were discussions on Aboriginal education, the role of civil society, the role of major multilateral banks in promoting and implementing educational reforms, and around a multilateral educational reform program led by the Inter-American Dialogue in Washington.[38] While education reform in the Americas is designed within the framework of a market democracy, there are social issues in the civil society that policy makers need to address with some eclecticism if member countries are to avoid social upheavals.

Iris Young conceptualizes the privatized notion of democracy as interest-based democracy, which she describes "as a process of expressing one's preferences and demands, and registering them in a vote."[39] In her view, in this kind of process individuals and interest groups vote for policies which they perceive to serve their interests, with the aggregated outcome constituting the public interest. This approach to democracy minimizes state participation, and individuals do not need to leave their subjective point of view or address collective issues as different to their individual needs and goals. It is important, however, to understand that, as Young indicates, pluralism can still have room in a privatized democracy since self-interest can be pursued in groups within an individualist frame of reference.[40] The privatized model of democracy corresponds to the market model of democracy described by Wilfred Carr and tends to be dominant in western liberal democracies.[41] But democracy can also be conceived of as a moral ideal, never fully achieved.[42] In our view, an ethic of care attentive to individual and social responsibilities should permeate forms of power in a democratic moral society, and we concur with Carr when he says that social rights are not only justified on humanitarian grounds, but they are also essential to deal with social and economic inequalities that are incompatible with the tenets of a moral participatory democracy.[43] This model, however, needs to be exercised across difference. Young proposes that differences of social position and identity "function as a resource for public reason," thus broadening the recognition of communicative forms beyond deliberation and allowing citizens to speak across difference where there is no shared understanding.[44]

New approaches to multicultural anti-racist education have made a strong argument in favour of questioning existing oppressive social and political structures, opening democratic spaces, and unveiling institutionalized racism in the classroom. In our view, teachers also need to consider the meanings of democratic citizenship in the Canadian context, the economic and political implications of emphasizing certain skills and outcomes, and the relevance of community building, "while seeking a regard for distinctiveness as well as reaching toward connectedness."[45] One of the main issues that has been raised but not fully addressed by multicultural/anti-racist educators is the danger of addressing issues of difference, but leaving the common ground to be eclectically defined by the market (corporate power). We use the term eclectic because we are aware of the fluid character of political life. At the core of multicultural/anti-racist education is the issue of citizenship and its articulation in educational discourse and practice.[46]

Ken Osborne has written in connection with citizenship and teaching that "[t]eachers must have a clearly articulated and ethically defensible vision of education and of citizenship and of the connection between the two."[47] This is one of the eight principles that, in his view, teachers should consider when selecting teaching strategies and organizing their classrooms. Although we can only initiate the pedagogical conversation here, we will add to Osborne's principles that, in light of the role of the market in every aspect of life and concomitant hegemonic values of self-interest and individualism, teachers should be able to understand critically the forces at play in a market and global society. The aim is to encourage a balanced and healthy view of market "efficiency" in relation to the other components of a free society. A statement by Charles Taylor is pertinent to our argument:

> We can't abolish the market, nor can we organize ourselves exclusively through markets. To restrict them may be costly; not to restrict them at all would be fatal. Governing a contemporary society is continually recreating a balance between requirements that tend to undercut each other, constantly finding creative new solutions as the old equilibria become stultifying.[48]

In light of the dangerous tendency to see democracy as neutral, teachers must be able to distinguish different concepts of democracy and concomitant values and explore the notion of public good in relation to the students' lived experience. This approach is motivated by relevant scholarship that calls attention to the increasing neglect of the common good in favour of self-interest.[49] Given the need to develop an inclusive disposition to citizenship in the Canadian context, teachers should understand Canada as a multi-nation and poly-ethnic state, as defined by Kymlicka, in a global context. The articulation of a citizen of Canada and the world as a doubter (a term coined by John Ralston Saul[50]) would set a basis to encourage a decentered humanism that rescues community sensitivity and restores ideas which are central to social solidarity. Within this frame of reference teacher candidates would be stimulated 1) to pay attention to forms of economic development that are ecologically sensitive; 2) to emphasize respect for human rights including recognition of racism, sexism, and classism as important categories in the analysis of systemic and individual forms of discrimination, in particular within the framework of teacher research; 3) to generate an understanding of civil rights and obligations; 4) to search for a dialogical approach to settling conflict (question violence); 5) to cultivate public participation as a moral imperative. Regrettably political commentators on neither the left nor the right have considered the place of difference and the construction of meanings in their analysis of schooling and globalization. Teacher researchers from the classroom, in partnership with university-based educators and other parties in the educational process, have the task of making difference a fundamental feature of our public culture.

Conclusion

While multiculturalism acknowledged diversity as a key element of Canadian identity, thus formally moving away from the Anglo-conformist ethos that had dominated Canadian education, in particular in English Canada, its implementation in the educational setting contained important limitations. Multicultural education did not address at all, or did so only in a fragmentary manner, the main issues concerning the national question with respect to the legitimate nationalist aspirations of the Aboriginal and Québéc peoples. Moreover, multicultural education tended to have a culturalist tone, and by and large treated ethnicity as a discrete social category not articulated with class and gender. Anti-racist education developed in the United States, Canada, and Great Britain as a reaction to the limitations of multicultural education and the persistence in schools of systemic racism along with social inequalities. Oppositional in character, it is concerned with the structures sustaining racism and the differential distribution of power. However, we think that the dominance of globalization as an economic ideology and the changes that are being brought to education in its name are generating new scenarios which demand careful consideration by multicultural/anti-racist educators. This situation needs to be addressed more fully.

Multicultural/anti-racist educators, in our view, must pay more attention in their pedagogic strategies to the new layer of meaning generated by globalization in the classroom and beyond. For example, the presence of upper class students from the third world in Canadian classrooms introduces a new dimension to the issue of diversity. Moreover, the development of a multicultural/anti-racist education is influenced by educational reform which has taken on a world character. We note in this paper with some concern that the discussion of educational reform in Canada does not include a meaningful analysis of its relation with the globalization process understood as an economic ideology. This is an ideology centred in the market, having little concern with conscious collective efforts to build a space to define and redefine a public good. There is no doubt that the economic agenda is influencing citizenship formation in our schools even as teachers and students mediate those influences.

Citizenship education is at the core of all educational processes. It is, therefore, important for educators to have an understanding of the various approaches to the building of a Canadian polity. Relevant to this end is the search for clarification of the concept of democracy in light of the market imperative which has permeated language and the construction of meanings. We advance as a pedagogical theme a Canadian polity based on a pluralistic moral democracy that recognizes a fluid concept of cultural retention, a decentered humanism, differentiated citizenship, as outlined by Kymlicka (based on an understanding of Canada as a poly-ethnic and multinational state), and a social ethic of care that aims at generating a common ground in the building of Canadian identity.

NOTES

1. A recent review discusses over three dozen books which have been published in the 1990s on the question of Canadian unity. Ian McKay identifies himself as a "lapsed Canadian" to underline his own sense of futility in ever finding a satisfactory resolution in the present circumstances. See his "After Canada: On Amnesia and Apocalypse in the Contemporary Crisis," *Acadiensis* 28, no.1 (1998): 76-97. The "Canada question" is hardly new. The first significant work on this issue was published by the British liberal philosopher Goldwin Smith, whose 1891 book advocated Canadian union with the United States. See Goldwin Smith, *Canada and the Canadian Question* (1891; reprint, Toronto: University of Toronto Press, 1971).

2. In a recent analysis, Will Kymlicka claims that the official multicultural policy has greatly enhanced the integration of immigrants into society. During the period in which Canada has become a poly-ethnic society, however, attempts to re-shape the constitution to reflect its multinational character have ended in failure. See his *Finding Our Way: Rethinking Ethnocultural Relations in Canada* (Toronto: Oxford University Press, 1998).

3. Charles Taylor, *The Ethics of Authenticity* (Cambridge: Harvard University Press, 1992).

4. Kymlicka, "The Theory and Practice of Canadian Multiculturalism" (speech at Breakfast on the Hill, Ottawa, 23 November 1998).

5. Kymlicka, "Three Forms of Group-Differentiated Citizenship in Canada," in *Democracy and Difference: Contesting the Boundaries of the Political*, ed. Seyla Benhabib (Princeton: Princeton University Press, 1996), 155.

6. Ibid.

7. See Benhabib, introduction to *Democracy and Difference*, 8, and chapters 12 and 20.

8. Chantal Mouffe, "Democracy, Power, and the 'Political,' " in *Democracy and Difference*, 248.

9. Heather-Jane Robertson, *No More Teachers, No More Books: The Commercialization of Canada's Schools* (Toronto: McClelland and Stewart, 1998). See also Marita Moll, ed., *Tech High: Globalization and the Future of Canadian Education: A Collection of Critical Perspectives on Social, Cultural, and Political Dilemmas* (Ottawa: Canadian Centre for Policy Alternatives; Halifax: Fernwood Publishing, 1997). A related theme to the new technology has been the new trading relationship with the United States which, critics argue, threatens Canadian sovereignty by exposing public institutions to the demands of American corporate interests. See John Calvert and Larry Kuehn, *Pandora's Box: Corporate Power, Free Trade, and Canadian Education* (Toronto: Our Schools/Our Selves Education Foundation, 1993); Maude Barlow and Heather-Jane Robertson, *Class Warfare: The Assault on Canada's Schools* (Toronto: Key Porter, 1994).

10. The literature on the historical development of schooling in Canada is voluminous. For a short synthesis of its early history, see Paul Axelrod, *The Promise of Schooling: Education in Canada, 1800-1914* (Toronto: University of Toronto Press, 1997). Most of the literature has been written from a provincial perspective. More recent works include Jean Barman, Neil Sutherland, and J. Donald Wilson, eds., *Children, Teachers, and Schools in the History of British Columbia* (Calgary: Detselig Enterprises, 1995); Nancy M. Sheehan, J. Donald Wilson, and David C. Jones, eds., *Schools in the West: Essays in Canadian Educational History* (Calgary: Detselig Enterprises, 1986); Susan E. Houston and Alison Prentice, *Schooling and Scholars in Nineteenth-Century Ontario* (Toronto: University of Toronto Press, 1988); Bruce Curtis, *Building the Educational State: Canada West, 1836-1871* (London, ON: Althouse Press, 1988); Dick Henley, "The Origins of State Schooling and the Design of Administrative Structure in Nova Scotia, 1850-1878," in *Papers on Contemporary Issues in Educational Policy and Administration in Canada: A Foundations Perspective*, ed. Rosa Bruno-Jofré and Lois Grieger, Monographs in Education 23 (Winnipeg: Faculty of Education, University of Manitoba, 1996), 3-31. Manitoba did not concede special status to the Roman Catholic minority. See Rosa del C. Bruno-Jofré, ed., *Issues in the*

History of Education in Manitoba: From the Construction of the Common School to the Politics of Voices (Lewiston, NY: Edwin Mellen Press, 1993); and Rosa Bruno-Jofré, "Citizenship and Schooling in Manitoba, 1918-1945," *Manitoba History* 36 (1998-1999): 26-36. The journal *Historical Studies in Education/Revue d'histoire de l' education* is also a valuable source.

11. Bruno-Jofré, "Citizenship and Schooling in Manitoba, 1918-1945," 35.

12. Ibid.

13. Rosa Bruno-Jofré, "Manitoba Schooling in the Canadian Context and the Building of a Polity: 1919-1971," *Canadian and International Education* 28, no. 2 (1999): 111.

14. Ibid.

15. Donald Wilson, "Multicultural Programmes in Canadian Education," in *Multiculturalism in Canada: Social and Educational Perspectives*, ed. Ronald J. Samuda, John W. Berry, and Michel Laferrière (Toronto: Allyn and Bacon, 1984), 62-77; and Marie McAndrew, "Ethnicity, Multiculturalism, and Multicultural Education in Canada," in *Social Change and Education in Canada*, ed. Ratna Ghosh and Douglas Ray, 3d ed. (Toronto: Harcourt Brace, Canada, 1995), 165-177.

16. From time to time, collections of works related to the developing conception of multiculturalism were published. See, for example, articles marking its tenth anniversary as an official national policy in *Education and Canadian Multiculturalism: Some Problems and Some Solutions*, ed. Daniel Dorotich, 8th yearbook (Saskatoon: Canadian Society for the Study of Education, 1981) and *History and Social Science Teacher* 17, no. 1 (1981). Probably the two most influential collections were: John R. Mallea and Jonathan C. Young, eds., *Cultural Diversity and Canadian Education: Issues and Innovations* (Ottawa: Carleton University Press, 1984) and Samuda et al., eds., *Multiculturalism in Canada*.

17. Jonathan C. Young, "Education in a Multicultural Society: What Sort of Education? What Sort of Society?" *Canadian Journal of Education* 4, no. 3 (1979): 6-7.

18. See Ken Osborne, "Class or Culture?" in *Intercultural Education and Community Development: Papers Presented at a Symposium at the Faculty of Education, University of Toronto*, ed. Keith Mcleod (Toronto: Guidance Centre, Faculty of Education, University of Toronto, 1980), 94-98; also Christopher Bagley, "Multiculturalism, Class, and Ideology: A European-Canadian

Comparison," in *Multicultural Education: The Interminable Debate*, ed. Sohan Modgil, G. Verma, K. Mallick, and C. Modgil (London: Falmer Press, 1986), 49-59.

19. Kymlicka, "The Theory and Practice of Canadian Multiculturalism."

20. For an analysis, see Kogila A. Moodley, "Multicultural Education in Canada: Historical Development and Current Status," in *Handbook of Research on Multicultural Education*, ed. James A. Banks (New York: MacMillan, 1995), 801-820. For an exploration of the meaning of multiculturalism in academic writing in Canada and the United States, see Helen Raptis and Thomas Fleming, "Unraveling Multicultural Education's Meanings: An Analysis of Core Assumptions Found in Academic Writings in Canada and the United States, 1981-1997," *Journal of Educational Thought* 32, no. 2 (1998): 169-194.

21. Jon Young, ed., *Breaking the Mosaic: Ethnic Identities in Canadian Schooling* (Toronto: Garamond Press, 1987).

22. We have already said that multicultural education in Canada had, from the beginning, been characterized by regional variations. *Breaking the Mosaic,* it should be noted, was largely a product of scholars associated with the Ontario Institute for Studies in Education (OISE), where professors Roger Simon and Philip Corrigan and a powerful cohort of students and former students, including Kari Dehli, Nancy Jackson, Enid Lee, Magda Lewis, Ann Manicom, and Roxana Ng, were regular participants in a blossoming critical pedagogy group. All subsequently became leaders in the anti-racist education movement in Canada.

23. Terry Wotherspoon, ed., *The Political Economy of Canadian Schooling* (Toronto: Methuen, 1987).

24. Goli Rezai-Rashti, "Multicultural Education, Anti-Racist Education, and Critical Pedagogy: Reflections on Everyday Practice," in *Anti-Racism, Feminism, and Critical Approaches to Education*, ed. Roxana Ng, Pat Staton, and Joyce Scane (Westport: Bergin and Garvey, 1995), 7.

25. George J. Sefa Dei, *Anti-Racism Education: Theory and Practice* (Halifax: Fernwood Publishing, 1996), 9. See also Patrick Solomon, *Black Resistance in High School: Forging a Separatist Culture* (New York: State University of New York Press, 1992); Carl E. James, *Perspectives on Racism and the Human Services Sector: A Case for Change* (Toronto: University of Toronto Press, 1996); Elizabeth McIsaac, George J. Sefa Dei, John Ogbu, Josephine

Mazzuca, and Jasmin Zine, *Reconstructing 'Dropout': A Critical Ethnography of the Dynamics of Black Students' Disengagement from School* (Toronto: University of Toronto Press, 1997); and Carl E. James, "Contradictory Tensions in the Experiences of African Canadians in a Faculty of Education with an Access Program," *Canadian Journal of Education* 22, no.2 (1997): 158-174.

26. In the context of educational reform, globalization refers to the market forces and their penetration everywhere, as well as the development of world media spaces. There is no analysis in most Canadian discussions of educational reform of the international migrations and consequent diversification of the population as a result of the economic process of globalization. For a discussion of globalization, see Charles Taylor, "Globalization and the Future of Canada," *Queen's Quarterly* 105, no.3 (1998): 331-332.

27. For example, Ben Levin mentions neoliberalism and acknowledges that the corporate global economy informed educational policy-making in Canada, but this insight is not integrated into the possibility for agency, thus making the analysis a functionalist one. See Jon Young and Ben Levin, "Education in Transition–Canada," in *The World Yearbook 2000: Education in Transition*, ed. David Coulby, Robert Cowen, and Crispin Jones (London: Kogan Page, forthcoming).

28. Dei raises the question of globalization in the context of anti-racist education in his 1996 book, for example, but does not fully develop the relationship. See Dei, *Anti-Racism Education*, 68-69. Since its publication, Canada has become very involved in hemispheric developments in education. Canada played a role in the development of the Plan of Action for Education, adopted by thirty-four heads of state at the Santiago (Chile) Summit of the Americas in 1998. At that meeting, participating countries agreed to negotiate the Free Trade Area of the Americas by the year 2005 and educational reform was identified as an essential component of the structural changes needed in advance of any hemispheric free trade agreement. The summit was followed by a conference, sponsored by the Canadian Foundation for the Americas, in Toronto in November, 1998, which was devoted to educational reform and included among its attendees representatives of Canadian provincial ministries of education, ministries of education from Chile and Argentina, the World Bank, the Inter-American Development Bank, the Canadian International Development Agency, federal departments, teachers' unions, professors, students

from the Ontario Institute for Studies in Education, a large group of Chilean school principals, and experts in education from across the Americas. See "Educational Reform in the Americas," *FOCAL Update* (January 1999):1.

29. For example, Trevor W. Harrison and Jerrold L. Kachur, eds., *Contested Classrooms: Education, Globalization, and Democracy in Alberta* (Edmonton: University of Alberta Press and Parkland Institute, 1999); Philip Brown, "The 'Third Wave': Education and the Ideology of Parentocracy," in *Education, Culture, Economy, Society,* ed. A.H. Halsey, Hugh Lauder, Philip Brown, and Amy Stuart Wells (Oxford: Oxford University Press, 1997), 393-408; Carol Anne Wien and Curt Dudley-Marling, "Limited Vision: The Ontario Curriculum and Outcomes-Based Learning," *Canadian Journal of Education* 23, no. 4 (1998): 405-420. For an analysis grounded in political economy, see Barlow and Robertson, *Class Warfare.*

30. Peter McLaren, "Revolutionary Pedagogy in Post-Revolutionary Times: Rethinking the Political Economy of Critical Education," *Educational Theory* 48, no. 4 (1998): 431-462; Peter McLaren, "Contesting Capital: Critical Pedagogy and Globalism: A Response to Michael Apple," *Current Issues in Comparative Education* 1, no. 2 (1999) [journal online]; available from <http:www.tc.columbia.edu>; Internet; accessed 26 October 2000; Peter McLaren and Rodolfo Torres, "Racism and Multicultural Education: Rethinking 'Race' and 'Whiteness' in Late Capitalism," in *Critical Multiculturalism: Rethinking Multicultural and Antiracist Education,* ed. Stephen May (London: Falmer Press, 1999), 42-76; and Michael W. Apple, "The Absent Presence of Race in Educational Reform," *Race, Ethnicity, and Education* 2, no.1 (1999): 9-16. An important Canadian book is David W. Livingston, *The Education-Jobs Gap* (Toronto: Garamond Press, 1999).

31. Michael Apple, "Rhetorical Reforms: Markets, Standards, and Inequality," *Current Issues in Comparative Education* 1, no. 2 (1999) [journal online]; available from <http://www.tc.columbia.edu/cice/vol01nr2/mwaart1.htm>; Internet; accessed 14 January 2000; and McLaren, "Contesting Capital."

32. There were almost 100,000 foreign students studying at all levels of education in Canada in 1997, generating a total revenue of $2.7 billion, behind only the export of wheat in terms of trade value,

according to a federal government report. See Department of Foreign Affairs and International Trade, *Overview of the Canadian Education Industry* (Ottawa: Department of Foreign Affairs and International Trade, 1998), 1-2 [online]; available from <http://www.dfait-maeci.gc.ca/culture/educationmarketing/menu-e.htm>; Internet; accessed 26 October 2000

33. See Alan Sears and Andrew S. Hughes, "Citizenship Education and Current Educational Reform," *Canadian Journal of Education* 21, no. 2 (1996): 123-142.

34. Jon Young and Robert J. Graham, "School and Curriculum Reform: Manitoba Frameworks and Multicultural Teacher Education," below, pp. 181-198.

35. For a discussion by Michael Ignatieff, John Ralston Saul, Mark Kingwell, and others about the threat posed to Canadian conceptions of the public good by the ideologically-driven global agenda, see *Toward the Common Good*, special issue of *Queen's Quarterly* 106, no. 1 (1999).

36. Laura Jones and Liv Fredricksen, "The Greening of Education: What are Grade School Textbooks Teaching Children about the Environment?" *Fraser Forum* (September 1997): 35 [journal online]; available from <http://www.fraserinstitute.ca/publications/forum/1997/September/coverstory.html#greening>; Internet; accessed 26 October 2000;. For a critique of the Fraser Institute and its educational policies, see Erika Shaker, "The North American Education Industry and Education Restructuring in Canada," *Education, Limited* 1, no.1 (1998): 41-47 [journal online]; available from <http://www.policyalternatives.ca/eduproj/index.html>; Internet; accessed 26 October, 2000.

37. Shaker, "North American Education Industry," 39.

38. See "Educational Reforms in the Americas," *FOCAL Update* (January 1999): 1. The Canadian Foundation for the Americas (FOCAL) is funded by the Department of Foreign Affairs and International Trade, the Canadian International Development Agency (CIDA) and other public and private sector organizations, as well as inter-American institutions.

39. Iris Marion Young, "Communication and the Other: Beyond Deliberative Democracy," in *Democracy and Difference*, ed. Benhabib, 122.

40. Ibid, 121.

41. Wilfred Carr, "Becoming a Citizen: Civic Education in a Democratic Society" (paper presented at the International Symposium on Human Development and Education, Universidad Complutense de Madrid, Madrid, October 1991).

42. Ibid.

43. Ibid.

44. Young, "Communication and the Other," 127.

45. Maxine Greene, "The Passions of Pluralism: Multiculturalism and the Expanding Community," *Educational Researcher* 22, no. 1 (1993): 13.

46. For a conceptual framework of citizenship that rests on national identity, social, cultural, and supranational belonging, an effective system of rights, and political and civic participation, see France Gagnon and Michel Pagé, *Conceptual Framework and Analysis*, vol. 1 of *Conceptual Framework for an Analysis of Citizenship in the Liberal Democracies* ([Ottawa]: Department of Canadian Heritage, Citizens' Participation, Multiculturalism, and Strategic Research and Analysis Directorates, May 1999). Also see Yvonne Hébert, "Citizenship Education: Towards a Pedagogy of Social Participation and Identity Formation," *Canadian Ethnic Studies/ Études ethnique au Canada* 29, no. 2 (1997): 82-96.

47. Ken Osborne, "Citizenship Education and Social Studies," in *Trends and Issues in Canadian Social Studies*, ed. Ian Wright (Vancouver: Pacific Educational Press, 1997), 57.

48. Taylor, *Ethics of Authenticity*, 110-111.

49. See, for example, Taylor, "Globalization and the Future of Canada."

50. John Ralston Saul, *The Unconscious Civilization* (Concorde, ON: House of Anansi Press, 1995); and his *The Doubter's Companion: A Dictionary of Aggressive Common Sense* (Toronto: Viking, 1994).

4 Pluralism, Corporatism, and Educating Citizens

ERIC W. STOCKDEN

ABSTRACT/RÉSUMÉ

Educating for citizenship is faced with many obstacles not the least of which is the ambiguity of citizenship itself. Problematic, too, are the possible forms such an education may take, since schooling is influenced by claims to political legitimacy and the varieties of civic initiation that evolve from such assertions. The disparate senses of public interest are noted as is the increasing role of corporatism in liberal democracies with its attendant claim to determine the scope of citizenship. Also discussed is the requirement of the state to provide an education for citizenship based on the notion that it ought to be one with a democratic society's basic ideals. But it is suggested that the pursuit of group interests significantly hinders the attainment of this objective. The work suggests that an education for citizenship in a democratic polity, where political legitimacy lies with individual citizens, will most likely be achieved through a liberal education designed for that purpose. However, the paper indicates that such an end will only be successfully pursued if the influence on public education of corporatism, and corporate capitalism in particular, is substantially diminished.

L'éducation pour la citoyenneté fait face à plusieurs obstacles, en particulier l'ambiguité de la citoyenneté elle-même. Ce qui est aussi problématique est les formes possibles que revêtira une telle éducation puisque l'instruction est influée par des prétentions à la légitimité politique et les variétés d'initiation civique qui se développent sur la base de telles assertions. On remarque aussi les sens disparates de l'intérêt public ainsi que le rôle croissant du corporatisme dans les démocraties libérales, avec sa prétention concomitante à déterminer l'étendue de la citoyenneté. On discute aussi l'exigence pour l'état de fournir une éducation pour la citoyenneté, basée sur la notion qu'elle devrait être d'accord avec les idéaux d'une société démocratique. Mais on suggère aussi que la poursuite des intérêts collectifs empêchent d'une façon significative l'acomplissement de cet objectif. L'article suggère qu'on atteindra une éducation pour la citoyenneté dans un régime démocratique, où la légitimité réside dans les citoyens individuels, avec la plus de probabilité, au moyen d'une éducation libérale conçue pour ce but. Cependant, l'article indique aussi qu'on poursuivra un tel but avec succès seulement si l'on diminue considérablement l'influence du corporatisme et, en particulier, le capitalisme corporatiste, sur l'éducation publique.

Introduction

It now seems banal to characterise contemporary western liberal democracies as societies facing a growing recondite and persistent tessellation, with its origin traced to a cultural fragmenting as citizens embrace diverse identities growing from ethnic allegiances, religious affiliations, personal perceptions of morality, and views about what may be valuable in life. Its impact is observed in an apparent decay in the ideal of commonality that, in turn, expands differences, for example, in interpreting moral and civic engagement. Evident, too, are differences in portraying liberal political theory, since liberals disagree about the concept of liberty with the consequence that the ideal of protecting freedom influences contrary conceptions of the role of government as well as interpretations of public interest. Plainly, these characteristics define conditions in Canada, but Cairns also suggests that in this country there is a further fragmentation of citizenship created by multiple nationalisms and by the politicized diversity of modernity.[1] Obviously, these factors raise particular problems for understanding the concept of "citizenship" and the means for its development through an appropriate education. Moreover, Cairns warns us that if Canada is to survive as one country, it will be necessary to respond to this variegated condition by accommodating diversity without eroding an interconnectedness essential for the collective undertaking of future civic tasks.[2] But the potency of corporatism, which contributes to this diversity, is inhibiting the achievement of this end, since it asserts that political legitimacy lies with the group, which leads, in turn, to the diminishing ability of the individual to exercise the rights and responsibilities of citizenship. It will be useful, therefore, to examine an understanding of citizenship within corporatism (while emphasizing corporate capitalism) with the intent of appraising its growing impact on schools and, consequently, its influence on the education of citizens. But, before this pursuit, it is appropriate to examine the ambiguity of citizenship itself.

The Ambiguity of Citizenship

It should be clear that the notion of growing differences in personal lives and commitments entail particular concerns for understanding citizenship. However, there still exists a general acceptance, as Lasch points out, that democratic societies are characterized as such because citizens are in some sense equal, since equality is conferred by citizenship itself and not its reverse, that is, citizenship bestowed because of some other quality or qualities already possessed.[3] From this perspective, citizenship grants some degree of legal and political equality with a democratic citizenry presumably expecting to share a common legal status and a formally defined set of rights and obligations. This suggests that democratic citizenship equalizes people otherwise unequal in their capacities, an idea that perseveres even as uncertainties remain concerning what it means to be a citizen of a democracy. It makes it legitimate, therefore, to query what rights and obligations ought to be included in the legal status so granted and to question how citizens ought to behave when fulfilling their roles in this capacity. However, even as diversities multiply, the appeal persists for some notion of a common citizenship envisaged as some form of integrative force. It is an idea that endures in an increasingly pluralistic and fragmented world, even if it is seemingly more difficult to realize as an ideal because of realities extant in contemporary liberal democratic states.

But if this condition proves a significant challenge in establishing an understanding of citizenship, it raises, in turn, particularly formidable obstacles for education if one task of schooling ought to be directed to engaging the young in some form of preparation for citizenship. Even so, it is claimed by Saul, for example, that the existence of a high-quality, national public education school system for the first dozen or so years of training is the key to a democracy where legitimacy lies with the individual citizen.[4] However, such an assignment is rendered problematic, first, by the uncertainty about what constitutes citizenship (perhaps best referred to here as a national citizenship) and, second, by further demands for instilling in the young a sense, too, of global citizenship, since this concept is also ambiguous. For instance, some refer to global citizenship in terms of developing the acceptance of democratic world institutions so that a world free from war, discrimination, human rights violations, and environmental destruction will evolve. Presumably the desired outcome would lead to the unification of the notion of global citizenship with that of some sense of world government, further encouraging some fundamental global extension of civic and legal rights and obligations, now conferred only on those citizens of democratic states. Such a view receives a powerful impetus from ethical theories that emphasize universalism which, as Miller indicates, suggest that the subject matter of ethics must be attached to persons considered as such, and independent of all local connections and relations like that of nationality.[5] It follows, then, that one could ask, "What obligations or duties do I owe to my fellow human beings?" and "What rights do they have against me?" It is questions such as these that hint at the sense of world citizenship intended in this interpretation.

But another view of global citizenship is being advanced. It originates not from ethical universalism, but from the notion of economic globalization. Perhaps it is possible to understand the latter in terms of four factors, namely, investments, industry, information technology, and consumers, all of which are now more mobile than ever before. As an example, investment is no longer bound geographically, since it flows where the best opportunities for profit exist and where there is minimum intervention from government. This can also be said of industry, where the methods of multinational corporations are moulded by their search for new markets and resources, wherever they may exist. No longer are they restricted by reasons of state, since their allegiances to host, and even home, governments have diminished. Obviously, this is true, as well, of information technology which makes it viable for companies to function in various parts of the world without the necessity of having to construct an entire business infrastructure in each country where they operate. Neither do companies have to transfer many experts or train a large local work force. It is also the case that individual consumers have become more global in orientation, and, as they receive the same information and television networks, they aspire to similar lifestyles and the possession of similar products. In combination, these four factors allow economic enterprises in virtually any part of the world to gather what is required for further development and exploitation of markets without any dependence on national governments and national sovereignty. Moreover, economic enterprises often consider it necessary to overcome the limitations that may be imposed by government claims to sovereignty because national cultures may inhibit the pursuit of the self-interest achieved through global transactions.

Yet, in light of this, it seems legitimate to ask whether this interpretation of global citizenship furnishes any rightful conception of legitimacy to citizenship at all? Furthermore, even though it seems reasonable to accept the view that having a nation is not an inherent property of humanity, does the very nature of economic globalization undermine the essence of national citizenship and the rights and obligations associated with it? And does this understanding of global citizenship merely reflect the fundamental political, social, and economic forces that are influencing and even establishing a claim to a legitimization of authority in society that is increasingly dominated by corporate capitalism and economic managerialism? In response, what seems essential is to consider the impact such influences are likely to have on the implementation of an education for citizenship within liberal democracies which are linked, in turn, to some sense of national identity and national citizenship.

Political Legitimacy and Civic Initiation

It is from our understanding of the legitimacy of authority that views about power, organizations, attitudes, both private and public, and ethics, admired or condemned or ignored, emanate. As Saul explains it, four possibilities (God, kings, groups, and individuals) emerge as sources of this legitimacy in Western history.[6] It is evident that although theocracies have sometimes been part of the Western tradition, none now function as the basis of legitimacy in Western nation-states. Of course, if they did, one would expect civic initiation in them to stress the importance of the Word in public and private life with any deviation from it being suppressed. Monarchs have frequently claimed direct inspiration and legitimacy from God, and civic indoctrination under monarchial rule gave prominence to this. Yet we could not argue that initiates being taught to accept the legitimacy of such supremacy were at the same time being prepared for democratic citizenship, since they were treated as mere subjects to the power of others.

Of course, it is also the case that modern dictators have claimed inheritance to the legitimacy of kings, with civic initiation reflecting this. For instance, although we can certainly speak of civic training in Nazi Germany, we also see citizens (if members of such states could be so characterized) as having obligations or duties to the state widely disproportional to their rights. Distastrously for many, any rights they may have possessed prior to Hitler's achievement of power were soon removed, with tragic consequences.

A similar understanding may be applied to the former Soviet Union. There the aim of what Grant refers to as moral teaching was to produce a person willing and able to put all of the effort of which he was capable into work for the common good, building the society under the guidance of the Communist Party. Moreover, it was believed that persons would find fulfillment and joy in the task.[7] This was a more ambitious objective than simply getting people to behave themselves, since it was also intended to encourage conformity in selflessness, in emphasizing collective action, and in instilling patriotic duty. But what we see advanced here, too, is the attempt to reduce the individual to a state of acquiescence. It may also be suggested that this is the purpose when the source of legitimacy is the group, whether in the form of a medieval guild or modern corporatism. For Saul, passivity, rather than participation, is required of the individual, and the result here, as well, is the eventual reduction of the individual to the status of a subject.[8]

Yet, in discussing these distinctions, it would seem obvious that contemporary democratic societies operate primarily on the relationships between groups, and although the notion of corporatism immediately brings to mind multinational corporations, the idea is broader than this since it includes, as Saul suggests, all the hierarchically organised interest and specialist groups in society.[9] Some are businesses, of course, but some are groupings of businesses, while others are narrow categories of intellectuals and professions and ethnocultural affiliations. Obviously, some are private and some public, but society is now seen as the sum of all the groups, and the primary loyalty of the individual may not be to society as a whole, but to the group to which he or she belongs. Therefore, decisions tend to be made, not through democratic discussion or participation, but through negotiation between the relevant groups based upon their expertise, their interests, and their ability to exercise influence. Consequently, more power is slipping toward groups, which limits the capacity of individuals to exercise the rights and duties of citizenship; this, in turn, decreases the opportunity for the development of the notion of a democracy of participating individuals.

Further support for such a conclusion is offered by the argument, presented by Dahl, that modern corporatism generates a fundamental hazard to liberty. It evolves from a special kind of freedom, one leading to inequality, since it permits, through corporate capitalism as an example, the accumulation of significant economic resources and the establishment of economic activity into hierarchically organized enterprises.[10] This implies that the modern system of ownership and control of organizations is deeply implicated in the creation of other forms of inequality, all of which threaten the extent of the practice of political liberty. It produces differences in wealth, income, education, status, access to the means of communication, and organizational resources, which result in significant inequalities among citizens in their capacities and opportunities for participating as political equals in governing the state.[11] Within this claim, Dahl concludes, modern corporatism develops inequalities in social and economic resources so significant that it gives rise to severe violations of political equality that breach the principles of democratic process.[12] Obviously, this refers to the oligarchic tendencies present within democracies, which discourage political participation while contributing, instead, to passivity and acquiescence — both of which defeat the perception of democracy as existing within a society of participating individuals. Clearly, this is a concern, as Held suggests, central to the whole tradition of democracy that emphasizes individuals as active citizens in their political order and not merely the subjects of the power of others.[13] Ideally, of course, a democratic system intent on individual participation would exist with a socio-economic arrangement established for a democracy of individuals, perhaps even taking the form of a self-regulating, egalitarian order; but, obviously, it does not as yet exist.

Corporatism's assumption, then, that legitimacy lies with the group and not the individual citizen emphasizes the idea that modern liberal democracy should be built on claims of group interest. Therefore, corporatism, since it is not devoid of self-interest, is unable to perform contentedly with a model of democracy seen as a polity of individuals. Instead, its actions are based on group interest, not on what could be considered the public interest or the common weal, which, according to Saul, are measures of disinterest or impartiality.[14] Corporate capitalism, as an example, unconsciously accepts the dominance of its interests, and this leads inevitably to its advocacy of a marketplace ideology that serves those interests. This also offers authorization to whatever forms modern globalization happens to take, since neo-market liberalism, economic managerialism, and economic globalization are simply judged to be advantageous to its narrower concerns. Whether such acceptance is in the public interest, the public good, or the common weal of a national citizenry matters not because such notions, to the corporatist way of thinking, cannot override its own compressed claims to pursue its own advantage.

The tessellation of contemporary society may, in part, be understood from this perspective of legitimacy, explained in terms of the pursuit of group interest. However, the impact of this condition is particularly troubling since it is evident that the notion of civil society constructed on the basis of public interest is unable to withstand the onslaught. Instead, it is being overwhelmed by the fragmentation that results, and this may explain why the view of citizenship as a unifying force in a divided world now appeals to political thinkers of various political camps, even if the motivations underlying the concerns may differ. From the political right, for example, the encouragement of citizenship arises from what could be considered the belated awareness that the individualism (frequently pursued through corporate entities) that drives the free market is insufficient to hold society together, since people take less interest in the welfare of others around them. This trend is characterized by the shrinking welfare state that was once seen as the operative representation of the principle of universally shared responsibility for individual well-being and affliction. As Bauman points out, its disassembling removes the institutionalized commonality of fate, the provisions of which were intended for every citizen in equal measure by balancing everybody's privations with everybody's gains.[15] To overcome these new circumstances, we hear calls for reasserting traditional moral values, for instilling social responsibility, and for acts of public service such as charity work. Yet the cries tend to take on the tone of mere moral exhortations even if some responses may reflect a genuine concern for others.

From the political left, immediate concerns regarding the nature of citizenship may be seen as a reaction to the general rejection of redistributive economic policies and a decrease in the provisions of social welfare which, when coupled with expanding economic competition, have led to growing economic disparities. Miller suggests that this viewpoint declares that even those deprived under such policies are, nonetheless, citizens and are entitled, by virtue of that citizenship, to particular provisions including services such as health care and other social benefits.[16] As a response, it can be seen, at least, as an attempt to protect the weak in an increasingly competitive world, but it also suggests citizens have particular kinds of rights as well as responsibilities regardless of their status in the market place. Moreover, these differences continue to reflect disagreement about the meaning of citizenship. For example, is citizenship shaped simply by legal rights and duties that do not extend beyond contractual obligations, or is there is an ethical component to it in terms of social and political practice as well? Furthermore, there seems to be disagreement about citizenship extending beyond civic rights to encompass obligations that advance the common good through purposive action. In other words, it suggests a notion not entailed by an Invisible Hand and indicating, in turn, as White delineates it, the distinction between the strong and weak senses of public interest respectively.[17] And, as already suggested, there is further uncertainty about what is implied by the notion of global citizenship, although there are obviously parallels with the distinctions regarding what has been referred to as national citizenship. Therefore, with these demarcations at least tentatively established, it seems reasonable to explore notions of citizenship and education for citizenship in the context of these diversities extant in modern liberal democracies, particularly of the interests pursued by modern corporatism with special reference to corporate capitalism.

Corporatism and Citizenship

One factor underlying the disagreement concerning citizenship and political legitimacy in liberal democracies is the discord among liberals concerning liberty, since the liberal idea of protecting freedom leads to different conceptions of the role of government. One understanding (rights-based liberalism) establishes the idea of liberty in emphasizing the absence of coercion by others. As Berlin has shown, it implies that if a person is prevented from doing what he could otherwise do, then a degree of constraint has taken place which indicates deliberate interference by others within the area in which that person could otherwise have acted with liberty.[18] In this understanding, the liberal state's responsibility is in protecting liberty by ensuring that citizens do not coerce each other unless there are compelling reasons for so doing. But another awareness of liberty (autonomy-based liberalism) is based on the notion that one is free only when one is self-directed, and offers a perspective incorporating the idea of free persons as those whose actions are their own since they are not disposed to compulsions. They would deliberate on their ideals and would not follow customs irrationally. Neither would they disregard long-term interests for short-term pleasures. It is a view offering the basis for justifying interference in individual liberty if it can be determined that such interventions are freedom enhancing — a position in sharp contrast to the limited role of government conceived in rights-based liberalism.

But adding to the complications regarding the education of citizens in a liberal democracy is the fact that the notion of "democracy" itself possesses ambiguities. Although it has been defined as a form of government in which the people rule, it is, nonetheless, problematic since definitional problems emerge concerning "rule by the people." For instance, "Who are to be considered 'the people'?"; "What kind of role is imagined for them?"; and "What conditions are assumed to be beneficial to participation?" Similarly, the idea of rule evokes a deluge of concerns such as, "How broadly or narrowly is the scope of rule to be interpreted?" and "What is the appropriate field of democratic activity?" These queries display the potential for disagreement and, therefore, the meaning of democracy and citizenship in a democracy is enigmatic; thus, the notion of rule by the people remains blurred. Does it imply, for example, that all should govern, or that all should be involved in crucial decision-making, or that rulers should act in the interests of the ruled? Inevitably, as Held points out, positions taken will obtain, in part, from the different ways of justifying democracy, since it is a system of government defended on the grounds that it consummates one or more basic values or goods which include equality, liberty, moral self-development, the common interest, private interest, social utility, the satisfaction of wants, and efficient decisions.[19]

In considering these ambiguities, what can be said of the evolution of contemporary democracy? As already implied, it appears to be a form of government unable to free itself from the tentacles of what corporatists refer to as interest representation and becoming, instead, a form of democracy that discourages individual participation, with legitimacy being exercised by the most influential groups. Moreover, as Held suggests, it exhibits oligarchic tendencies in which bureaucratic structures ossify and leaders become unresponsive elites in the public and private sectors.[20] This signals the danger, noted by Taylor, of "soft despotism" developed by the acceptance of the dark side of individualism which, when coupled with the inappropriate uses of instrumental reason, leads to individual powerlessness and demoralization.[21] Such criticism is extended further by the idea, offered by Lasch, that the elites have betrayed democracy and that conditions will only change if a public philosophy gives more weight to the community than to the right of private decision. It will also have to emphasize responsibilities rather than rights, and it will have to limit the scope of the market and the power of corporations.[22] Yet, this indicates the establishment of a sense of public interest in the strong sense at the expense of the increasing influence of public interest in the weak sense, even though its agency, an Invisible Hand, now commands through group or corporatist interests. Moreover, the translation of this view into an accompanying educational policy would require a significant reduction in the growing influence of those who wish to see schools more closely tied to specific group concerns, among which are those of corporate economic and managerial interests.

In considering such interests it is clear already that contemporary society is permeated by the values of business, particularly those of corporate capitalism. This perspective already influences schools with the purpose of such institutions seen in terms of preparing the young to assume their future economic roles. This direction is conceived on the premise that schooling is not primarily a social and political and moral concern, but principally an economic matter linked directly to global competitiveness. For example, we see in Canada encouragement for schools to form partnerships with business, apparently to foster learning that will ensure the country's corporations success in the global economy. However, its underlying purpose, surely, is to unite work, career awareness, and job preparation with classroom experiences. Its emphasis is on the categories of skills that it deems essential to employability where the focus is on observable and measurable outcomes.[23] One consequence of such "engagements" is the introduction of outcomes-based learning despite criticisms, such as those of Wein and Dudley-Marling, that these approaches are simply mechanisms to ensure that teachers carry out the instructions of others, while withholding the development of the characteristics required for full participation in a democratic process that could otherwise educate its members for full citizenship and responsibility in adult life.[24]

Obviously, it is beyond dispute that corporate capitalism and economic managerialism produce an organizational culture that is hierarchical, competitive, self-interested, and task-oriented, as is the view, set out by Codd, that its application to schools is not new, with its employment to public schools being traced to the United States during a twenty-year period after 1910.[25] Its purpose then was to bring about a business influence to schools with the intent of creating an appropriately prepared workforce during a period of rapid transformation from an entrepreneurial, individualistic (and familial) capitalism to that of a hierarchical, corporate capitalism. Surely, it bears considering that we are witnessing a similar urgency as businesses expand from national or even continental limits to a globalized economy. As Codd points out, it was not until the 1930s that the liberation of schools came with the introduction of ideas developed, for example, by Dewey and others. Only then was economic managerialism defeated, with schools attempting to reconstruct themselves on the basis of democratic educational values.[26] Of course, if ideas of economic managerialism had been soundly vanquished, they would not be reasserting themselves again, and we would not be witnessing the demands that schools respond to these requirements with an understanding of citizenship, according to Miller, underlined by the intention to alter the relationship between the individual and the state so that it becomes explicitly contractual.[27] Citizenship, in this understanding, is not valued for its own sake, since individuals are seen as citizens only in the sense that they demand goods that require public provision. In reference to schools, this means that those who now pursue outcomes-based learning will be seen in a particular light, that is, a contractual one. Therefore, children and their parents are to be seen as clients or customers and even consumers of services provided by schools. Within this viewpoint, teaching is to be understood as the "delivery of curriculum," implying that it is akin to the delivery of a business service, the outcome of which is assured or at least readily measurable to determine whether the "transaction" has been successfully completed or not. But this view can never align itself with the idea, expressed by Orteza y Miranda, for example, that knowledge is a human construct subject to continuous inquiry and examination,[28] or to the perspective, offered by Postman, that one end of education ought to be the encouragement of scepticism.[29] Both positions are antagonistic to a view of teaching as some form of serial performance apparently certain in its outcome. They offer instead a conception of education conceived on the grounds that citizens need to be prepared to play an active role in shaping the direction of society. By extension, such points of view imply that the state be required to provide an education that serves the broader public interest and reject notions of schooling aimed at narrow individual or group interests if they interfere with the establishment of this obligation.

The Requirement for Providing an Education for Democratic Citizenship

Barber argues that the fundamental task of education in a democracy is the apprenticeship of liberty, that is, in learning to be free.[30] This applies, White claims, regardless of what may be seen as the good life, since a democracy will survive only if its citizens value such a political system and know how to operate and control its institutions.[31] But human beings are born ignorant, and, unless they receive some education in human affairs, they will continue to remain uninformed. It follows, then, that an education for democratic citizenship is in the public interest in the strong sense, since it is judged to benefit all members of society at large. This stands, argues Gutmann, even if a democracy is committed to allowing its citizens the freedom to pursue their own concerns in a wide range of matters. It cannot escape its responsibilities in ensuring the young receive an adequate education that initiates them into citizenship. But, she also says, this should not be construed as a mere process of socialization. Rather, it is a commitment concerned with developing citizens who will be involved in consciously shaping a society's future, since the distinctive feature of democratic societies is that they authorize their citizens to influence how the society reproduces itself.[32]

This, then, delineates what may be considered an important purpose of public schools, suggesting, too, that this aspiration must be one with a democratic society's basic ideals, since an education for citizenship is a deliberative enterprise for the realization of such ends. It also implies that such an education is not, and cannot be, a neutral, quiescent arrangement in which the individual is left alone to grow and develop. Instead, it must be seen as an organized social effort attempting to bring about changes in human beliefs and behaviour that would otherwise not occur. This, of course, rejects the notion that it should be built upon the ideal of impartiality, to an unprejudiced individual freedom, and offering a superficial dichotomy between the development of civic virtue and the exercise of freedom, even if it is sometimes claimed that such an attempt to cast the mind of the young is immoral. Instead, it should be clear that the problem of developing an appropriate education for citizenship is not one of patterning or not patterning, but rather one of the means to be employed so that the development of the young is one of enrichment and liberation, not of exploitation and subjugation.

Ideally, then, an education for citizenship in some form of liberal democracy would be one that leads to the exercise of liberty and the development of civic virtue, and is not a choice between liberty and civic virtue since neither alternative is sufficient on its own. Therefore, it appears legitimate to claim that democratic societies must establish and maintain schools with the intent of insuring that the raising of future generations is not left to chance, since it is through an education for citizenship that society consciously seeks to pattern or change human beings in preparing citizens for a role in determining that society's future.

Group Interests and Education for Citizenship

One assumption about an education for citizenship within a pluralistic society, governed through some arrangements reached between competing group interests, is that children will already be members of one or more of the diverse groups that constitute society. Certainly, their parents may be members of such entities as community associations, social and recreation clubs, religious bodies, trade unions, and business organizations, some of which may slice across various lives, perhaps even connecting them in complex ways to a variety of institutions including, obviously, government and its agencies (including schools). But, unlike the notion that the importance of democratic politics reflects the individual citizen's relation to the state, we see here concern with factions (or interest or pressure groups) and their relationship to the state founded on the value of free association whereby individuals will form groups to pursue their common interests. The result, indicated by Held, is the existence of multiple power centres, diverse and fragmented interests, the propensity for one group to offset the power of another, and a "transcendent" consensus which binds state and society, the state being judge and arbitrator between factions.[33] This is a characterization of democracy in which the government is responsible to groups rather than to individuals. Its task is to act like a "referee," ensuring rules are obeyed according to the principle of tolerance, since its essential role is to protect the liberty of groups so that they may further their interests. As Held explains it, the emphasis is on group rights with its efficacy displayed, according to its supporters, by the political stability it creates, since the existence of diverse competitive interests provide the basis for a democratic equilibrium and a favourable means for developing public policy.[34]

Assuming, then, that the preceding description of group interest politics is a reasonable representation, an education for citizenship would require, at least, that children learn to relate to government and the state through the group and come to acquire forbearance and open-mindedness toward other groups with different interests and values. They will have to learn tolerance and respect for others as freely choosing persons with the capacity to determine their own ends (even though achieved through the group) and come to understand the means of operating the various mechanisms which will institutionalize these beliefs. And, as White determines it, they will eventually be required to grasp how and when to place pressure on a government, and, because such demands are applied through group politics, they will have to learn to function effectively within such factions.[35] But the existence of active groups of disparate types is critical if this form of democratic process is to be maintained and if citizens are to further their interests. However, involvement in collectively formulating public policy is not compulsory, since people are free to organize or not, at liberty to press factional interest or not, or even to vote in elections or not. Decisions to participate in the democratic process and the world of democratic institutions is the citizen's prerogative with some theorists, Held suggests, even seeing this as advantageous, since a degree of inaction or apathy might even be functional for stability in the political system.[36] Children will learn this, too.

But the foregoing characterization assumes that the competing interest groups are in a sense in balance and that there is an impression of symmetry. However, there are systematic imbalances in the distribution of power, influences, and resources employed in determining public policy, an asymmetry creating political inequality which leads to public policy that is biased in favour of group interest of the most powerful and influential. This is why the establishment of public interest in the strong sense is increasingly defenceless before the most potent forces, including that of self-interested economic managerialism exemplified in corporate capitalism and its lobbying arms. This influence is clearly applicable to public policy concerning schools. Codd offers an example in his examination of the restructuring of primary and secondary education in New Zealand between 1987 and 1990. He argues that the country became the site for a struggle between competing political, ideological, and educational beliefs, between the instrumental values of economic managerialism and the intrinsic values of educational democracy.[37] Whichever dominates will determine what form an education for citizenship takes. If economic managerialism and corporate capitalism prevail, then the state will invest in education on the grounds of improving overall economic performance, since the aim of neo-market liberalism and economic globalization is to achieve maximum return on investment. But even if, under these very specific pressures for conformity, it is still claimed that schools have objectives other than simply preparing the young for the world of work and a consumer culture, the trend is, nevertheless, toward impelling schools to give priority to economic concerns with, as Saul sees it, the elites of corporate capitalism urging governments to strike further in this direction.[38] It is likely, therefore, that goals such as developing moral autonomy and independent thought will diminish in importance, with the result that the oligarchic tendencies in both public and private organizations will be reinforced, with schools, as Codd points out, acting as an instrument for social control committed to the dominant political values and the perpetuation of the existing economic order.[39] Furthermore, schools will not abandon their role as the agencies employed in determining who will enter the meritocracy, an elitism based on the specific talents desired by corporate capitalism and economic managerialism.

It should be obvious, then, that political cultures, which emphasize the political process as competition between unequal factional interests while accepting the authority and legitimacy of the most powerful and influential groups, lead to forms of democracy which inhibit widespread engagement in establishing public policy in a broad participatory sense. Also undermined is the implementation of a democratic theory of education established only in a democracy where legitimacy lies with individual citizens. Nevertheless, even under such conditions, the requirement will remain that children learn tolerance as the foundation of an education for citizenship, since this is a guiding principle in a political system dominated by competing factional interests, even if those groups are unequal in power and influence.

Tolerance as a Guiding Principle in a Democracy of Factional Interests

In exploring tolerance, it is important at the outset to distinguish between freedom of thought and freedom of action, since it is reasonable to conclude that whereas the right of the former is absolute, the right of the latter is contingent upon the possible harm one could do to others if all actions and practical opinion were unrestrained. But what belief reins in an unrestricted pursuit of interests to the detriment of others? Within a political culture espousing the virtue of self-interested group politics, tolerance is essential if perpetual hostility is to be avoided and factions with competing interests are to be accommodated. Although one would imagine that no hard and fast rules can be established, accepting the value of tolerance is critical in resolving frictions that may arise between the pursuit of liberty and the consideration of the group or factional interest of others. But what is also clear is that the pursuit of liberty and the consideration of other group interests can conflict if intolerance predominates. Therefore, in a political system of group politics, it is assumed that the government will intervene (or establish constitutional means) to ensure that antagonisms are minimalized. But, as Lasch makes clear, there is a tendency to be far too tolerant and sympathetic for our own good, since this leads to the acceptance of the second-rate.[40] The implication, he suggests, is that democracies require a more invigorating ethic than forbearance, since tolerance is only the beginning of democracy, not its destination.[41] Nonetheless, we may see our "times" as an era of unadulterated individualism but pursued through group politics and interests. At the same time, if we seem to be searching for our own interpretations of the good life limited only by the demand for tolerance in circumstances of scruple-free self-celebration, then the demand for forbearance may result in expressing itself merely as indifference to others. In opposing this perspective, Fletcher suggests the application of three qualifications: first, arguments against intolerance; second, assertions against the moral failing of indifference; and, third, claims against the desire to respect and accept everyone and everything.[42]

The freedom, then, to pursue one's interests with like-minded people, while being tolerant of others (or even indifferent if they do not interfere with one's own goals), who behave similarly in pursuing their interests, is the ethos of democracy interpreted as the expression of group politics. Yet it is a limited perception of democracy on two counts. First, factions are unequal. Therefore, the most robust and influential will possess greater authority. Secondly, another outlook involving citizens as individuals requires concern not only with liberty and tolerance, but also, as White suggests, with concepts such as equality, justice, and consideration of interests even of a minority of one.[43] Inclusion of (and acting upon) these tenets would more closely resemble the requirements for establishing a democracy where legitimacy lies with individual citizens. Yet, this requires an understanding of responsibilities to others as well as an appreciation of one's rights and interests (whether as an individual or as one who is a member of a faction), since only then will it be possible to consider public policy in the public interest in the strong sense. However, an accent on responsibilities and an emphasis on our existence within some kind of community, with a desire to strengthen some sense of citizenship entailed in that community, is clearly at odds with the now dominant view of democracy, including its seemingly exclusive reliance on tolerance as its guiding principle. It is this influence that directs approaches to the education of citizens within corporatism, along with ideas that entrench inequality which, in turn, establish and reinforce a form of meritocracy which fits only with the dominant political and economic order.

Inequalities and Meritocracy

How can the move toward the further development of a meritocracy, which places impediments in the path of the means of creating a democracy where legitimacy lies with individual citizens, be diminished? One response may be to allocate resources in such a way that all children are provided with a reasonable foundation in school so that their chances for eventual participation in a participatory democracy are improved. Advocacy of such appropriations is based on an acceptance of the principle of equalization. Gutmann claims that, within this understanding, a democratic state is required to take steps to overcome the inequalities that deprive children of educational attainment adequate to their participation in the political process.[44] But the idea of equalization also reveals a flaw in meritocracy applied in the strong sense, a defect contained in the understanding that meritocracy in this form is committed to disbursing all educational resources in proportion to natural ability and a readiness to learn. However, this approach gives an unequivocal answer to the question, "Who should receive an education for citizenship?" since only members of the meritocracy, or those who may enter it, will be so prepared, with the rest, it is assumed, encouraged to be passive in political affairs.

But an alternative to this narrow view of the education of citizens has been suggested, and it requires an education committed to a broader task. From this perspective, it is reasonable to insist that such an education be fairly and universally distributed so that all children come to possess the means by which they will be able to participate, eventually, in the democratic process. This view may be developed upon the principle of distributive justice which claims that unequals should be treated unequally and implying, in turn, that more educational resources need to be directed to those considered educationally disadvantaged. Of course, it is possible to argue from the same tenet that the talented and the motivated should receive more because they are likely to give more back to society. Nonetheless, whatever they get should not be at the expense of an education for citizenship for all children under the principle of equality. Therefore, what must be avoided is an approach that fails to meet the required minimum for all, while providing so excessively for the talented and diligent that a meritocracy in the strong sense prevails. Only then will one be able to reply, "All children," to the query, "Who should receive an education for democratic citizenship?"

But what are the characteristics of an education for citizenship in a democracy where legitimacy resides with individual citizens? Three factors seem immediately evident. First, an education for citizenship must be distributed in such a way that no child is prevented (unless there are convincing arguments to the contrary[45]) from eventual participation in a democracy of individual citizens. Second, it seems clear that such an education must be democratically organized, and, third, the content and the means by which such an education is taught and learned is critical to an education for a democracy of individual citizens. This last condition suggests something of a liberal education (an education for liberty), but not in the form in which it has been frequently cast as an intellectual training for a few.

Liberal Education as a Preparation for Citizenship

Our grasp of the origins of liberal education extends to fifth and fourth century Greek culture, where we see enunciated a connection for such an education for a ruling elite striving to understand the nature of the individual, the nature of society, and the nature of knowledge. As Beck explains it, this association is evident, for example, in the oratorical tradition in which Isocrates argued that the aim of education lies in the production of civic efficiency and political leadership, and with those qualities that demand the power to judge wisely and to make right decisions. It is concerned, too, with relationships with others, the development of temperance within oneself, and with the unfolding of character and virtue.[46]

For Plato, too, the goal of education was the formation of citizens able to play their part in the life of the civic community. Attached to this was the belief that the matter and methods of education must be calculated so as to realize this practical ideal, and suggests, as Beck points out, why Plato's discussion of education was not established in a separate discourse, but, rather, in his works on the Ideal State, where the individual would live the fullest life in the service of his city.[47] But there is in this the indication that civic virtue can be taught along with the implication that it is achieved through the process of acquiring knowledge. This is the means by which character is cultivated and civic virtue encouraged. However, it must be understood, as Beck argues, that the acquisition of knowledge demands intellectual effort, and it is this that has educational significance, rather than the mere practical utility of possessing knowledge itself.[48] It is also for this reason, suggests Frankena, that Aristotle linked politics, education, and ethics in the belief that the main duty of the statesman was to make citizens good, that is, to educate them.[49]

These initial developments in what we may call liberal education took place in the newly evolving democratic institutions of the Greek city-states and especially in the assemblies of free citizens. They overturned the Homeric tradition of noble and valorous leadership in war that once shaped the character of the ruling elite, replacing it with a democratic polity at a time which coincided with the flourishing of Hellenic culture. For the Greeks, and particularly the Athenians, this meant devoting a great deal of effort in trying to understand their cultural development and deliberating on how it should be transmitted to new generations of citizens being readied to participate in governing the city-state.

It is out of these concerns that we see the development of two traditions trying to answer questions concerning the comprehension and transmission of culture. Kimball claims that for the "orators" this would be accomplished through rhetoric and the ability to persuade, emphasizing the pronunciation of words, the faculty of talking, and the formal art of communication, including the skills of composing, delivering, and analyzing speeches.[50] Here, according to the "orators," is the legitimate response to their central concern. Yet the ambiguity concerning liberal education, not only in specific purpose but also in method of transfer, is evident in the criticisms of rhetoric as being imprecise and merely a practical tool which only shadowed the true essence of education. For the "philosophers," mathematics and syllogistic logic held the key in the pursuit of the essential nature of things. Therefore, we see the origin of the debate between the advocates of grammar and rhetoric on one side, and mathematics and logic on the other, and representing the critical distinctions between the traditions.

The contemporary understanding of the philosophical tradition lies in the search of the liberal-free ideal, that is, in free academic inquiry and research in pursuit of truth. But it may be expressed in schools, for example, in the demands for encouraging higher order thinking skills. The rhetorical tradition, in contrast, announces that education is a moral enterprise and that learning has to make a moral difference. It declares, too, that institutions intended for this purpose must become learning communities in which the development of character and civic virtue are the central concerns, a position, it claims, neglected in the pursuit of the liberal-free ideal. Seemingly, then, there exists an unbridgeable gap existing since the traditions first developed. Yet there may be a way out of this discord by accepting that the "philosophers" are right about the pursuit of truth and the "orators" are correct about the need for community. It may create a tension but not an unacceptable one, since the assumption of the liberal free ideal that knowledge is objective and neutral needs to be questioned, as does the nature of the communities to be established, to ensure, as Giroux asserts, that the behaviour of students so developed is not adaptive and conditioned, but rather active and critical.[51] It may be possible, then, to create environments in which the young are engaged in the search for understanding, but in settings committed to the development of civic virtue and in the encouragement of a citizenship that is participatory and emancipatory. Schools could become places devoted to the pursuit of the common good (in the strong sense) and with the nurturing of self-determination (by developing autonomy and wholeness[52]) worked out through an understanding of the nature of knowledge and advanced in such a way that together they assist in the evolution and maturing of a democracy of participating citizens.

One approach for teaching that may assist in achieving this idea is suggested by Gardener and Boix-Mansella in their proposal that the curriculum should be based on the enduring traditions of civilization represented by the scholarly disciplines and the world of disciplined scholarship.[53] But how should we perceive knowledge within the context of these disciplines? One indication offered by Schwab is that a liberal education should be developed emphasizing knowledge as a process, and this is why science should be included since it possesses an unavoidably revisionary character.[54] To learn science, for example, is not simply to remember a litany of facts. In contrast, it would have, as its goal in a liberal curriculum, the task of developing intellectual skills and habits and attitudes, as well as bodies of information. Other disciplines, seen in this way, would play an important part as well, including history, although Postman indicates that we ought to refer to the notion of "histories" instead, so that the young come to understand that what has happened has been observed from different points of view, by different people, each with a different story to tell.[55] Clearly such an understanding has importance for a pluralistic society, but so, too, does the view presented by Nussbaum expressing support for the arts and humanities, since, she argues, they foster imaginative abilities central to political life by cultivating the capacity to imagine the experiences of others and to "participate" in their sufferings.[56] She also argues that such an education for citizenship would be aimed, too, at developing compassionate citizenship and should, therefore, also be considered a multicultural education.[57]

Since a formal education may be seen as a deliberative enterprise for the realization of a democratic society's basic ideals, it is reasonable to conclude that educational objectives ought to be one with such ends. And if we are to determine the education of citizens in Canada's liberal democracy, it seems reasonable to elucidate the country's basic ideals, since these will provide the foundation for the education of citizens that follows. It is not my intent here to elaborate on those ideals, but merely to suggest that the articulation of a liberal education is the likely result of such deliberations. Such a claim is developed on the assumption that Canadian society ought to be constructed along democratic lines with all playing a part as citizens in its development. The liberal education advanced for such a task would assert itself as an education in the public interest in the strong sense. It would contradict, in the process, a system of public schooling subject to the oligarchic tendencies extant in all democracies and influenced by the interests of corporate capitalism and economic managerialism. But the prospects for such an ideal will become increasingly remote unless we begin to accept that an education for citizenship of individual citizens ought to be the primary goal of our schools as opposed to the demands of powerful corporate interests.

NOTES

1. Alan C. Cairns, "The Fragmentation of Canadian Citizenship," in *Reconfigurations: Canadian Citizenship and Constitutional Change: Selected Essays*, ed. Douglas E. Williams (Toronto: McClelland and Stewart, 1995), 159.

2. Ibid., 185.

3. Christopher Lasch, *The Revolt of the Elites: And the Betrayal of Democracy* (New York: W.W. Norton, 1995), 88.

4. John Ralston Saul, *The Unconscious Civilization* (Concord, ON: House of Ananasi, 1995), 65.

5. David Miller, "The Ethical Significance of Nationality," *Ethics* 98 (1987-1988): 647.

6. Saul, *The Unconscious Civilization* , 30.

7. Nigel Grant, *Soviet Education*, rev. ed. (Harmondsworth: Penguin, 1968), 50.

8. Saul, *The Unconscious Civilization* , 30-31.

9. Ibid., 31.

10. Robert A. Dahl, *A Preface to Economic Democracy* (Cambridge: Polity Press, 1985), 50.

11. Ibid., 55.

12. Ibid., 60.

13. David Held, *Models of Democracy* (Stanford: Stanford University Press, 1987), 179.

14. Saul, *The Unconscious Civilization* , 32-33.

15. Zygmunt Bauman, *Postmodernist Ethics* (Oxford: Blackwell, 1993), 243.

16. Miller, "Citizenship and Pluralism," *Political Studies* 43, no. 3 (1995): 433.

17. Patricia White, "Education, Democracy, and the Public Interest," in *The Philosophy of Education*, ed. R.S. Peters (Oxford: Oxford University Press, 1973), 221-222.

18. Isaiah Berlin, "Two Concepts of Liberty," in *Four Essays on Liberty* (London: Oxford University Press, 1969), 122.

19. Held, *Models of Democracy*, 3.

20. Ibid., 195.

21. Charles Taylor, *The Malaise of Modernity* (Concord, ON: House of Ananasi, 1991), 9-10.

22. Lasch, *The Revolt of the Elites: And the Betrayal of Democracy*, 113.

23. See, for example, Mary Ann McLaughlin, *Employability Skills Profile: What Are Employers Looking for?* (Ottawa: Conference Board of Canada, 1992).

24. Carol Anne Wein and Curt Dudley-Marling, "Limited Vision: The Ontario Curriculum and Outcomes-Based Learning," *Canadian Journal of Education* 23, no. 4 (1998): 418.

25. John A. Codd, "Managerialism, Market Liberalism, and the Move to Self-Managing Schools in New Zealand," in *A Socially Critical View of the Self-Managing School*, ed. John Smyth (London: Falmer Press, 1993), 159-160.

26. Ibid., 161.

27. Miller, "Citizenship and Pluralism," 443.

28. Evelina Orteza y Miranda, "Autonomy and Education," In *Teaching, Schools, and Society*, ed. Evelina Orteza y Miranda and Romulo F. Magsino (London: Falmer Press, 1990), 120.

29. Neil Postman, *Building a Bridge to the Eighteenth Century: How the Past Can Improve Our Future* (New York: Alfred A. Knopf, 1999), 159-163.

30. Benjamin R. Barber, *An Aristocracy of Everyone: The Politics of Education and the Future of America* (New York: Oxford University Press, 1992), 4.

31. White, "Education, Democracy, and the Public Interest," 227.

32. Amy Gutmann, *Democratic Education* (Princeton: Princeton University Press, 1987), 15.

33. Held, *Models of Democracy*, 195.

34. Ibid., 187-188.

35. White, "Education, Democracy, and the Public Interest," 229.

36. Held, *Models of Democracy*, 191.

37. Codd, "Managerialism," 153-154.

38. Saul, *The Unconscious Civilization* , 65-67.

39. Codd, "Managerialism," 168.

40. Lasch, *The Revolt of the Elites and the Betrayal of Democracy*, 107.

41. Ibid., 89.

42. George B. Fletcher, "The Case for Tolerance," *Social Philosophy and Policy* 13, no. 1 (1996): 229-239.

43. White, "Education, Democracy, and the Public Interest," 229-230.

44. Gutmann, *Democratic Education*, 133-134.

45. See, for example, Richard M. Hare, "Opportunity for What? Some Remarks on Current Disputes about Equality in Education," *Oxford Review of Education* 3, no. 3 (1977): 207-216.

46. Frederick A.G. Beck, *Greek Education: 450-350 B.C.* (London: Methuen, 1964), 255-256.

47. Ibid., 199.

48. Ibid., 201.

49. William K. Frankena, *Historical Philosophies of Education: Artistotle, Kant, and Dewey* (Glenview: Scott Foresman, 1965), 269-270.

50. Bruce A. Kimball, *Orators and Philosophers: A History of the Idea of Liberal Education* (New York: College Entrance Examination Board, 1995), 269-270.

51. Henry A. Giroux, "Critical Theory and Rationality in Citizenship Education," *Curriculum Inquiry* 10, no. 4 (1980): 336.

52. Wholeness suggests linking thought and action, and autonomy refers to acting on one's volition when one is free to act. Of course, when I write here of autonomy I am referring to moral autonomy. It is clear that the autonomous person without morality is a danger to us all.

53. Howard Gardener and Veronica Boix-Mansilla, "Teaching for Understanding in the Disciplines — and Beyond," *Teachers College Record* 96, no. 2 (1994): 198-218.

54. For a discussion of science within the context of liberal education, see J.J. Schwab, "What Do Scientists Do?" in Joseph J. Schwab, *Science, Curriculum, and Liberal Education; Selected Essays*, ed. Ian Westbury and Neil J. Wilkof (Chicago: University of Chicago Press, 1978), 184-228.

55. Postman, *Building a Bridge to the Eighteenth Century*, 173.

56. Martha Nussbaum, "Compassion: The Basic Social Emotion," *Social Philosophy and Policy* 13, no.1 (1996): 50.

57. Ibid., 51.

5 Examining Higher Education and Citizenship in a Global Context of Neoliberal Restructuring

JAMIE-LYNN MAGNUSSON

ABSTRACT/RÉSUMÉ

My paper begins by articulating a neo-Gramscian framework to conceptualize issues of citizenship and the recent changes to Canadian higher education. This framework is adopted from the writing of Jacob Torfing who provides a critical integration of the work of Laclau, Mouffe, and Zizek. Within this framework, political economies are conceptualized as discursive formations, within which higher education is constituted in specific ways to achieve expansion of practices consistent with, and supportive of, strategies of capital accumulation. Using this framework, I develop a sketch of the ways Canadian higher education evolved within the Keynesian welfare state during the postwar era and was influenced by the development of the U.S. higher education system, which was conscientiously sculpted as an extension of the capitalist nation-state. Then I outline how Canadian higher education is being reshaped during the period of economic restructuring, which involves replacing Keynesian-like economics with neoliberal strategies within a global economic context. Finally, I discuss the implications of neoliberal restructuring of higher education in terms of issues of identity formation, citizenship, and the role of higher education with respect to equity, social justice, and the democratic imperative.

Mon article commence par articuler un cadre néo-gramscien pour conceptualiser les problèmes sur la citoyenneté et les changements récents à l'éducation supérieure canadienne. Ce cadre est adopté des écritures de Jacob Torfing qui fournit une intégration critique du travail de Laclau, Mouffe et Zizek. A l'intérieur de ce cadre, les économies politiques se conceptualisent comme des formations discursives, à l'intérieur desquelles l'éducation supérieure se constitue de façons spécifiques pour atteindre l'expansion de pratiques compatibles avec des stratégies de l'accumulation du capital qui les soutiennent. En utilisant ce cadre, je développe un aperçu des manières dont l'éducation supérieure canadienne s'est développée à l'intérieur de l'état-providence keynésien pendant l'époque d'après-guerre et qui a été influée par le développement du système d'éducation supérieure des États-Unis, qui a été consciencieusement sculptée comme une extension de la nation en tant qu'état capitaliste. Ensuite, j'expose dans ses lignes générales comment on est en train de réorganiser l'éducation supérieure canadienne pendant la période de la restructuration économique, qui a entraîné le remplacement des économies politiques "néo-keynésian" par des stratégies néolibérales dans un contexte économique global. Enfin, je discute des impliciations de la restructuration néolibérale de l'éducation supérieure en termes de problèmes de la formation d'une identité, de la citoyenneté et du rôle de l'éducation supérieure par rapport à l'équité, à la justice sociale et à l'impératif démocratique.

A Neo-Gramscian Perspective on Citizenship

A great deal of the recent literature on citizenship and education focuses on questions of identity and difference. One large body of work exemplifying this emphasis is that of radical democracy, which evolved to a large extent from the writings of Laclau and Mouffe.[1] The major project of radical democracy, according to Torfing, is to extend egalitarian participation and emancipatory struggle to all social spheres in such a way as to recognize plurality of identity, not as essential or transcendent, but as socially constructed. That is, social identity is conceptualized as constituted in and through discourse which, in turn, is theorized as a system of signifying practices. Without delving too deeply into discourse theory, the implication of this perspective for understanding citizenship is that notions of citizenship are realised ontologically and epistemologically in terms of discursive practises through which social identity is constructed. This conceptualization is used here because it does not fix citizenship to pre-existing, or essentialist categories such as nation-state; rather, it permits social identity to be viewed as constitutive rather than transcendent.[2]

Radical democracy has been offered as a somewhat problematic alternative to liberal democracy, which suffers a plethora of difficulties primarily due to its rigid demarcation of, on the one hand, a public sphere of democratic politics and, on the other, a private sphere of economic liberalism.[3] Liberal democratic discourse constructs the democratic project so that it supports the major discursive features of capitalist social organization, including private property, free enterprise, and protection of individual freedom through a political framework of "democratic" practice that is inherently elitist. However, some of the literature on radical democracy has been criticized for its near exclusive emphasis on post-structuralist analysis of difference and identity without embedding these within a broader discussion of political and economic implications and global perspectives.[4]

I will review three versions of this type of criticism that are aimed primarily at the post-structuralist writings on radical democracy emphasizing cultural politics. First, Epstein argues that post-structuralist versions of radical democracy confuse ascendant forms of global capitalism with radicalism, precisely at a time when these should be challenged and attention turned to developing progressive alternatives. Epstein feels that the gaze has shifted from questions related to capitalist exploitation — the working class and poverty, for example — toward issues that are more interesting to the intellectual elite, who write about cultural politics in/a way that is aesthetically sophisticated but politically empty.[5]

Another critique, offered by Dahliwal, addresses Mouffe's notion that democracy needs to be extended through a view of citizenship that entails a political identity able to construct social relations that are responsive to a plurality of social movements.[6] Dahliwal argues that this view retains liberal conceptions of difference and a modernist understanding of democracy, and is, therefore, a version of liberal democracy, rather than an alternative. She further points out that because liberal democracy was constituted through the colonialist, bourgeois nation-state, it is productive of racist relations predicated on nationalism and imperialist expansion. She concludes, then, that, although radical democratic theories discuss categories of difference, including race and ethnicity, they fail to articulate "with any concreteness how radical democracy would deal with these social relations better than non-radical democracy."[7] That is, radical democracy fails to discuss and challenge the racial history of modern democracy.

A third critique, developed by Giyatri Spivak in an interview with David Plotke, suggests that the "Left's" adoption of radical democratic theory is a provincialism in that there is a failure to acknowledge the cultural specificity of the theory.[8] In her discussion of the enthusiastic embracing of radical democratic theory among leftist intellectuals in the U.S., Spivak points out that there is little recognition or understanding of "existing models of economic resistance to the U.S. (a metonym for the forces of the North) in the South."[9] Thus, the discourse of radical democracy creates an aporia between the vision of U.S. leftist intellectuals and the vision of progressive politics informed by a more global vision.

The current paper attempts to avoid these criticisms by theorizing political economies themselves as discursive formations, thereby linking, for the purpose of this discussion, issues of identity and difference to their political and economic implications. This framework is one that is developed by Torfing in his critical integration of the works of Laclau, Mouffe, and Zizek.[10] As Torfing explains,

In the second phase of their intellectual development, Laclau and Mouffe (1982:92) came to see the space that traditional Marxism designated "the economy" as a discursive formation: a terrain for the articulation of discourses of authority and management, technical discourses, discourses of accountancy, discourses of information, etc. Replacement of the traditional Marxist notion of the economy with a theory of discursive construction of the economic might seem a rather drastic step. Yet the logic of the eradication of the essentialist remnant in Gramsci and the early works of Laclau and Mouffe leads directly to a theory of discourse.[11]

This formulation can be viewed as neo-Gramscian to the extent that it retains a reformulated understanding of hegemony, social identity, and economics. Torfing argues that Gramscian theory of hegemony was embedded within the base-superstructure model within which the economic (i.e., modes of production) served as an ontological underpinning of the political, which was the sphere within which contingent struggles for hegemony were played out. He argues that one of Laclau and Mouffe's contributions was to point out that this framework, which cast the superstructure as relatively autonomous, left intact a traditional Marxist version of economy.

It is exactly this implicit, though strictly necessary, reliance upon a traditional Marxist notion of the economic in terms of a specific logic of market production which constitutes the essentialist remnant in Gramsci and in the early works of Laclau and Mouffe. ... The economy is described merely in terms of the formal combination of certain pregiven elements of production and is thus conceived in total abstraction from economic regimes.[12]

It would be impossible to argue that Gramsci failed to acknowledge the political, and therefore contingent, nature of the economy; after all his legacy is a theory of ideology that explains reproduction of modes of production through dynamics taking place within the political, or superstructural, sphere. However, Laclau and Mouffe's contribution was to extend Gramsci's theory by specifically articulating the economic as the political and the political as the economic by conceptualizing political-economies as discursive formations.

Within this neo-Gramscian framework, hegemony is theorized as a historically contingent expansion of a discourse or discourses supporting a dominant social orientation and social actions. Establishment of hegemonic discourse occurs through a process of articulation, which is defined by Laclau and Mouffe as practices that establish "relations among elements such that their identity is modified as a result of the articulatory practice."[13] For example, conflating certain ethnic groups with social class categories achieves a rearticulation of both the ethnic identity and the social class identity. Or, within neoliberal hegemonic discourse, as another example, the interventionist state is articulated as a curtailment on individual freedom, thereby achieving a rearticulation of the relation between the state and civil liberties.

Hegemonic discourse is always established through political struggle, and, therefore, involves oppression and repression. Laclau and Mouffe develop this characteristic of hegemonic process through their notion of social antagonism which, according to Torfing, was reconceptualized by Zizek.[14] Zizek's major contribution on this topic, with respect to the discussion in this paper, is his argument that social identity is constituted *through* social antagonism. Therefore, social identities constructed through hegemonic discourses, for example, necessarily involve oppression and repression. If hegemonic discourse is theoretically embedded within political-economy as discursive formation, then the neo-Gramscian framework described here can assist in theorizing social identity and social practices associated with citizenship as political struggle within contingent relations of power. However, this conception avoids the difficulties of Marxism, which was unable to address questions of identity and difference that mattered, including race and gender and ethnicity. Moreover, by rearticulating discourse in terms of neo-Gramscian political theory, identity and difference can be framed as political-economic discourse. Thus, marginality, in this sense, is linked to *economic* and *political* marginality.

Before moving to a discussion of higher education, the notion of ideology needs to be developed a bit further. Once again using Torfing's critical integration of Mouffe, Laclau, and Zizek, ideology is theoretically constructed as a totalizing discourse. Hence, ideology is critical in the formation of hegemony which, as discussed above, involves "expansion of a particular discourse of norms, values, views and perceptions through persuasive redescriptions of the world."[15] However, rather than viewing ideology as "false consciousness" or "social totality," concepts based on essentialist conceptions of society, it is viewed as a will toward discursive forms that attempt to describe the social realm in totalizing terms. For example, ideology constructs social identity not as discursive categories, but as essential realities with universalistic tendencies.

Neoliberalism as hegemonic discourse is ideological when it constructs the deregulated market as the purest form of democracy and social justice, for example. However, as Zizek asserts, these ideologies are never quite totalizing because most people do not take ideological truths seriously. Nevertheless, we act "as if" the ideological proposition were true — a kind of ideological fantasy. For example, although we may not believe that women are less equal than men, we may, in fact, behave as if they are. That is, we move through the social field as if the ideological fantasy were true, thereby structuring our social reality along patriarchal relations. A final comment on this reconceptualization of ideology is that the meanings constituted through ideology or ideological fantasy are institutionally mediated. That is, institutions actively construct social identity, not as contingent but, rather, as fixed, transcendental categories with essentialist tendencies. In this sense, institutions such as education — and, of course, higher education — can be viewed as critical with respect to ideological formation.

Applying the Neo-Gramscian Framework to Canadian Citizenship: Analysing Multiculturalism as Keynesian Capitalist Discourse

Briefly, to capture the utility of neo-Gramscian concepts, consider the Canadian capitalist welfare state as a discursive formation within which certain notions of citizenship and entitlements are constructed through liberalist hegemonic discourse. Within this discursive field, citizenship is linked to the nation-state as a matter of national identity with notions of entitlements constructed through a liberal democratic discourse of equality. That is, everyone is treated the same by the welfare state regardless of other discursively constituted categories such as race or ethnic origin or social class. Canadian multiculturalism is an institutionally mediated discourse by which identity and difference are ideologically cast as liberal and democratic practice bounded by the nation-state as a natural, essentialist category. Multicultural discourse constructs hyphenated social identities, reinforcing the nation-state as the primary or privileged discursive framework within which identity and citizenship is constituted: Ukrainian-Canadian, Icelandic-Canadian, Jamaican-Canadian, and so on. Social identities that represent categories of political-economic marginalisation are constructed as equivalent (i.e., equal) to social identities of relative economic privilege.

Multicultural discourse, then, legitimates practices that actively structure relations in ways that are raced, classed, and gendered, and help us construct our participation in these relations as enjoyable. As a post-ideological society, we do not really "buy into" the discourse of equality; yet we continue to maneuver through social reality as if, for example, racial discrimination did not exist. The hyphenated social identity of Canadian multiculturalism is constructed antagonistically through hegemonic discourses of liberalism and nationalism that are oppressive and violent. That is, the hyphenated social identity and its rearticulation of citizenship necessarily entails oppressive social relations that are productive of economic and political marginalization.

An important dimension to this analysis is the linking of multicultural discourse to the expansion of the capitalist welfare state as a discursive formation. This linking permits us to explore multiculturalism and its implications for social identity and citizenship in terms of capitalist strategies of accumulation, for example. The discourse of multiculturalism that emerged during the expansion of the social welfare state not only eased social antagonisms, but assisted in legitimating discursive practices useful in achieving further expansion. As neoliberal restructuring began, multicultural discourse was rearticulated as postmodernist discourse consistent with globalizing economic practices that forced an examination of cultural politics. Like Epstein and Dahliwal, I situate Canadian and U.S. radical democratic discourse within this formation.

My use of neo-Gramscian analysis, then, does not imply a radical democratic project in the sense described by Mouffe. However, the framework is very useful in theorizing the connection between higher education and issues of citizenship within a political-economic discursive field. Rather than focus on the possibilities of pluralistic democracy, my intention is simply to use the framework to examine Canadian higher education as constituted through political-economic formations, with particular attention to issues of citizenship.

The neo-Gramscian framework used in the current discussion will foreground economic restructuring of the Keynesian welfare state within a neoliberal paradigm. It urges an exploration of issues of citizenship and higher education that is contextualized and analyzed in terms of economic restructuring and neoliberal discourse. The framework developed here views the intellectual work of Canadian universities as embedded within discourses constituted through the discursive formation of political economies. For example, discourses constructed through social science practices, or professional education, can create interpellation of subjectivities and construction of social identities consistent with the political economy. In a welfare state formation, these can be consistent with sensibilities and dispositions associated with Fordist production, social rationality, and so on. Within a neoliberal formation, interpellated subjectivities may be consistent with the diminishing of the social welfare state; notions of citizenship and entitlements may emphasize individual responsibility and consumerism with respect to health services, for example.

Development of Canadian Higher Education
within a Capitalist Welfare State

An important point to note about the development of Canadian higher education in this century is that it is characterized by the construction of universities that adopted the institutional form of the typical U.S. research university. In the U.S. context, the shaping of the university as a research institution with its departmental structure affiliated with a particular discipline or field was deliberately and systematically carried out. According to Geiger, the period between the 1880s and 1920s was marked by various kinds of changes to American institutional, political, and cultural life that impacted the evolution of the higher education system.[16] These changes included, according to Barrow, the development of the national railway system that provided an important infrastructure to support the nationalization of capital.[17] Local economies became grafted onto parts of national economies that were regulated through particular centers of economic control, not the least of which were located in the northeast, especially in New York.

Barrow's historical analysis of the U.S. higher education system involved demonstrating the co-development of this system with that of the capitalist nation-state, with the latter influencing important features of universities including curricula, research agenda, governance, and ties to the political and economic communities. The important implication of Barrow's work for this paper is his systematic mapping out of the relation between higher education and the needs of capital organized at the level of nation-state in the earlier part of this century. Using his analysis, one can argue that the national system of higher education that eventually emerged was an important and conscientiously constructed apparatus by which the capitalist state could regulate production of identities, attitudes, dispositions, skills, etc., critical in advancing, as Noble stated, an industrial nation of people.[18]

By the 1940s, according to Geiger, the higher education system had developed many of the characteristics recognizable in universities and colleges today. Modeled after the Humboldt institutions of higher education, universities in the U.S. were reshaped by capital to emphasize research and graduate education. This was carried out quite systematically through block transfer grants from major foundations and offered to key institutions that were to use the funds to develop the research and graduate education infrastructure to support technology and innovation in both the sciences and social sciences.[19]

The departmental governance structure common to U.S. institutions emerged as an aspect of the above funding strategy which favored formation of centres and departments with, as noted above, impressive infrastructure to support research. The typical institutional organization involved a network of departments (organized according to discipline or field) that have closer links with research and professional societies, in terms of regulation of curricula and research, than with the central administration.

Barrow suggests that this departmental structure, leading to what would now be considered the current institutional form of U.S. universities, was further reinforced by Cooke, who was hired by the Carnegie Foundation to undertake a major study of U.S. higher education from the vantage point of Taylor's scientific management. Cooke, an engineer by training, was a disciple of Taylor and developed social engineering and statistical concepts published in his report "Academic and Industrial Efficiency" that achieved for the first time the proletarianization of academic faculty. His notion was to move away from the individual professor as arbiter of curricula and producer of undirected scholarship and develop a tighter accounting of what was taught, how it was taught, and what type of research was conducted. The departmental structure, then, afforded an organizational framework to achieve greater regulation of the work of the faculty.

At the same time, national societies and councils emerged, and these were influenced by national agendas via governing bodies that represented corporate interests.[20] In this manner, the interests of the capitalist state could steer the curricula of undergraduate, professional, and graduate education according to the needs and imperatives of corporate players. The societies, then, represented a substantial source of external control on the departmental structure: they constituted the major scholarly venues and organizational framework within which national interests could regulate knowledge production.

As industrialism proceeded within a Keynesian political-economic formation in the post-war years, the institutional form of the research university was established and could be regulated according to the needs of the capitalist welfare state. The major implication, in terms of ideological formation and citizenship, was that the expanding higher education system could, through social science practice, professional training, and so forth, extend hegemonic discourses of progressivism.

Progressivism refers to a conservative program of reform that achieves improvements in labor through regulated business practices and the like, but at the same time leaves intact the basic economic framework characterized by "private property, free markets, and the emphasis on individual achievement."[21] That is, progressivism is ideologically aligned with corporate interests and the corporate establishment, but is cast as a liberal democratic discourse. Thus, democratic discourse was constructed in a way that was entirely consistent with the interests of the capitalist state. I have argued elsewhere that various social science discourses have emerged recently signifying the "new progressivism": a movement away from ideologies supporting the capitalist welfare state to those supporting neoliberal paradigms of global capital.[22]

In Canada, the higher education system was developing just as the U.S. was undertaking a nationally orchestrated reform of its universities. The institutional form of the research university with its departmental structure was convenient. First, as with its U.S. counterpart, the intellectual work of the Canadian university was subject to external influence. The external influence could take the form of a combination of U.S.-mediated economic interests, organized through the steering effects of American research associations, and particularistic national concerns, organized through national funding agencies. In this way, higher education could serve a similar function in the development of the Canadian capitalist state to that which the U.S. research institution has served within the U.S. economic agenda.

The discursive formation of the Canadian university and the role it played in terms of ideological formation was, therefore, shaped by how it was constituted through the development of the Canadian capitalist welfare state which, in turn, was mediated by U.S. economic interests. Hegemonic discourses and discursive practices could be expanded through programs of teacher education, social work, health education, business management, sciences, and so on. Higher education, then, was used by the state to cultivate skills, dispositions, and social identities consistent with the imperatives of the capitalist state. As well, the intellectual work of the universities had become proletarianized and was useful in its own right in terms of innovations that could be applied in industry or in the management of social institutions. However, as neoliberal economic restructuring began to take place, the intellectual work of universities began to reflect this discursive shift. The next section explores this change.

The Restructuring of Intellectual Work in Canadian Universities: The Case of Ontario

In this section I review the work of Goyan[23] and Fisher and Rubenson[24] who extend the analysis provided by Slaughter and Leslie in 1997, which concludes that Canadian universities, unlike universities in the U.S., United Kingdom, and Australia, have resisted subordinating intellectual work to market imperatives.[25] According to Goyan, Slaughter and Leslie's conclusions are an accurate depiction of the Canadian higher education landscape in terms of the time frame within which they were working, which extends up to the early 1990s. During that period a national commitment with respect to nurturing connections between universities and industry had been established through position statements and initiatives such as the Corporate-Higher Education Forum established under the Mulroney government. These position statements were an extension of the neoliberal ideology promoted by the Mulroney government with respect to the reshaping of the Canadian economy. The neoliberal rhetoric of the Mulroney government involved representing the interventionist state as decidedly against the best interests of citizens. Within this rhetoric, the forces of globalization compelled strategies of economic development emphasizing free trade and an entrepreneurial spirit, both of which, according to neoliberal ideology, were hampered by an indulgent social welfare state. However, in spite of this rhetoric, the Mulroney government, in fact, did little in terms of radical cutbacks to the social welfare state. As Fisher and Rubenson suggest, "[t]he Conservative government's approach was incremental and favored greater selectivity, setting ceilings on program costs and, in some instances, making them self-financing."[26] The cumulative effect was that, in spite of strong talk concerning the importance of reducing the deficit, little action was actually taken.

The Progressive Conservative regime came to an end in 1993 with the election of the Liberal Party under Jean Chrétien. In contrast to the Mulroney government, the Chrétien government has expended relatively fewer words on position statements and party rhetoric, but has implemented a program of budget reduction that, nevertheless, achieves, in a much more radical way, a neoliberal agenda. Legitimized within the economic and social policies encapsulated within the free trade agreements (the Canada-United States Free Trade Agreement [FTA] and the North American Free Trade Agreement [NAFTA]), the Liberal government proceeded to introduce radical reductions in transfer payments to the provinces.[27] These transfer payments included, for example, funding for income assistance, health, and post-secondary education. These kinds of strategies represent an alternative, neoliberal, economic model to the Keynesian welfare state paradigm.

In terms of Slaughter and Leslie's conclusions, much of their analysis ended at the time that the Liberal government came to power. Their analysis of the impact of restructuring on intellectual work in Canada had taken place prior to the federal cutbacks enacted under the Liberal government beginning in 1993. Indeed, much of their analysis was grounded in the writings of Skolnik and Jones from 1983 to 1992. Slaughter and Leslie write:

> Throughout the 1980s business and government leaders in Canada proposed initiatives to create industry-higher education-academic partnerships (Skolnik, 1983a; 1983b; 1987). However, this policy direction was never adopted; instead Canada gave the highest priority to increasing and widening access, overtaking the United States in terms of

participation rates in 1988 (Skolnik and Jones, 1992). Although Canadian scientists view themselves as doing more applied work, for the most part Canadian academics have resisted rapproachment with business, despite promptings from some several agencies. In the words of Glen Jones (1991) there have been "modest modifications and structural stability." Canadian academics have perhaps been able to resist pressures by both business and federal government because Canada has by far the most decentralized higher education system of the four countries (Skolnik and Jones, 1990; Jones and Skolnik, 1992).[28]

Hence, according to Slaughter and Leslie, Canada, unlike the other countries they examined (U.S., United Kingdom, and Australia), has been able to resist the pressure to align higher education more closely with market imperatives. However, the analyses developed by Jones and Skolnik over several papers is in contrast to that provided by, for example, Newson and Buchbinder[29] or Buchbinder and Rajagopal.[30] These authors argue that throughout the 1970s and 1980s higher education enrollments continued to increase in spite of a lack of corresponding increases to operating grants. According to this analysis, the stage was already being set, in terms of increasingly constricted operating budgets, for the transformation of the university. Fisher and Rubenson and Goyan suggest that this transformation accelerated under the Chrétien government as a result of implementing a number of deficit reduction strategies. As Goyan points out,

> Serious effort to reduce the federal deficit began with the Social Security Reform process announced by Lloyd Axworthy in October 1994. First, the government revised the Unemployment Insurance Act to reduce entitlement and benefits substantially. Then, it announced that it would eliminate the Canada Assistance Program (for welfare and daycare) and Established Programs Fund (EPF). It proposed a new combined program, the Canadian Health and Social Transfer (CHST), which would reduce cash transfers to the provinces by $4.3 billion (37%) by 1997/98, including a $2 billion reduction for higher education. The implementation of the CHST gave the provinces the necessary impetus to commence cutbacks to higher education in earnest.[31]

The impact that these attacks to the social welfare state had on higher education systems varied somewhat across the different provinces according to the political and economic agenda at that level. In the case of Ontario, the cutbacks coincided with the election of a populist New Right provincial government in 1995 under the leadership of Mike Harris. The attack on the provincial social welfare state under the Harris regime has been systematic and relentless. The ideology is explicitly neoliberal, emphasizing tax reductions, free trade, and the disassembling of the interventionist state. According to Harris,

> History placed us at the centre of the continent's richest markets. As we approach the 21ˢᵗ century, our challenge is to continue to be North American's leading environment within which to live, work and invest. And the world is watching: Ontario is cutting taxes, restructuring government, scrapping barriers to investment and unleashing our entrepreneurial energies. Add to that our leading-edge workforce, high-tech industries, gleaming cities, unparalleled quality of life and unmatched natural resources, and you'll get the message: **Ontario isn't just open for business. In Canada, Ontario *is* business.**[32]

The Ontario government responded to the federal cutbacks by reducing the amount of its operating grants to universities by fifteen percent and at the same time allowed institutions to increase tuition fees. For graduate and professional programs, tuition fees were deregulated to allow institutions freedom to decide the level of increase on a program by program basis. Of the increased revenue generated by higher tuition fees, thirty percent is to be redirected back to student financial assistance with an overall effect of increasing competition among the province's universities to attract the best students.[33] The effect of these strategies with respect to quality of education, accessibility, and so on, seriously undermines the equity framework for higher education participation.[34]

At the same time that it reduced operating grants, the Ontario government began to reinvest in universities through targeted initiatives and matching grants. The three billion dollar Challenge Fund introduced in 1997 involved a provincial government contribution of up to $500 million toward research and development. To access these funds, universities are required to shift some of their operating revenues toward research and secure at least a one-third contribution from the private sector. In addition, Goyan cites the following examples of reinvestment strategies:

1. The Ontario Business-Research Institute Tax Credit was introduced in 1997 for business-sponsored research and development carried out by universities, teaching hospitals, and nonprofit research centres.

2. At the request of the Canadian Advanced Technology Association, the government introduced a $150 million dollar initiative in 1998 that aims to double enrollments in computer science and engineering programs over a three-year period.

3. Also in 1998, the provincial budget dedicated $29 million dollars toward higher education accessibility, $75 million dollars over a twenty-year period toward graduate scholarships, and $75 million toward research excellence awards.[35]

Thus, the conclusions reached by Slaughter and Leslie with respect to Canadian resistance to "academic capitalism" no longer hold true. On a province by province basis, and in particular after the Chrétien government came to federal power in 1993, higher education has undergone extensive restructuring throughout Canada. The restructuring of intellectual work that began in the Mulroney era has now been reinforced through the elaborate orchestration of budget cuts, performance based funding, and reinvestment through targeted initiatives. Through these tactics of financial leveraging, position statements, garnered through various task forces and commissions and promoted as state policy, have been enacted as institutional policy. Without these tactics, the push to shape intellectual work to emphasize, for example, "new products, processes, or services that can be commercialized by firms operating in Canada,"[36] would not have been realized.

Hence, the shaping of intellectual work in Canadian universities through the discourse and discursive practices of neoliberal restructuring can no longer be denied. Within this discourse, conceptions of quality and excellence are linked to economic development through innovation and training of knowledge workers. Restructuring practices such as performance based funding, institutional funding contingent on business partnerships, and curricula jointly developed and delivered by the public and private sector are transforming the university in terms of its institutional form. Deregulated tuition fees for designer degrees (such as executive MBAs and infotechs) set the stage for commodity fetishism with regard to higher education as a consumer commodity. Publicly traded universities such as Phoenix have experienced incredible growth over the past two years, and now the province of Ontario has taken the unprecedented step of sanctioning degree-granting for-profit private institutions such as Phoenix.

Perhaps most serious is the social legitimation of academic knowledge constructed primarily within an unregulated terrain of unfettered corporate interests, creating a situation within which intellectual work predominantly supports neoliberal capitalist ideology. "Advances" in biotechnology, agricultural and food sciences, forestry sciences, engineering, information technology, pharmaceuticals, economic theory, and so on, have immediate commercial potential and are, therefore, highly valued and supported within the restructured academic environment. However, this knowledge has devastating consequences when examined through the lens of global emancipatory interests and environmental sustainability. The work of scholars writing from a location outside imperatives of the so-called first world, such as Shiva, Amin, or Mah, illustrate the ways in which such "advances" reinscribe global inequities through neocolonial practices that are raced, gendered, and classed.[37] The restructured academic environment has even further shifted intellectual work away from the participation of the public and the imperatives of public interests. The production of knowledge within the imperatives of transnational strategies of capital accumulation succeeds in bringing higher education more effectively, and more insidiously, within relations of ruling that support global, interlocking systems of oppression and exploitation.

The Question of Citizenship

Clearly, Canadian universities are being discursively reconstituted within a neoliberal political-economic formation. The neo-Gramscian framework described earlier is helpful in terms of developing a discourse, or version of events, that runs counter to two prevalent themes in the higher education literature related to recent changes. The first theme is one articulated by a conservative reading of the changes to Canadian higher education since the Chrétian government came to power. According to this reading, in spite of evidence of restructuring, the overall impact on Canadian higher education systems is minimal. This reading is informed by an examination of institutions that look to be very similar in spite of some restructuring; shifts in curricula and research agenda are read as subtle and expected given other minor shifts that have occurred over the century. In contrast to this view, the neo-Gramscian framework situates the changes in Canadian higher education within a much broader political-economic discursive formation that is strategically being reshaped to emphasize neoliberal globalizing strategies that serve, in an unregulated way, the corporate interest rather than the public interest. According to the neo-Gramscian view, then, the restructuring of Canadian universities involves much more than minor changes at a system level.

The other theme is one articulated by a more progressive reading of changes to Canadian higher education. According to this reading, universities are undergoing corporatization, thereby aligning the agenda of the university in an unprecedented way with corporate interests.

According to the analysis provided here, the degree to which Canadian universities are aligned with capitalist imperatives has not changed much. As institutions, they were constituted in and through the capitalist state and now that this political-economic formation is changing through neoliberal structuring, universities are also undergoing changes. This reading of neoliberal restructuring of Canadian higher education suggests that political resistance to these changes should not be inspired by what the university used to be. Rather, a new vision is required that takes into account the role that higher education could play within a global context and that provides a clear alternative to notions of citizenship constituted through Keynesian and neoliberal political-economic formations.

However, the degree to which universities can articulate and mobilize new social movements, in my view, is increasingly threatened. Universities, already elitist institutions, are quickly becoming more so. Cuts to government transfer payments have led universities to balance their operating budget by increasing tuition fees. In Ontario, the University of Toronto, which prides itself on being an elite research institution, played a significant leadership role with respect to lobbying the provincial government to deregulate tuition fees for professional programs. The movement in Ontario is toward a higher education landscape within which universities and colleges compete with one another for enrollments and for corporate funding. This discursive shift has curricular and research implications.

Shanahan, for example, has compared the graduate curricula of a traditional law degree program offered in a campus-situated school to that of a more recent off-campus, part-time program from the same law school.[38] She shows that the off-campus courses offered in downtown office space are more oriented to practical skills, legal needs of corporations, and so on. In addition, these courses are taught on a contract basis by practicing lawyers who do not necessarily have advanced degrees themselves. The focus on pragmatic skills, she thinks, is a shift away from understanding law practice within a broader framework of social justice, civic life, etc. Similarly, programs of various kinds are becoming more entrepreneurial in terms of packaging curricula in ways that bring in revenues; these are marketed to professionals with ample financial means who are willing to pay high tuition fees.

The restructured academic environment has institutional forms that blend with and complement the new corporate culture.[39] My own academic context serves as a convenient illustration of the reshaping of the institution as a discursive formation. In this context an institutional merger took place along with departmental restructuring and downsizing. Devolution of various kinds of functions related to day-to-day operations has been completed. The unions have come under serious, systematic attacks with the faculty union finally succumbing by giving up its certified status shortly after the merger, which was interpreted by labour law as a "bill of sale." The struggle to maintain democratic decision-making in various arenas has been ongoing. Many academic and administrative staff alike have taken the view that democratic process is cumbersome — a view that supports the rise of managerialism whereby the leadership functions of universities are taken up by professional managers.[40] The support of managerialism is also indicative of an academic culture that views the democratic process as anachronistic and clumsy in an environment within which universities, as corporations, must be able to respond quickly.

Although the institutional arrangements for management and decision-making have moved away from democratized structures, there has nevertheless been an appropriation of democratic discourse in the formation of new structures. Terms such as "devolution," and "flattened hierarchies," for example, suggest more equitable distribution of power. The use of "teams" within which each member, regardless of organizational rank, can contribute to the discussions and decision-making appears to represent a shift toward empowering decision-making. However, the rise of managerialism, on the one hand, and the use of small teams, rather than broad-based institutional discussion and debate, on the other, reveal, in fact, the lack of democratic process in restructured environments. Bakker's analysis showing the gendered and classed consequences of Canadian economic restructuring further emphasizes the lack of equity and democratic imperative in the new order.[41]

The impact of these organizational changes on intellectual work has been captured to some extent within the higher education literature. Fisher and Rubenson and Axelrod, for example, suggest that the critical social function of universities within Canadian civic life is being threatened through a restructured notion of the liberal arts.[42] Ball has suggested that academics will experience "an intensification of work practices, loss of individual autonomy, closer monitoring and appraisal, less participatory decision-making, and a lack of personal development."[43]

Newson, in particular, has developed a number of insightful discussions concerning the transformation of Canadian universities in terms of: (1) the deterioration of collegial decision-making, (2) the adoption of corporate culture and institutional forms, (3) the subordination of democratic process to market imperatives, and (4) the pervasive impact of globalizing practices on intellectual work.[44] Polster and Newson provide a thoughtful analysis of performance indicators that is grounded in the work of Dorothy Smith.[45] They suggest that performance indicators are textual practices that coordinate our academic work in ways that are consistent with the organizational practices of ruling apparatuses. The province of Alberta, for instance, has followed countries such as the United Kingdom and Australia in terms of linking performance indicators to performance based funding. This type of disciplining strategy ensures compliance with a state agenda — in this case a neoliberal agenda — to regulate higher education as an extension of corporate needs. The province of Ontario has implemented performance contingent funding in the community college sector, further increasing the competitive landscape that already exists in that sector as a result of funding that is contingent on student enrollments.

Yet another feature of the changes of intellectual work concerns the explicit ordering of knowledge according to market relations. This ordering is accomplished through accounting practices and internal reallocation of resources: research and academic programs that are most aligned with market relations are not only able to receive relatively more external funding, but also relatively more institutional support. The types of programs that could stimulate critical scholarship, such as equity studies, are increasingly compromised in the restructured institutions. Faculty and student work that is aligned with market relations is rewarded, and work that challenges capitalist agenda is marginalised.

Universities, then, may not be best situated to mobilize social movements that challenge neoliberal transnational interests. The student population in the graduate and professional programs is increasingly elitist and the intellectual work of Canadian universities is increasingly consistent with a neoliberal agenda. The focus of the university elites on cultural politics that have erased issues of poverty,[46] on biotechnologies that reinscribe colonial patterns of domination,[47] on professional knowledge that emphasizes pragmatics over social reflection,[48] and so on, leads me to conclude that the pressure to mobilize change will not occur inside academia. The social identity inscribed through participation in Canadian universities is often an elitist one, and the citizenship practices that are shaped within the discursive forms of the institutional practice are those that are consistent with neoliberal economics.

There appears to be much more possibility for pressure, resistance, and change within a broader context and definition of post-secondary institutions. When one considers the substantially larger percentage of students attending community colleges, many of which are articulated with universities and more closely situated to the interests of the working class, the possibility for change, coalition building, and expansion of populist hegemony appears to be greater in the college than in the university sector. However, this notion punctures a mythic bourgeois construction of the leftist intellectual being groomed inside liberal arts departments. It suggests, rather, the enormous potential for cultural work and cultural leadership being groomed in those institutions that have been constructed as "less": less intellectual, less critical, less able.

Interestingly, though, it is precisely within this sector that one sees the statist/corporatist agenda advanced within institutional structures noted for their lack of autonomy and democratic decision-making. These characteristics of institutional citizenship have always been exclusively reserved for universities and have been constructed within liberal democratic, progressive discourses of academic freedom and such. If higher education is to play a role in advancing social justice and democracy, then, it will need to occur by expanding democratic discourse and discursive practices within all parts of the system, rather than locating these only in that part of the higher education system that is inherently elitist. That is, higher education must be restructured once more, but this time through expansion of a populist discourse that is formed within imperatives of social justice and democracy.

NOTES

1. See, for example, Chantal Mouffe, "Feminism, Citizenship, and Radical Democratic Politics," in *The Return of the Political*, ed. Chantal Mouffe (London: Verso, 1993), 74-89; and Ernesto Laclau and Chantal Mouffe, *Hegemony and Socialist Strategy* (London, New York: Verso, 1985).

2. Jacob Torfing, *New Theories of Discourse: Laclau, Mouffe, and Zizek* (Oxford: Blackwell, 1999).

3. Amarpal K. Dahliwal, "Can the Subaltern Vote? Radical Democracy, Discourses of Representation and Rights, and Questions of Race," in *Radical Democracy: Identity, Citizenship, and State*, ed. David Trend (London: Routledge, 1996), 42-61.

4. Barbara Epstein, "Radical Democracy and Cultural Politics: What About Class? What About Political Power?" in *Radical Democracy*, 127-139.

5. Ibid.

6. Dahliwal, "Can the Subaltern Vote?"

7. Ibid., 56.

8. Gayatri Chakravorty Spivak and David Plotke, "A Dialogue on Democracy," in *Radical Democracy*, 209-222.

9. Ibid., 210.

10. Torfing, *New Theories of Discourse*.

11. Ibid., 41.

12. Ibid., 37-38.

13. Laclau and Mouffe, *Hegemony and Socialist Strategy*, 105.

14. Torfing, *New Theories of Discourse.*

15. Ibid., 302.

16. Roger L. Geiger, *To Advance Knowledge: The Growth of American Research Universities, 1900-1940* (Oxford: Oxford University Press, 1986).

17. Clyde W. Barrow, *Universities and the Capitalist State: Corporate Liberalism and the Reconstruction of American Higher Education.* (Madison: University of Wisconsin Press, 1990).

18. David F. Noble, *America by Design: Science, Technology, and the Rise of Corporate Capitalism.* (Oxford: Oxford University Press, 1979).

19. Geiger, *To Advance Knowledge.*

20. Barrow, *Universities and the Capitalist State*; Noble, *America by Design.*

21. Barrow, *Universities and the Capitalist State*, 49.

22. Jamie-Lynn Magnusson, "Restructuring the Social Sciences within a Neoliberal Agenda of Global Capital" (paper presented at the joint meeting of the Socialist Studies Society and the Canadian Anthropology and Sociology Society, University of Sherbrooke, May 1999).

23. Paul Goyan, "Slaughter and Leslie's Academic Capitalism and Canadian Higher Education in the 1990s," working paper, Ontario Institute for Studies in Education/University of Toronto, 1998.

24. Donald Fisher and Kjell Rubenson, "The Changing Political Economy: The Private and Public Lives of Canadian Universities," in *Universities and Globalization: Critical Perspectives*, ed. Jan Currie and Janice Newson (Thousand Oaks, CA: Sage Publications, 1998), 77-98.

25. Sheila Slaughter and Larry L. Leslie, *Academic Capitalism: Politics and the Entrepreneurial University* (Baltimore: Johns Hopkins University Press, 1999).

26. Fisher and Rubenson, "The Changing Political Economy," 80.

27. Maude Barlow and Bruce Campbell, *Take Back the Nation* (Toronto: Key Porter, 1991).

28. Slaughter and Leslie, *Academic Capitalism*, 54.

29. Janice Newson and Howard Buchbinder, *The University Means Business: Universities, Corporations, and Academic Work* (Toronto: Garamond, 1988).

30. Howard Buchbinder and Pinayur Rajagopal, "Canadian Universities: The Impact of Free Trade and Globalization," *Higher Education* 31 (1996): 283-299.

31. Goyon, "Slaughter and Leslie's Academic Capitalism and Canadian Higher Education in the 1990s," 14.

32. Premier Mike Harris <http://www.gov.on.ca/MBS/english/premier/message.html>; Internet; accessed 15 March 1999. Emphasis retained from the original.

33. Goyan, "Slaughter and Leslie's Academic Capitalism."

34. See, for example, Philip Brown and Hugh Lauder, "Education, Globalization, and Economic Development," *Journal of Education Policy* 11 (1996): 1-25.

35. Goyon, "Slaughter and Leslie's Academic Capitalism."

36. National Centres of Excellence Program Guide <http://www.nce.gc.ca/en/index.htm>; Internet; accessed 27 October 2000.

37. Vandana Shiva, *Biopiracy: The Plunder of Nature and Knowledge* (Boston: South End Press, 1997); S. Amin, *Capitalism in the Age of Globalization: The Management of Contemporary Society* (London: Zed Books, 1997); and A. Mah, "Biocolonization in the Age of Globalization: Biotechnology and 'Developing' Societies" (paper presented at the Biology as if the World Mattered Conference, Ontario Institute for Studies in Education/University of Toronto, May 2000).

38. Theresa Shanahan, "Corporate Influence on Professional Curriculum: A Case of the Professional Development Program at Osgoode Hall Law School" (paper presented at the annual meeting of the Canadian Society for Studies in Higher Education, University of Alberta, May 2000).

39. Currie and Newson, *Universities and Globalization.*

40. Jan Currie and Lesley Vidovich, "Micro-Economic Reform through Managerialism in American and Australian Universities," in Currie and Newson, *Universities and Globalization,* 153-172.

41. Isabella Bakker, ed. *Rethinking Restructuring: Gender and Change in Canada* (Toronto: University of Toronto Press, 1996).

42. Fisher and Rubenson, "The Changing Poltical Economy"; and Paul Axelrod, "Changes to Liberal Education in an Age of Uncertainty," *Historical Studies in Education* 10 (1998): 1-19.

43. Stephen J. Ball, ed. *Foucault and Education: Disciplines and Knowledge* (London: Routledge, 1990).

44. Some of the works that make these points include: Newson and Buchbinder, *The University Means Business*; Janice Newson, "The Decline of Faculty Influence: Confronting the Effects of the Corporate Agenda," in *Fragile Truths: Twenty-Five Years of Sociology and Anthropology in Canada*, ed. William K. Carroll, Linda Christianson-Ruffman, Raymond F. Currie, and Deborah Harrison (Ottawa: Carleton University Press, 1992), 227-246; and Janice Newson, "Subordinating Democracy: The Effects of Fiscal Retrenchment and University-Business Partnerships on Knowledge Creation and Knowledge Dissemination in Universities," *Higher Education* 27 (1994): 141-161.

45. Claire Polster and Janice Newson, "Don't Count Your Blessings: The Social Accomplishments of Performance Indicators," in Currie and Newson, *Universities and Globalization,* 173-192.

46. Epstein, "Radical Democracy and Cultural Politics."

47. Shiva, *Biopiracy.*

48. Shanahan, "Corporate Influence on Professional Curriculum."

6 Canadian Pluralism, the Charter, and Citizenship Education

ROMULO F. MAGSINO, JOHN C. LONG, AND RAYMOND THÉBERGE

ABSTRACT/RÉSUMÉ

As the constitutional document defining the entitlement of Canadians, the Charter of Rights and Freedoms establishes the legal parameters of citizenship in Canada. Since its adoption in 1982, not only individuals but members of cultural groups have gone to the courts to ascertain their entitlements as citizens. Thus, Francophones have litigated their linguistic educational rights particularly on the basis of section 23 of the Charter. Litigation across Canada affirms that mother tongue instruction in schools has a fundamental role to play in maintaining the vitality of official language minorities in the country. This affirmation is accompanied by court rulings on, among others, educational services for Francophone students, management and control of educational facilities, and allocation of financial resources. Religious minorities have also tested the extent of their rights in the courts and have received a mixed message. The imposition in the classroom of any religion other than their own has been confirmed as constitutionally impermissible. Yet, their entitlement to government support for religious schools intended to preserve their religions has been denied. Like the minority religious groups, ethnocultural groups have received protection against hate and discrimination on account of their culture or cultural practices. Legal parameters are now evident but further group litigation may be expected. The confirmation of group rights in Canada through Charter litigation makes it necessary that group rights become part not only of the management and administration of schools, but also of the activities and the curriculum for study by all children. In a culturally diverse society such as Canada, study of the extent and limits of rights by future citizens is vitally important.

La Charte canadienne des droits et libertés est le document constitutionnel qui définit les droits des canadiens et établit les paramètres de la citoyenneté au Canada. Depuis son adoption en 1982, non seulement des individus, mais aussi des membres de groupes culturels se sont présentés devant les tribunaux pour revendiquer leurs droits en tant que citoyens. En ce qui concerne, les communautés francophones, leurs actions juridiques sont fondées sur l'article 23 de la Charte. La jurisprudence canadienne affirme que l'enseignement dans la langue de la minorité joue un rôle prépondérant dans le maintien de la vitalité des groupes minoritaires de langue officielle. Cette affirmation est appuyée par un ensemble de décisions, portant entre autres, sur les services éducatifs destinées aux élèves francophones, la gestion et le contrôle des établissements scolaires et l'allocation des ressources financières. Les minorités religieuses ont aussi vérifié l'étendue de leurs droits devant les tribunaux et elles ont reçu un message mitigé. Leur droit à la liberté de religion empêche qu'on leur impose une religion autre que la leur dans la salle de classe. Cependant, leur droit à l'appui gouvernemental pour des écoles religieuses en vue de maintenir leur religion n'a pas été reconnu. Tout comme les groupes religieux minoritaires, les groupes ethnoculturels profitent d'une protection contre la haîne et la discrimination culturelle. Les paramètres légaux sont maintenant clairs, mais on peut s'attendre à d'autres revendications juridiques. La confirmation des droits de divers groupes au Canada en vertu des litiges soulevés par la Charte fait en sorte que les droits des groupes doivent non seulement faire partie de la gestion et de l'administration des écoles, mais aussi des activités et des programmes d'études de tous les enfants. Dans la société pluraliste canadienne, l'étude de la portée et de la limite des droits par les futurs citoyens est très importante.

Introduction

The Canadian Charter of Rights and Freedoms undoubtedly occupies a prominent role in any discussion of citizenship and citizenship education in Canada. Waldron[1] points out that citizenship is uncontentiously conceived, in part, to involve individuals' entitlement to certain rights in the body politic. Thus, what it means to be a citizen in the Canadian context, what framework constrains the exercise of one's citizenship, and how one is to be prepared for citizenship participation become quite abstract without reference to the documents which outline the rights of citizens in a given jurisdiction. In Canada, the controlling document is the Charter of Rights and Freedoms.

Not surprisingly, the Charter has been described as the single most important innovation in the constitutional changes of 1982 in the country.[2] Cairns went so far as to claim that, over time, "the cumulative results of its application will reach deeply into our innermost being, manipulating our psyche, and transforming our self-image,"[3] and that our children "will be very different people because of this Charter."[4] This prediction may or may not come true. Nonetheless, we can agree that, with full knowledge of more than ten years of Charter-based litigation, Cairns is justified in pointing to the Charter's profound impact on citizenship. This impact was amply demonstrated by the prominent role of many Canadian citizens' groups in the Meech Lake and the Charlottetown Accord debacles.[5] Citizens coming to realize that they are important elements in the constitutional life of the country and their testing the extent of their rights in the body politic have led to what Cairns calls "constitutional minoritarianism"[6] and the "fragmentation of Canadian citizenship."[7]

The Charter has, in the minds of its critics, also been the culprit in the disturbing development of litigiousness in Canada. Critics with communitarian tendencies[8] have deplored what is perceived to be the problematic individualistic ideology underlying the document. As proof of this problem, it has been noted that, during the first year of the Charter's existence, hundreds of Charter-related cases were lodged in courts across the country. This indicates that Canadians have not been slow in seizing a powerful tool in their quest of their own interests.

Welcome or not, the reality is that the Charter has stimulated the unleashing of the militant pursuit of individual rights through the process of litigation. This appears readily understandable in light of the language of the Charter itself. The dominance of such words as "everyone," "every citizen," "every individual," "anyone," and "any person" overwhelms the infrequent references to groups. This is no accident. For the Charter's primary proponent Pierre Elliott Trudeau, this is the quintessential embodiment of his political philosophy. He stated:

> The very adoption of a constitutional charter is in keeping
> with the purest liberalism, according to which all members
> of a civil society enjoy certain fundamental, inalienable
> rights and cannot be deprived of them by any collectivity
> (state or government) or on behalf of any collectivity
> (nation, ethnic group, religious group or other).
>
> It follows that only the individual is the possessor of rights.
> A collectivity can exercise only those rights it has received
> by delegation from its members. ...[9]

Nonetheless, the document's individualistic language is more a reflection of what Trudeau would have preferred the Charter to be. The story of the Charter is a saga of struggle between Trudeau and his Liberals, on the one hand, and the provinces and groups with strong commitment to their respective interests, on the other.[10] Trudeau's victorious patriation of the Canadian constitution with an entrenched Charter was achieved only through accommodation with the collectivistic interests of his antagonists. As Monahan[11] insists, the aspect of the Charter oriented to the individual accounts for only half of the document. The other half "contains provisions which are distinctively Canadian (vs. American),"[12] that is, in his view, community oriented. Included in the latter are the official and minority language rights provisions (Ss. 16-23), the interpretive provisions affecting the Aboriginal groups and the ethnic minorities (Ss. 25 and 27), and the guaranteed rights of denominational groups (S.29). As Monahan sees it, these provisions enjoin the courts to avoid protecting individuals at the expense of destroying the capacity of communities to define their common identity and enrich the lives of individuals in those communities. In his reassessment of the Charter seven years later, Monahan concludes, as follows:

> It is in the wider political realm where the idea that the Charter protects "group rights" has attained a greater degree of prominence. This was most obvious in the drafting and the debate on the proposed "Canada Clause" in the Charlottetown Accord. The proposed Canada Clause was primarily organized around the concepts of group identity and collective rights. It referred to the fact that aboriginal peoples were the first peoples to govern Canada; to the fact that Quebec constitutes a "distinct society"; to the commitment to the development and vitality of minority language "communities"; to a commitment to racial and ethnic equality; ... to the equality of female and male persons.[13]

In the sections which follow, we focus on the rights claims advanced by certain groups, namely, the official language minority outside Quebec, minority religious communities, and ethnic or racial minorities. We highlight particularly the claims that have been litigated in the courts in order to determine the status of those claims. Having surveyed the Charter litigation, we analyze the impact of the judicial decisions on different aspects of schooling in Canada, giving special attention to the implications of this litigation for citizenship education.

The Charter and Minority Language Educational Rights

The Francophone Concern for Language Rights in Education

Language and language conflict is a defining characteristic of the Canadian identity. For nearly a century Canada's Francophone minority communities have struggled to obtain control of French language education. Minority language education rights have been argued by, or on behalf of, the Anglophone minority in Quebec and the Francophone minority in Canada's provinces and territories. The focus of this section is the Francophone minority in light of the distinct and separate nature of the two groups. Also, much of the case law dealing with S.23 of the Charter involves Francophone communities.

Francophone minorities have always argued the need to have and manage their own schools in order to ensure the continued survival of their communities. The prevailing view is that the ethnolinguistic vitality of Canada's Francophone and Acadian communities is very much dependent upon the establishment and control of schools that allow for the transmission of cultural values and language.[14] Some question the minority schools' ability to counter the societal factors that influence the rate of assimilation.[15] Nonetheless, for many Francophones, schools represent one sphere of activity where sociolinguistic behaviours can be impacted. In 1996, 970,190 Francophones lived outside Quebec; of these, 76 percent lived in New Brunswick and Ontario, and 618,526 spoke French at home. Though this number is substantial, there is concern that the number of French speakers outside Quebec will constantly and disturbingly diminish. The use of French as a language of communication outside the school is, in many communities, restricted to the home environment. Provinces, as well as municipal governments, have been slow to provide French language services to official language minorities. The resulting weakness of the institutional infrastructure, as Breton has observed,[16] limits the opportunities of using French in meaningful contexts.

These sociolinguistic factors coupled with negative demolinguistic trends such as linguistic exogamy have greatly affected the development of official language minorities. With the exception of the New Brunswick Acadian community, Canada's Francophone minorities are characterized by high rates of linguisitic and cultural assimilation. Assimilation rates range from as low as 6 percent in parts of New Brunswick to as high as 70 percent in certain Western provinces. The presence of Francophone minorities in most of the provinces outside Quebec contrasts with the monolithic nature of "la nation canadienne-française" which existed prior to Quebec's Quiet Revolution. "La nation canadienne-française" transcended Quebec's borders to encompass all those who shared a common language and religion and viewed education as the means to ensure that the next generation would be French-speaking. During the sixties, Quebec's nationalists concluded that it was no longer possible to ensure the continued existence of "la nation canadienne-française"; therefore, they retreated within the borders of the province of Quebec. Today we find a Québécois nation and numerous Francophone (Franco-Manitoban, Franco-Ontarian, etc.) and Acadian communities where language maintenance and cultural retention are under the purview of the educational system.

In varying degrees in different regions, two major historical developments common to all provinces and territories have marked the evolution of school instruction in French and school management by this linguistic minority. Each development entailed a period of restriction followed by a period more favourable to the development of the French language minority: (1) withdrawal of rights, sometimes including prohibition of French language instruction followed by a gradual recognition of the education rights of the Francophone minorities; and (2) consolidation of school districts, entailing loss of the de facto local control which Francophone communities had established, followed by the establishment of new management models to accommodate the Francophone minorities. In the first instance, these developments included the partial or complete substitution of programs of instruction in the mother tongue designed for the French minority by "second language" French immersion programs designed for the majority; in the second instance, an official differentiation between these programs resulted only after some struggle.

Restoration of Francophone Rights through Charter Litigation

Section 23 of the Charter guarantees the educational rights of English and French official language minorities. The provision provides for a novel form of legal right quite different from the type of legal rights which courts have traditionally dealt with. Both its genesis and its form are evidence of the unusual nature of S.23:

> The set of constitutional provisions was not enacted by the framers in a vacuum. When it was adopted, the framers knew, and clearly had in mind the regimes governing the Anglophone and Francophone linguistic minorities in various provinces in Canada so far as the language of instruction was concerned. ... Rightly or wrongly ... the framers of the Constitution manifestly regarded as inadequate some and perhaps all of the regimes in force at the time the Charter was enacted, and this intention was to remedy the perceived defects of these regimes by uniform corrective measures, namely, those contained in S.23 of the Charter, which were at the same time given the status of a constitutional guarantee.[17]

Section 23 confers upon a group a right which places positive obligations on government to alter or develop major institutional structures sensitive to the linguistic minority's ambitions and circumstances. The Court itself observed: "Careful interpretation of such a section is wise; however, this does not mean that the courts should not breathe life into the expressed purpose of the section, or avoid implementing the possibly novel remedies needed to achieve that purpose."[18] Understandably, then, the interpretation of S.23 — its meaning and application in specific circumstances — has in large part been left to the courts, especially as provincial governments have generally interpreted S.23 in such a way as to limit the scope of application. Given the reluctance of most provinces to broadly interpret S.23 in accordance with the aspirations and expectations of the Francophone minorities, citizens and groups have launched a series of court challenges which sought a more generous application of S.23.

Two landmark decisions have established the principles and rules of interpretation of section 23: *Mahé v. Alberta* (1990)[19] and Reference Re *Public Schools Act (Man)* (1993).[20] The Mahé case established a set of general principles that govern the interpretation of Section 23, and in doing so the Court has dealt with the following issues: the underlying purposes of S.23; the scope of educational services to be made available; clarification of the provision "where numbers warrant"; governance, that is, the management and control of facilities; and the allocation of financial resources for the operation of minority language schools. As the Court stated:

> The foregoing textual analysis ... is strongly supported by a consideration of the overall purpose of S.23. That purpose, as discussed earlier, is to preserve and promote minority language and culture throughout Canada. In my view, it is essential, in order to further this purpose, that, where the numbers warrant, minority language parents possess a measure of management and control over the educational facilities in which their children are taught. Such management and control is vital to ensure that their language and culture flourish. It is necessary because a variety of management issues in education, e.g., curricula, hiring and expenditures, can affect linguistic and cultural concerns. I think it is incontrovertible that the health and survival of the minority language and culture can be affected in subtle but important ways by decisions relating to these issues.[21]

The principles implied in the Court's statement reflect the body of literature dealing with ethnolinguistic vitality and the pivotal role of education and schooling in language maintenance and cultural retention in minority language communities. Specifically, the court recognized that there are links between language and culture and that mother tongue instruction and minority schools play a fundamental role in the maintenance and vitality of official language minorities. The Supreme

Court confirmed its position this way:

> My reference to cultures is significant: it is based on the fact
> that any broad guarantee of language rights, especially in
> the context of education, cannot be separated from a
> concern for the culture associated with the language.
> Language is more than a mere means of communication, it
> is part and parcel of the identity and culture of the people
> speaking it.[22]

With respect to educational facilities, the Court took the view that it was reasonable to infer that some distinctiveness in the physical setting is required to fulfil the cultural role of the French minority language.[23] In many jurisdictions this has meant the transfer of existing schools to a newly established Francophone authority. In many Francophone communities the school is also the cultural and community centre, the only Francophone *milieu de vie*.

The issue of sufficient numbers of students has been broadly interpreted by the Court. The relevant figure for Section 23 purposes corresponds to the number of persons who will eventually take advantage of the contemplated program or facility.[24] This interpretation takes into account the differences between the actual number of students and the potential number of students. The Summerside decision by the Court in January, 2000[25] reaffirms this approach to calculating sufficient numbers — in this case the number of children was between 49 and 155. In part, this flexible approach reflects the fact that the participation rate of official minority language children in Francophone education varies widely. In Manitoba, for example, roughly 35 percent of eligible students are registered in Francophone schools compared to 10 percent in British Columbia. Further, it is likely that the current participation rates are largely the result of decades of a lack or a limited number of Francophone schools in many provinces.

For Canada's official language minorities, Section 23 of the Charter represents the culmination of decades of constant litigation and conflict in order to secure the schools that conform to their aspirations for the maintenance of their language and culture. All of Canada's Anglophone provinces have implemented educational reforms that attempt to meet the standard set by S.23. Certainly, Section 23 and the judicial decisions on the litigation related to it have contributed to the strengthening of Canada's linguistic duality. However, there are still several unresolved issues as evidenced by the recent decision in Summerside, Prince Edward Island and the continuing legal action in Manitoba by a group of Francophone parents in the community of St. Claude.[26] These issues mainly concern access to schools and the quality of programs and services. Section 23 confirms that official language minorities are entitled to special consideration and treatment in order to foster their development, and it is a clear attempt to engineer Trudeau's particular vision that it was truly possible to create viable Francophone communities from coast to coast.

Surprisingly, the establishment of Francophone educational structures has been met with indifference by most groups. It could be argued that other ethnolinguistic communities are bolstered in their efforts to obtain schooling in their language by the success of Francophone groups. Interestingly, in Canada, Chinese will replace French as the most common language other than English outside Quebec. This development, associated with the increased immigration from Asia, can be viewed positively or, perhaps, as a sign of Canadians' weariness with issues of national identity. Nevertheless, Section 23 has forever altered the Canadian educational landscape. It may be too early to tell whether the application of S.23 will have the desired long-term impact of strengthening Canada's Francophone linguistic minorities or whether it is simply the linguistic equivalent of a life-support system.

Needless to say, Section 23 does nothing to address the needs of other ethnolinguistic communities which are also interested in enhancing their cultural vitality through language retention. A fundamental question is, "To what degree can multiculturalism flourish in the absence of linguistic anchors?" Since the Charlottetown Accord, there has been no attempt to undertake, at least politically, a public debate dealing with Canada's linguistic diversity. Therefore, the answer to this question will have to wait.

The Charter and Religous Minorities

Introduction

Traditionally, schooling has been regarded as a mechanism of socialization and has been perceived as bearing part of the burden for the acquisition of knowledge and the inculcation of dispositions, norms, and values which could represent and sustain a common national culture or, at least, a majoritarian civic ethos. Any resistance to this ethos by parents on behalf of their own or other children was, until the advent of the Canadian Charter of Rights and Freedoms, necessarily political since legal efforts were largely ineffective. Since 1982, and especially within the last decade, litigation has been an effective form of resistance to majoritarian school practices, particularly those anchored in a Judeo-Christian religious outlook. This Charter-inspired litigation, and the emerging judicial doctrine regarding the intersection of religion and schooling, clearly reflects the Canadian context of cultural diversity, and, in one aspect, the emergent Charter doctrine might be described as strongly protective of minority rights, as revealing a wholesale rejection of religious majoritarianism. In short, the legal rulings so far on religious exercises and curricula in Canadian schools sound the death knell of Anglo-conformity; Christian prayer and a curriculum of religious education may not be upheld as demonstrably justified in a free and democratic society merely on the grounds that they promote moral values in a predominantly Christian country. Such promotion, in the face of culturally diverse groups and competing social and moral values, has no overriding constitutional validity when it comes to deciding how individual rights to freedom of religion and conscience (in Section 2 [a] of the Charter) and guarantees of non-discrimination and equal benefit and treatment before and under the law (in Section 15 of the Charter) shall be protected and secured.

However, in another respect, this emergent Charter doctrine does not necessarily reflect a thorough or unambiguous embrace of multiculturalism or pluralism in public schooling arrangements or structures. Might not the courts favour the fuller exercise of minority rights by, for example, entitlements in regard to funding and the governance of schools comparable or similar to the rights of Roman Catholics to public denominational schools? On these structural issues — financing and governance — the judicial result of Charter-inspired litigation is proving paradoxical, indeed disappointing, for minority groups. An examination of the litigation concerning the intersection of religion and schooling in Canada, and the emergent judicial doctrine, yields some specific implications for public policy and educational practice and suggests something of the serious challenge involved, in an increasingly pluralistic society, of viewing the public school as a vehicle for the formation of the citizen and the practice of multiculturalism. Certainly, citizenship and citizenship education are, as Sears[27] has argued, highly contested concepts. And certainly, as Magsino has argued, multiculturalism is under siege and, recently, its espousal has been muted in the face of an undeserved backlash.[28] It seems clear that the traditional Canadian discourse of dualism and regionalism is not adequate to the realities of contemporary Canada. Indeed, according to Cairns, Canadian citizenship already can be described as fragmented, and constitutional minoritarianism — "the orientation of minority groups unremittingly to their own precise constitutional concerns, not to the larger claims of the community or to the overall health of the constitutional order" — is already upon us.[29] Majoritarian and minority interests must somehow be reconciled in Canada. Otherwise, a viable or realistic conception of citizenship and citizenship education, of multiculturalism and multicultural education, sensitive to both diverse cultural realities and ambitions and common public purposes and values, may not be possible.

Recent Charter Litigation and Emergent Judicial Doctrine

Public schools in Canada have been and continue to be faced with some conflicting expectations of their social role. For Hurlbert and Hurlbert, the ambiguity is this:

> Public education in Canada bears much of the burden and responsibility for instilling society's morals and dictums into the youth of today in an attempt to realize our aspirations for the world of tomorrow. Young people must be taught to respect the laws and customs of our land and to appreciate the country in which they live. With this educational task, however, comes the unenviable job of ascertaining not only which morals and dictums of our pluralistic society should be taught but also how they will be taught. In meeting this challenge, educators must often tread on the fine line separating secular from non-secular subjects and methods. For example, should students be taught competition or cooperation? never to lie? never to kill? and not use the Lord's name in vain? If they are to be taught these values, may they be taught in the context of the Ten Commandments? If they are so taught, how will a non-Christian pupil participate?[30]

It is in this social context, and upon rights claims anchored in the Canadian Charter of Rights and Freedoms, that certain key Canadian court cases concerning school-based religious exercises, religious education, and the funding of religious schools have been launched and adjudicated. In *Zylberberg v. Sudbury (Board of Education)* (1988),[31] Ontario's regulations on religious exercises in public schools were found unconstitutional by the provincial Court of Appeal. Following the lead of the Ontario Court of Appeal in ruling religious exercises unconstitutional, the British Columbia Supreme Court, in *Russow v. British Columbia (Attorney General)* (1989),[32] and the Manitoba Court of Queen's Bench, in *Manitoba Association for Rights and Liberties Inc. v. Manitoba (Minister of Education)* (1992),[33] found in favor of complainants who presented very similar Charter-inspired challenges in each of these provinces. Similarly, in *Canadian Civil Liberties Association v. Ontario (Minister of Education)* (1990),[34] the legal challenge to the religious education curriculum of the Elgin County School Board and the provincial Regulation underpinning the curriculum was successful in the Ontario Court of Appeal; that is, the curriculum was struck down as unconstitutional. In all of these court cases — none of which reached the Supreme Court of Canada — we encounter legal reasoning which goes clearly in the direction of the American constitutional tradition of maintaining a wall between church and state.[35]

More recently, the ruling by the Supreme Court in *Adler v. Ontario (Minister of Education)* (1996)[36] brought judicial closure to a decade-long dispute in the Ontario courts in regard to the funding of private religious schools. That ruling embodied this same principle of the separation of church and state and, indirectly, suggested the ultimate outcome of another case at the intersection of religion and schooling, namely, *Bal v. Ontario (Attorney General)* (1994).[37] The claims of the minority religious groups in *Adler* and *Bal* were essentially parallel. They claimed a violation of their rights to freedom of conscience and religion and a denial of their right to equal benefit of the law given the requirement that they personally finance their children's education in private religious schools since, for reasons of conscience, they could not send their children to schools which taught, at least implicitly, beliefs and moral values incompatible with the parents' beliefs and values. The aggrieved applicants pointed to the advantaged position of Roman Catholics in Ontario in respect of their entitlement to religious schooling and argued for the same treatment to ensure that the principles of free religious exercise, equality, and non-discrimination would be respected in their case. In the majority judgment in *Adler*, the Supreme Court ruled against the applicants, essentially saying that Ontario's funding of Roman Catholic separate schools does not open a constitutional door for other religious groups. The only voice fully consonant with the voice of religious minorities was the dissenting view of Mme L'Heureux Dubé:

> At issue here are the efforts of small, insular religious minority communities seeking to survive in a large, secular society. As such, the complete non-recognition of this group strikes at the very heart of the principles underlying S.15. This provision, more than any other in the Charter, is intended to protect socially vulnerable groups from the discriminatory will of the majority as expressed through state action. The distinction created under the Education Act gives the clear message to these parents that their beliefs and practices are less worthy of consideration and value than those of the majoritarian secular society. They are not granted the same degree of concern, dignity and worth as other parents. I conclude that the Education Act funding scheme results in a *prima facie* violation of S.15's guarantee of equal benefit of the law without discrimination.

> ... [W]e cannot imagine a deeper scar being inflicted on a
> more insular group by the denial of a more fundamental
> interest; it is the very survival of these communities which
> is threatened.[38]

In the wake of *Zylberberg, CCLA,* and the *Adler* ruling in the Ontario Court of Appeal in 1994,[39] the province of Ontario amended its own Regulations (#298) so as to prohibit any funding of independent religious schools at school board discretion, a discretion some Ontario boards had exercised. The *Bal* case was essentially a challenge to the Ontario government's decision to eliminate this discretion by school boards. The applicants in *Bal* were Christian Reformed, Hindu, Mennonite, Muslim, and Sikh parents who, prior to the change in the regulation, had their children in religious alternative schools within the public system or who desired to enroll their children in such schools. In 1997, the Ontario Court of Appeal dismissed the application for leave to appeal by the *Bal* applicants,[40] in effect adopting the legal reasoning of the lower court decision in 1994. "To grant the relief sought in this application would require that the court undo what the Ontario Court of Appeal has decided in Zylberberg, Elgin County and Adler,"[41] said the lower court. On February 12, 1998 the Supreme Court of Canada also dismissed the application for leave to appeal by the *Bal* applicants from the Court of Appeal for Ontario,[42] echoing the longstanding reasoning of the Ontario courts: the effective legal secularization of the public school cannot countenance the applicant's ambitions for religious schooling within a public system nor support for religious schooling by public funds.

What are the important implications for educational policy and practice which emerge from the legal decisions and doctrines recently advanced by the Canadian courts concerning the right to religious exercise in Canadian public schools? Have Charter-inspired rulings and the emergent judicial doctrine altered the legal posture of the public school? Indeed, why might the Charter-inspired rulings and doctrine be described as paradoxical and disappointing for minority groups?

First, it appears that anyone's freedom to manifest his/her religious beliefs in public, non-sectarian schools, or to have the school officially sponsor or express such beliefs, on the basis of the argument that they are the preferences of the majority, would be constrained by the legal interpretations which have been given to the Charter guarantees of "freedom of conscience and religion" (Section 2a) and by the prohibitions against discrimination on the basis of religion (Section 15(1)). Second, it appears that the principle of exemption from religious practices in schools is insufficient as a protection to religious minorities or those of no particular religious persuasion; indeed, such a principle is considered discriminatory and is constitutionally impermissible. Third, the protection of the constitutional rights of everyone would seem to require that the public school not attempt to teach morality or civic values by means of a program of religious studies which has, in any aspect, a sectarian purpose or a predominant representation of the beliefs of either the religious majority or a religious minority, except in the case of Roman Catholics, where they have a constitutional entitlement to denominational public schools. In short, the public (non-denominational) school in the age of the Charter must be officially secular. For religious minorities these results are paradoxical. While the applicants in *Zylberberg* (and in the cases in British Columbia and Manitoba) and *CCLA* succeeded in gaining judicial supression of majoritarian religious exercises and "indoctrinating" religious education, respectively, the *Adler* and *Bal* applicants found themselves "out in the cold," so to speak, because the judiciary seems to have accomplished a thorough secularization of the school system, such that it must be inhospitable to religious groups. Especially as a result of the Supreme Court ruling in *Adler,* it is now judicially clear that the Ontario government is not required to support any religious schools apart from its constitutional obligation to support denominational schools for Roman Catholics — an increasingly controversial anomaly. And largely on the basis of the reasoning and outcome in *Adler* and *Bal,* the challenge to only Christian holidays in the school year for Ontario schools by the Islamic Schools Federation of Ontario failed in the Ontario Court of Appeal in 1997.[43]

While the results of these several legal cases may be seen as judicially consistent — a liberal approach which emphasizes individual rights and an apparent state neutrality in the face of religious pluralism — they are not morally appealing from the point of view of the fair treatment of minorities. Further, politically, they fuel resentment and encourage a "political minoritarianism" as a substitute for what appears, so far, as an unsuccessful constitutional minoritarianism or at least a constitutional minoritarianism of limited scope. Concerning this development as it has occurred in Ontario especially, it is the view of Dickinson and Dolmage that "Ontario's education system reflects an uneasy relationship between the corporate dualism (linguistic and religious) of the Constitution Act, 1867 and the cultural pluralism of federal and provincial policies of official multiculturalism."[44] The judicial result here is clear, they say:

> ... [T]he inevitable conclusion [is] that the [Ontario] courts favor a liberal-pluralist approach. ... [S]uch a position ... has, to this point, fallen distinctly short of any active attempt to promote ethnic and cultural diversity.[45]

We can see the main outlines of the emergent Charter-inspired judicial doctrine easily: when the religious freedom of individuals was threatened by educational policy (*Zylberberg* and *CCLA*, for example), the courts have struck down the policy; when group-based religious rights were claimed (as in *Adler* and *Bal*), these rights were not recognized. Thus, as Dickinson and Dolmage have observed, "[t]here is sparse evidence of judicial support for ... court-ordered official recognition of ethnic or religious groups within the education system."[46] Further, they say:

> The four cases dealing with religion in Ontario's public schools reveal a clear judicial predilection towards enforcing a "benign neutrality" on the part of the state. Where the government's laws, policies, or practices appeared to give prominence to the religion of the majority, violations of the religious freedom and equality rights of minority persons were found. By requiring the public system to be entirely secular, the courts have removed the temptation — and indeed the very ability — to argue from a corporate-pluralist platform that neutrality should be achieved by the state's permitting and funding religious education and schools, for *all* religious groups, both inside and outside the public system. ...[47]

For religious minorities in particular, the judiciary's definition of state neutrality seems hardly benign, and its secularist posture of church-state separation is very challenging to their aspirations and ambitions. These fault lines in the Canadian constitutional order seem to call for a different and tougher task according to Cairns, namely, "the elaboration of a political theory appropriate to the need for rapprochement between the majoritarian and minoritarian elements in contemporary Canada, and the devising of institutional arrangements for its expression."[48]

Nourishing Citizenship through the Canadian Policy of Multiculturalism

The Canadian Conception of Multiculturalism

A citizen is, by definition, one who possesses rights and corresponding obligations in society. It is a lesson in political history, however, that these rights and obligations do not get established in ways that ensure fair entitlement for all. The veil of ignorance, which John Rawls[49] prescribes in the formulation of impartial principles of justice, which are needed to guide the initiation and operation of societal arrangements and institutions, is nowhere available to us mortals now or at any time in the past or the future. The reality is that each state has to work out its own set of principles governing the life of its people and its institutions.

In pursuit of justice for minority cultural groups, Canada has decided to formulate and implement a multiculturalism policy. The country has, as a consequence, been rightly praised for undertaking a bold experiment in the management of its culturally diverse people through the policy. But even as the policy seeks justice for minority groups, its main goal is the attainment of national unity, which, for Trudeau, would result from the accommodation of the sentiments expressed passionately by determined ethnocultural groups that made presentations and submitted briefs to the Royal Commission on Bilingualism and Biculturalism in the 1960s.

Whether it is frequently realized or not, the Canadian policy of multiculturalism is also a major political statement supporting full citizenship status for members of ethnocultural communities in the country. As Jacques Hébert points out, the policy "recognized the right of each Canadian to live and be fulfilled in his or her chosen culture and of every ethnic group ... to preserve its own cultural and linguistic heritage while respecting the rights of others. ..."[50] The policy, he added, espoused the principle that "a free and just society must accept pluralism and allow each citizen to make a personal choice of suitable lifestyle, customs, and culture, whether or not these flowed from his or her own ethnicity."[51]

To understand and appreciate the rights and obligations espoused in the Canadian policy of multiculturalism, it is important to examine it closely. Clearly it is intended as an instrument for ethnic groups' integration through the legitimization and sustenance of the aspirations of their members to participate in society even as they retain elements of their cultural heritage. Trudeau initially stipulated the Canadian conception of multiculturalism in his statement in the House of Commons on October 8, 1971. Not long after declaring that his government had accepted the recommendations of the Royal Commission on Bilingualism and Biculturalism, as contained in its *Volume IV Report* and as directed to government departments and agencies, he said: "The individual's freedom would be hampered if he were locked for life within a particular compartment by the accident of birth or language."[52] To emphasize the policy's intent, he reiterated it in the last paragraph of his declaration, as follows:

> ... I wish to emphasize the view of the government that a policy of multiculturalism within a bilingual framework is basically a conscious support of individual freedom of choice. We are free to be ourselves. But this cannot be left to chance. It must be fostered and pursued actively. If

freedom of choice is in danger for some ethnic groups, it is in danger for all. It is the policy of this government to eliminate any such danger and to "safeguard" this freedom.[53]

In adopting a policy which assures the "cultural freedom of Canadians," Trudeau also stated, as follows:

Such a policy should help to break down discriminatory attitudes and cultural jealousies. National unity, if it is to mean anything in the deeply personal sense, must be founded on confidence in one's own individual identity; out of this can grow respect for that of others and a willingness to share ideas, attitudes, and assumptions. A vigorous policy of multiculturalism will help create this initial confidence. It can form the base of a society which is based on fair play for all.[54]

These two quoted statements contain the specification of three value assumptions or principles which he finds justifiable in a culturally diverse society such as Canada: (1) freedom of choice, which includes cultural retention; (2) mutual respect, arising from confidence in one's cultural identity and from cultural sharing; and (3) equality, or fair play for all.

Having stated the values underlying the policy, Trudeau stated the general strategy of the policy as follows:

The government will support and encourage the various cultures and ethnic groups that give structure and vitality to our society. They will be encouraged to share their cultural expression and values with other Canadians and so contribute to a richer life for us all.[55]

This general statement of strategy was explicitly presented in the form of a four-point plan for the federal government and its agencies.

It took seventeen years before the federal government could translate the policy of multiculturalism within a bilingual framework into legislation. However, the passing of time did not diminish governmental commitment to fundamental Canadian values enunciated in the original statement. In 1988, the House of Commons passed the *Act for the Preservation and Enhancement of Multiculturalism*.[56] It states, among other provisions, the following:

3. (1). It is hereby declared to be the policy of the Government of Canada to ...

    (c)   promote the full and equitable participation of individuals and communities of all origins in the continuing evolution and shaping of all aspects of Canadian society and assist them in the elimination of any barrier to such participation ...;

(e)   ensure that all individuals receive equal treatment and
        equal protection under law, while respecting and valuing
        their dignity;
(f)   encourage and assist the social, cultural, economic, and
        political institutions of Canada to be both respectful
        and inclusive of Canada's multicultural character;
(g)   promote the understanding and creativity that arise
        from the interaction between individuals and
        communities of different origins.[57]

These provisions are echoed by those found in pieces of legislation or
policy statements passed earlier by different provincial governments.[58] A
later provincial piece of legislation in Manitoba highlights the same
values, as follows:

It is hereby declared to be the policy of the Government of Manitoba
to ...

(b) recognize and promote the rights of all Manitobans,
    regardless of culture, religion, or racial background, to ...
        (i) equal access to opportunities,
        (ii) participate in all aspects of society, and
        (iii) respect for their cultural values, and
(c) enhance the opportunities of Manitoba's multicultural
    society by acting in partnership with all cultural
    communities and by encouraging cooperation and
    partnership between cultural communities.[59]

Needless to say, the proclamation of the multiculturalism policy has
led not only to federal and provincial legislation on multiculturalism but
also, more importantly, to the incorporation of the policy of
multiculturalism into the supreme law of the land. As an entrenched
element of the Canadian Constitution, the Charter of Rights and
Freedoms mandates in Section 27 that "[t]his Charter shall be interpreted
in a manner consistent with the preservation and enhancement of the
multicultural heritage of Canadians."[60]

Charter Litigation on Ethnic Rights

Section 27 has clearly yielded some protection to cultural minorities
in the country. Thus, in the *R. v. Big M Drug Mart Ltd.* decision, which
involved violation of the federal *Lord's Day Act*, the Supreme Court held
the Act unconstitutional because it infringed on the accused's freedom of
conscience and religion. In holding unconstitutional the Act's requirement
that all stores close on Sunday as a day of rest, the Court ruled that the
majoritarian (Christian) practice may not be imposed on citizens who
take a contrary view. As Justice Dickson put it,

I agree ... that to accept that Parliament retains the right to compel universal observance of the day of rest preferred by one religion is not consistent with the preservation and enhancement of the multicultural heritage of Canadians. To do so is contrary to the expressed provision of S.27.[61]

Aside from enabling minority cultural groups to express their cultural practices, the Charter provision has also helped to protect the integrity of minority cultural groups. Thus, in *R. v. Keegstra*,[62] involving alleged violation of the *Criminal Code* which forbids the wilful promotion of hatred against an identifiable group, the Supreme Court of Canada confirmed the decision of the Alberta Court of Appeal which applied S.27 in interpreting S.2(b), freedom of speech and expression of the Charter. Upholding the provision of the *Criminal Code* which penalizes wilful promotion of hatred, the Court declared as follows:

The value expressed in S.27 cannot be casually dismissed in assessing the validity of S.319(2) (of the Criminal Code) under S.1 (of the Charter), and I am of the belief that S.27 and the commitment to a multicultural vision of our nation bears notice in emphasizing the acute importance of the objective to eradicating hate propaganda from society.[63]

The thrust of the Keegstra decision clearly has been maintained by the Supreme Court in *Canada (Canadian Human Rights Commission) v. Taylor* (1990)[64] which dismissed the appellants' challenge against a provision of the Canadian Human Rights Code, under which their conduct was classified as exposing a group of people to hatred or contempt on the basis of race and religion. In *R. v. Andrews* (1991),[65] the court confirmed that the Charter has embraced the richness, depth, and vibrancy of Canadian society through Section 27 and has constitutionalized its importance. This Section has given a clear direction on how Section 1 of the Charter should be applied such that appropriate laws protecting multiculturalism become reasonable limits upon free expression. The protective stance of the Supreme Court has also been expressed in *R. v. Tran* (1995),[66] in which the Court ruled that failure to provide full translation of all evidence at trial to an accused constitutes an infringement of Section 14 of the Charter. For the Court, the right to an interpreter is linked to the right of an accused to benefit from a fair and impartial trial, and also to our society's claim to be multicultural, as expressed in S.27 of the Charter. Indeed these decisions at the highest judicial level have necessarily reverberated in cases adjudicated at the lower levels. Clearly, the Canadian policy of multiculturalism, first espoused officially in policy pronouncements and legislation and then entrenched in the Charter of Rights and Freedoms, has yielded concrete benefits for Canadian citizens belonging to ethnocultural communities.

Implications for Citizenship Education

Citizenship education, which implies individual participation in the body politic, cannot afford to slough over the development of participatory skills demanded of the citizen. Therefore, the renewed interest in the study of children as participating citizens (for example, Cogan,[67] Hahn,[68] Holden and Cough,[69]) — the study of the processes by which their abilities and inclinations to discuss, question, debate, and actively participate; and the conditions under which these processes are promoted — is certainly to be appreciated. Needless to say, much has been written and still more will be written to focus on this matter.

However, the substantive content of the citizen's abilities and the fullest understanding of the rights and responsibilities of the citizen are equally important and cannot be neglected. Curriculum developers who hope to provide for citizenship education must ensure the inclusion of materials and experiences that will foster, to the fullest degree, the development of informed and perceptive citizens who are cognizant of the contexts, privileges, and demands of citizenship. Thus, a full-blown proposal for citizenship education cannot but be a comprehensive effort at curriculum development, which is not only beyond the scope of this paper but also beyond the ability of its authors. However, a few important implications deriving from the foregoing analyses can be identified and addressed. We identify and address these implications, first, in relation to the status of French language rights, then in relation to an emergent hegemony of secular values in public schooling, and, finally, in regard to the distinctively Canadian conception of multiculturalism.

Following the Summerside decision by the Supreme Court in January 2000, a decision which resulted in victory for a group of Francophone parents seeking confirmation of their minority language rights under the Charter, a columnist in the *Globe and Mail* observed as follows:

> The Supreme Court, however, is bound to uphold the Constitution which, along with its nobler aspects, codifies the fruits of ancient grievances and unseemly political accommodations. And so this court once again affirmed the iniquitous principle that, in Canada, some citizens, for the sole reason that they speak an official language in a minority setting, are entitled to rights not shared by others.[70]

In the same commentary the author likely encapsulates the thoughts and attitudes of many Canadians when he states: "Our greatest strength is that people come here from everywhere, and everyone has an equal chance to fashion a good and just life. It's getting in the way of our future."[71] This view exemplifies the failings of our education system with respect to citizenship education; it attempts to trivialize the legitimate cultural aspiration of a significant group.

However, some would argue that Section 23 establishes an entitlement to separateness. The challenge for citizenship education is to foster an understanding of Canada's linguistic duality within a multicultural framework, as originally intended. Without an appropriate curriculum of citizenship education, the separateness will be emphasized and bridge-building reduced to symbolic gestures. Further, language must be seen as more than a means to communicate. French immersion programs have been extremely successful in teaching hundreds of thousands of Anglophone children to communicate in French with very little understanding of Canada's official language minorities. The strengthening of official minority language rights by Section 23 must be matched by an increased understanding by Canada's Anglophone majority through a culturally appropriate curriculum. Conversely, an inclusive curriculum should also be the foundation of citizenship education for the Francophone school systems.

There are also important questions to address in citizenship education pertaining to the rights of religious minorities. In taking up the challenging theoretical and practical task of justifying and devising institutional arrangements for the expression of a rapprochement between majoritarian and minoritarian elements of Canadian society, schooling and its relationship to cultural retention and citizenship must surely come to mind. It appears that judicial activism on individual rights at the intersection of public schooling and religion has resulted in the hegemony of secular values in schooling. If schooling is always or inescapably about the inculcation of values and the formation of the young for citizenship, on what basis do we choose the particular values to be sponsored in schooling? By the distaste of a minority for those values sponsored by the majority? By allowing the sponsorship of minority values — including religious values — only in the form of private schooling, with the financial burden being left to parents of conscience and means? Is a wall between church and state on the American constitutional model a result we can live with? Is such a wall not an especially awkward fit with the Canadian policy of multiculturalism and its embrace of cultural retention as an important feature of this social policy? Does not education for citizenship require that cultural pluralism be taken seriously? And how should the justification and orchestration of citizenship education be approached in schools where the curriculum must reflect the reality — achievements and failures — of the Canadian experience in attempting to deal with the fact of cultural pluralism, diversity, and competing identities?

Perhaps the core of these several questions, at least from the viewpoint of legally constrained religious minorities in Canada, is the issue of equal right to free religious exercise on the part of individuals or groups. The Canadian courts have proven unsympathetic to parents wanting opportunities for religious exercise or instruction in schools. Given the secular character of Canadian public schools and a predominant worldly ethos of social and economic life, parents of religious persuasion may well argue that secular schooling places unjustifiable burdens on their religious values and religious freedoms. The fact that religious or denominational schools exist privately as an alternative is no help to parents who cannot afford the additional expense; it is for them an unjust circumstance, inconsonant with the notion that parents have a prior right to choose the kind of education that shall be given to their children, a principle embedded in Article 26 of the Universal Declaration of Human Rights, adopted by the United Nations and to which Canada is a signatory. Despite the majority legal reasoning of the Canadian courts, including that of the Supreme Court in *Adler*, Canadian schooling arrangements are far from ideal in relation to the equal treatment of religious minorities if only because provinces differ in their financial support for parental ambitions to secure religious schooling for their children. It may be a matter of contention but, in the name of fairness, public and governmental leaders might have to explore ways by which religious exercise and equal protection of the law are institutionalized in our educational systems. Where parents have the unburdened, real choice of schools consistent with their religious or secular persuasions, those who send their children to public schools may legitimately expect non-sectarian schooling for their children. On the other hand, parents who find secular schooling offensive and threatening should enjoy the right to the free exercise of religion by sending their children to appropriate religious schools. It would appear that the real enjoyment of such a right requires the elimination of the onerous financial burden which, in effect, penalizes religious parents who send their children to religious schools; in effect, they pay twice for schooling. In a democratic society which treats religious pluralism and freedom seriously, serious accommodation, rather than grudging concessions, should be explored.

Such an accommodation will signal a significant commitment to Canada as a pluralistic society; it will represent an embrace of "meaningful pluralism," such as is contemplated by this Canadian citizen:

> [Meaningful pluralism] is diversity about things that matter to people. ... I have never understood why it is more consistent with the civil libertarian approach to exclude all religion from education rather than to create a system which makes religious instruction possible for all faiths. It

seems to me that pluralism, properly understood, must be meaningful, demanding equal respect for each viewpoint. That respect is due each of us in our inherent dignity. It is not accorded when we are obliged to forsake our faith in exchange for a public benefit.[72]

This view essentially accords with the legal reasoning of Justice L'Heureux Dubé's dissent in *Adler*— reasoning which, in our view, is the most ethically cogent and the most judicially responsive to the real circumstances of religious minorities in relation to secular public schooling. The only arena left for such argumentation now is the political arena, arguably a more fluid arena for discourse, even moral discourse. Is it time for a new politics in Canada which will engage seriously the plight of new religious minorities in relation to public schooling? We say, yes. In this discussion, will the secular state or majoritarian community continue to insist that children of parents of religious persuasion be sent to schools pervaded by the beliefs, values, and inclinations of the secular world? Or will the state and those who favour and dominate public schooling concede that the public school, as it has developed, is not a neutral or non-predisposing form of socialization[73] and is, perhaps, in its own way, indoctrinating? Will the accommodation that religious minorities seek be achieved? Who can say? In our view, it would be just if that were the outcome of such a public discourse.

In regard to matters of multiculturalism, a very important issue, deriving especially from the critiques of Gairdner,[74] Granatstein,[75] and Gwyn,[76] needs to be addressed. Would a multiculturalism-oriented citizenship education skew the schooling of children toward a curriculum which is biased against the western tradition? The answer, without doubt, is no. The multicultural citizens in Canada are Canadian, not Filipino, or Chinese, or East Indian, citizens. Canadian young people will live in Canada unless they adopt a new citizenship and live elsewhere. The educational character and the sum total of students' experiences cannot but prepare them for life in Canadian society. Thus, multiculturally oriented schooling which is intended to promote citizenship education will necessarily have to maintain much that has been provided in Canadian schools. Not only should that curriculum aim at the growth of educated individuals (who are developing citizens), as R.S. Peters characterizes them[77]; it should also initiate young people into those skills, attitudes, and habits that will promote responsible and satisfying involvement in the world of work and in participatory political and social life within the Canadian framework. Therefore, a multiculturally oriented education fostering citizenship does not require a total overhaul of schooling as presently constituted. It does not call for the withdrawal of the standard Canadian subjects. The curriculum called for will be an inclusive curriculum, one which is devised creatively to accommodate, within the standard curriculum, the study of diverse cultures in the country and of the entitlements and responsibilities of citizenship for every individual and group in society. It will also call for varied experiences — curricular and co-curricular — that will foster the interaction of individuals from different cultural groups in ways that provide opportunities for cooperative learning, understanding of and respect for one another, and exercise in the art of participatory democratic living.

Will the education for citizenship in a multicultural society, so envisaged within the Canadian context, impede the development of cosmopolitanism which now seems required by the globalization of the different aspects of human life, at least in the economically advanced societies? The answer may very well be, not necessarily. Insofar as schooling promotes education which, among others, our model requires, those educated within Canadian schools may be expected to possess breadth of understanding and perspectives that will enable them not only to make sense of human life in the complex and intertwined contemporary world, but also to meet its demands in a satisfactory manner. It may be that, because of its emphasis on the study of cultural diversity, education for citizenship in a multicultural society will positively contribute toward the development of young people, who are adept at meeting the challenges of working and living in different cultural environments, at home or abroad. It is also worth noting that the principles embedded in the Canadian multiculturalism policy, not to speak of the fundamental rights and freedoms entrenched in the Canadian Constitution, are the very same principles, rights, and freedoms heralded by the international documents on human rights espoused by the United Nations. Serious study of the curriculum required by the Canadian model may, therefore, be expected to satisfy the requirements of an emergent cosmopolitanism.

NOTES

1. Jeremy Waldron, *Liberal Rights* (Cambridge: Cambridge University Press, 1993), 271-308.

2. Keith Banting and Richard Simeon, eds. *And No One Cheered: Federalism, Democracy, and the Constitution Act* (Toronto: Meuthuen, 1983), 21.

3. Alan C. Cairns, *Reconfigurations: Canadian Citizenship and Constitutional Change; Selected Essays*, ed. Douglas E. Williams (Toronto: McClelland and Stewart, 1995), 8.

4. Ibid., 8.

5. Alan C. Cairns, *Disruptions: Constitutional Struggles, from the Charter to Meech Lake*, ed. Douglas E. Williams (Toronto: McClelland and Stewart, 1991), 159.

6. Cairns, *Reconfigurations*, 119-141.

7. Ibid., 156-185.

8. Rainer Knopff and F.L. Morton, *Charter Politics* (Scarborough: Nelson Canada, 1992); Peter H. Russell, "The Political Purposes of the Charter: Have They Been Fulfilled? An Agnostic's Report Card," in *Protecting Rights and Freedoms: Essays on the Charter's Place in Canada's Political, Legal, and Intellectual Life,* ed. Philip Bryden, Steven Davis, and John Russell (Toronto: University of Toronto Press, 1994), 33-44.

9. Thomas S. Axworthy and Pierre Elliot Trudeau, eds., *Towards a Just Society: The Trudeau Years*, trans. Patricia Claxton (Markham: Viking, 1990), 363-364.

10. David Milne, *The New Canadian Constitution* (Toronto: James Lorimer, 1982).

11. Patrick Monahan, *Politics and the Constitution: The Charter, Federalism, and the Supreme Court of Canada* (Toronto: Carswell, 1987), 111-115.

12. Ibid., 111.

13. Patrick Monahan, "The Charter Then and Now," in *Protecting Rights and Freedoms*, 124.

14. See G. Duquette and C. Cléroux, "Vivre en milieu minoritaire: principes théoriques, possibilités et limites, recommandations pratiques," *Canadian Modern Language Review/La revue canadienne des langues vivantes* 49, no. 4 (1993): 770-786; M. Heller, *Crossroads: Language, Education, and Ethnicity in French Ontario* (New York: Mouton de Gruyter, 1994); Rodrigue Landry, Réal Allard, and Raymond Théberge, "School and Family French Ambiance and the Bilingual Development of Francophone Western Canadians," *Canadian Modern Language Review/La revue canadienne des langues vivantes* 47, no. 5 (1991): 878-915; Rodrigue Landry and André Magord, "Vitalité de la langue française à Terre-Neuve et au Labrador: les rôles de la communauté et de l'école," *Education et francophonie* 20, no. 2 (1992): 3-23; and Raymond Théberge and Jean Lafontant, eds., *Demain, la francophonie en milieu minoritaire* (Winnipeg: Centre de recherche du Collège universitaire de Saint-Boniface, 1987).

15. Roger Bernard, "Les contradictions fondamentales de l'école minoritaire," *Revue des sciences de l'éducation* 23, no. 3 (1997): 509-526.

16. Raymond Breton, "Institutional Completeness of Ethnic Communities and the Personal Relations of Immigrants," *American Journal of Sociology* 70 (1964): 193-205.

17. *Mahé v. Alberta*, [1990] 1 R.C.S. 342 at 363.

140 Romulo F. Magsino, John C. Long, and Raymond Théberge

18. Ibid., at 365.

19. *Mahé v. Alberta.*

20. Reference Re *Public Schools Act (Man)*, [1993] 1 S.C.R. 839.

21. *Mahé v. Alberta*, at 370.

22. Ibid., at 362.

23. See Reference Re *Public Schools Act (Man)*, at 855.

24. *Mahé v. Alberta*, at 384.

25. *Arsenault-Cameron v. Prince Edward Island*, [2000] S.C.J. No. 1.

26. Paul Samyn, "High Court Ruling Hailed in St. Claude," *Winnipeg Free Press*, 14 January 2000, sec. A, p. 3.

27. Alan Sears and Murray Print, eds., *Citizenship Education: Canadian and International Dimensions*, special issue of *Canadian and International Education* 25, no. 2 (1996).

28. Romulo F. Magsino, "Multiculturalism in Canadian Society: A Re-Evaluation" (paper presented at the conference of the Canadian Society for the Study of Education, Memorial University of Newfoundland, June 1997).

29. Cairns, *Reconfigurations*, 131.

30. Earl Leroy Hurlbert and Margot Ann Hurlbert, *School Law under the Charter of Rights and Freedoms*, 2d ed. (Calgary: University of Calgary Press, 1992), 157.

31. *Zylberberg v. Sudbury (Board of Education)* (1988), 65 O.R. (2d) 641 (C.A.).

32. *Russow v. British Columbia (Attorney General)* (1989), 35 B.C.L.R. (2d) 29 (S.C.).

33. *Manitoba Association for Rights and Liberties, Inc. v. Manitoba (Minister of Education)* (1992), 82 MAN. R. (2d) 39

34. *Corp. of the Canadian Civil Liberties Assn. v. Ontario (Minister of Education)* (1990), 71 O.R. (2d) 341.

35. For a fuller analysis of this "Americanization" of Canadian legal reasoning in these early Charter cases concerning religion and education , see John C. Long and Romulo F. Magsino, "Legal Issues in Religion and Education," *Education and Law Journal* 4 (1993): 189-215.

36. *Adler v. Ontario*, [1996] 3 S.C.R. 609.

37. *Bal v. Ontario (Attorney General)* (1994), 21 O.R. (3d) 681.

38. *Adler*, Dubé J dissenting, at 664.

39. *Adler v. Ontario* (1994), 19 O.R. (3d) 1 (C.A.).

40. *Bal v. Ontario (Attorney General)* (1997), 34 O.R. (3d) 484 (C.A.).

41. *Bal v. Ontario (Attorney General)* (1994) at 715.

42. *Bal v. Ontario (Attorney General)* (1997), (C.A.), leave to appeal to S.C.C. refused (1998) 49 C.R.R. (2d) 188.

43. *Islamic Schools Federation of Ontario v. Ottawa Board of Education* (1997), 145 D.L.R. (4th) 659, (sub. nom. *Islamic Federation of Ontario v. Ottawa Board of Education*) (ONT. GEN. DIV.) leave to appeal refused (July 29, 1997), DOC.CA M20514 (ONT. C.A.).

44. Greg M. Dickinson and W. Rod Dolmage, "Education, Religion, and the Courts of Ontario," *Canadian Journal of Education* 21, no. 4 (1996): 378.

45. Ibid., 379.

46. Ibid., 379-380.

47. Ibid., 381.

48. Cairns, *Reconfigurations*, 141.

49. John Rawls, *A Theory of Justice* (Cambridge: Belknap Press of Harvard University Press, 1971).

50. Jacques Hébert, "Legislating for Freedom," in *Towards a Just Society*, 138.

51. Ibid., 138.

52. Pierre Elliot Trudeau, "Statement by the Prime Minister in the House of Commons, October 8, 1971," in *Cultural Diversity and Canadian Education: Issues and Innovations*, ed. John R. Mallea and Jonathan C. Young (Ottawa: Carleton University Press, 1984), 518.

53. Ibid., 520.

54. Ibid., 519.

55. Ibid.

56. House of Commons, Bill C-93, *An Act for the Preservation and Enhancement of Multiculturalism in Canada*, 2D Sess., 33rd Parl., 1988, cl. 3 (1) (Assented to 21 July 1988 S.C. 1988, c.31).

57. Bill C-93, *Multiculturalism in Canada Act*.

58. Romulo Magsino and Amarjit Singh, *Multicultural Education in Newfoundland and Labrador: A Survey of Practices, Policies, and Conceptions in Canada* (St. John's: Memorial University of Newfoundland, 1986).

59. Manitoba Legislative Assembly, Bill 98, *The Manitoba Multiculturalism Act*, 3rd Session, 35th Parl., 1992 (assented to 24 June 1992, S.M. 1992, c.56).

60. House of Commons, *Canadian Charter of Rights and Freedoms*, s.27, Part I of the *Constitution Act*, 1982, being Schedule B to the *Canada Act 1982* (U.K.), 1982, c.11.

61. *R. v. Big M Drug Mart Ltd.*, [1985] 1 S.C.R. 295 at 337-338.

62. *R. v. Keegstra*, [1990] 3 S.C.R. 697.

63. *R. v. Keegstra*, at 757.

64. *Canada (Canadian Human Rights Commission) v. Taylor* (1990), 75 D.L.R. (4th) 577.

65. *R. v. Andrews* (1991), 77 D.L.R. (4th) 128.

66. *R. v. Tran* (1995), 117 D.L.R. (4th) 7.

67. John J. Cogan and Ray Derricott, eds., *Citizenship for the 21st Century: An International Perspective on Education* (London: Kogan Page, 1998).

68. Carol L. Hahn, *Becoming Political: Comparative Perspectives on Citizenship Education* (Albany: State University of New York, 1998).

69. Cathie Holden and Nick Cough, eds. *Children as Citizens: Education for Participation* (London: J. Kingsley, 1998).

70. John Ibbitson, "Down With History," *Globe and Mail*, 17 January 2000, sec. A, p. 11.

71. Ibid.

72. Peter Lauwers, a Toronto lawyer, quoted in Lois Sweet, *God in the Classroom: The Controversial Issue of Religion in Canada's Schools* (Toronto: McClelland and Stewart, 1997), 237-238.

73. Elmer John Thiessen, *Teaching for Commitment: Liberal Education, Indoctrination, and Christian Nurture* (Montreal: McGill-Queen's University Press, 1993).

74. William D. Gairdner, *The Trouble with Canada* (Toronto: General Paperbacks, 1990).

75. J.L. Granastein, *Who Killed Canadian History?* (Toronto: Harper-Collins, 1998).

76. Richard Gwyn, *Nationalism without Walls: The Unbearable Lightness of Being Canadian* (Toronto: McClelland and Stewart, 1995).

77. R.S. Peters, *Ethics and Education* (London: Allen and Unwin, 1966).

7 Multiculturalism and Citizenship: The Status of "Visible Minorities" in Canada

BERYLE MAE JONES

ABSTRACT/RÉSUMÉ

It is never a strongly contested view that Canada has "grown up" as a multicultural society. Canada's dynamic process of growth in ethnocultural relations has largely been influenced by three principal forces — the indigenous peoples, variegated patterns of immigration, and the accommodation of minority nationalities. For the most part, multiculturalism has been distinguished by peaceful social co-existence, underpinned by experience in collective problem solving and passionate public discourse. These frameworks of order and co-operation, characteristic of the Canadian identity, have led to a pragmatic approach in public policy and institution building. Issues relating to multicultural citizenship and integration-assimilation, as well as the need for appropriate citizenship education, have been important by-products of this process of growth. The latter, however, are in need of theoretical refinement and a sharper focus on socio-historical points of reference from the minority perspective.

On n'a jamais fortement mis en doute l'opinion que le Canada "s'est développé" comme une société multiculturelle. Son processus dynamique de croissance dans les rapports ethnoculturels a été en grande partie influé par trois forces principales — les peuples autochtones, les caractéristiques bigarrées d'immigration et l'accommodation de nationalités minoritaires. Dans l'ensemble, le multiculturalisme émergent a été distingué par la coexistence sociale pacifique, soutenue par l'expérience dans la résolution des problèmes collectifs et un discours public véhément. Ces cadres d'ordre et de coopération, caractéristiques de l'identité canadienne, ont produit beaucoup de pragmatisme dans la politique publique et la construction des institutions. Des problèmes qui portent sur la citoyenneté multiculturelle et l'intégration-assimilation, ainsi que le besoin pour l'éducation sur la citoyenneté convenable, ont été des conséquences secondaires importantes du processus de croissance. Ce sont, cependant, des questions en grande partie disputées. Beaucoup de ces questions ont besoin d'être théoriquement raffinées et concentrées d'une façon plus pénétrante sur les points socio-historiques de référence de la perspective minoritaire.

Introduction

Increasingly multiculturalism is being perceived in terms of colour, focusing on "visible minorities." This, of course, is a particular perception implicitly accommodated in the language of Canadian public policy and reflected as well in certain of the social demands of the minority constituency. The common currency is acceptance of "cultural diversity" or "cultural pluralism" and the search for solutions to its resulting challenges.

According to Kymlicka, multiculturalism in Canada typically refers to the rights of immigrants to express their ethnic identity without fear of prejudice or discrimination.[1] Thus, for visible minorities multiculturalism translates into demands for the recognition of their cultural differences. It represents a desire to integrate into Canadian society and to be accepted as full members of it. It means ensuring their survival as a distinct community without becoming a "separate society." From this perspective, multiculturalism may be seen as a process-driven concept or movement aimed at modifying Canadian laws, institutions, thinking, and other aspects of mainstream society to make them more accommodating to cultural differences. In this sense, multiculturalism may be seen as a social engineering process to shape ethnocultural relations, relying on the central building blocks of "integration," the manipulation of theories of "citizenship,"[2] and changing educational philosophy and strategies.[3] Reinforcing effects may have come from contemporary concepts of "social capital" and "democratic governance" which, in practice, are presumed to be able to mitigate problems of identity and allegiance.

In practice, the fact that both social capital formation and democratic governance may be able to adjust the terms of integration and build allegiance for social capital reflects the idea of people working together for collective economic and socio-cultural purposes, sacrificing some individual and group interests in the process. Inherently a dialectical process, social capital expands with the number of opportunities for collective engagement on fundamental matters and becomes more difficult to forge where such opportunities are lacking. Obviously, it requires mutual trust as well as frameworks for meaningful social interactions. For such interactions to be meaningful, there must be a partnership of equals in which roles, responsibilities, and accountabilities are clearly defined. Further, accommodation of social differences requires both a sense of interdependence and a feel for the future. Relatedly, democratic governance is essentially about building systems of "co-management" within policy frameworks that emphasize participation on mutually acceptable terms, transparency, and accountability. Because such frameworks are essential pre-conditions for building trust and a stable climate of expectation, when established, they are likely to promote social commitment, support, and allegiance whether in institutional or national settings.[4] Canada has implicitly and explicitly drawn on these conceptual frameworks to strengthen multicultural imperatives, using the institutional vehicles of community organizations and educational policy with mixed results.

Ethnic minorities, including "visible minorities," have been convenient points of official intervention aimed at advancing the goals of multiculturalism. These communities have been, and continue to be, important transmission belts of the values, messages, symbols, and ideas on which multiculturalism and its preferred strategies thrive. Socio-political demands and desires with respect to recognition, accommodation, and the more tangible outputs of public policy are typically channeled through community organizations. This reality makes a necessary symbiotic relationship between community and officialdom inevitable. Yet, as we shall see, the dominant official responses — laws, ameliorative policy action in education, employment, and other areas; symbolic recognition of community leaders; sponsorship of community projects and programs and the like — have not been problem-free. Perhaps the most challenging of these responses relates to issues of multiculturalism/multicultural education and citizenship/citizenship education.

The Search for Deeper Understanding:
A "Visible Minority" Perspective on Multiculturalism

The intent is not to give a historical development of citizenship education in Canada (which itself has been described as complex and diverse, yet conservative, and as an agent for preserving the status quo[5]). The issues, then, appropriately start at a point in Canadian immigration history where minority groups, especially the so-called "visible minorities," have had a new and persistent impact on Canadian policy relative to "multiculturalism for all" and "citizenship for all."[6]

The official declaration of the policy of multiculturalism within a bilingual framework and its unanimous acceptance in the House of Commons in 1971, which affirmed Canada as a multicultural nation, not only meant an official recognition of minority groups, but was also viewed as a vast improvement on former notions of bilingualism and biculturalism. "What this policy does is to fundamentally assure, within a bilingual framework, the cultural freedom and equality of all Canadians."[7] The declaration of Canada as a multicultural society became enshrined in the new Charter of Rights and Freedoms which guarantees equality of rights for all Canadians — "equal protection and equal benefit of law without discrimination based on race, national or ethnic origin, color, religion, sex, age or mental or physical disability."[8] It became further extended in the Charter through Section 27 which requires interpretation of charter provisions to recognize the cultural heritage of Canadians. The rights and freedoms of minority groups received additional guarantees from the 1988 Canadian Multicultural Act, which, among other clauses, stated two affirmations particularly pertinent to this discussion: first, that "multiculturalism is a fundamental characteristic of our Canadian identity"; and, second, that Canada's culturally diverse communities and their contribution to Canadian society should be recognized in federal law.[9]

That Canada's concept of multiculturalism is rooted in the notion of ethnicity is illustrated by the emphasis on promoting harmonious ethnic/ race relations as one of the three areas of social concern identified by the Multiculturalism Directorate, which is part of the machinery responsible for implementing the policy on multiculturalism.[10] A number of nation-wide activities prevailed. These focused on developing harmony across and within the different ethnic groups. In 1983 the Canadian government created a Special Parliamentary Committee on the Participation of Visible Minorities in Canadian Society, and the report, entitled *Equality Now!*, was submitted to Parliament in 1984.[11] In essence, the report chronicled the participation, under-participation, and non-participation of "visible minorities" in both the private and public sectors. Subsequent efforts to implement employment equity, including the concept of affirmative action and the practice for minority groups to declare their status on application forms, became contentious issues among both the mainstream and minority groups.

More significant is the fact that multiculturalism in Canada, with its unique constitutional status, moves the concept beyond ethnicity (in terms of language and culture) to include broader "human rights" with the principle of equal opportunity relative to issues of race, class, gender, age, sexual orientation, and the physically and mentally challenged. It is not surprising, then, that the Directorate believed that immigrant women —"one of Canada's most isolated groups"— should be another area of concern and should be on the priority list for receiving special assistance toward their integration into Canadian society.[12] Consequently, a National Conference on Immigrant Women in 1981, which was also part of the assessment of the impact of the Multicultural Policy in its tenth year, precipitated a number of projects for language training for immigrant women, as well as assistance to women "pressing for changes in laws and administrative practices that mitigate against equal opportunity."[13] The conference also ushered in the beginning of the establishment of organizations to support immigrant women in their unique struggles for integration into Canadian society. These organizations mushroomed in many provinces across the country (e.g., the Immigrant Women's Association of Manitoba [IWAM] formed in 1982) and thrust themselves actively into feminist politics.

The concept of multicultural education, or "multiculturalism in education," followed swiftly as the third area of concern, for it was thought that "the most effective way of ensuring tolerance and mutual respect for our diversity [was] by reaching Canada's youth. Teacher training, special events, the publication of materials, and the support of innovative projects are aimed at having the concept of multiculturalism pervade *all* aspects of education."[14]

Although education in Canada falls within provincial jurisdiction, the formation of the Canadian Council for Multicultural and Intercultural Education (CCMIE), a network of educators and interest groups across Canada, initiated provincial action designed to actualize the educational ideals outlined above. The 1980s and the first half of the 1990s witnessed vigorous attempts to "multiculturalize" school curricula, as well as develop some kind of guiding principles to socialize students into a new paradigm shift in public education. These innovations were especially characteristic of urban schools in the inner-city with large concentrations of diverse ethnic groups, but were less evident in suburban and rural schools. This situation began to set the stage for multicultural education for the "others," even in the presence of provincial multicultural education policy/act, as is the case in Manitoba.[15]

Broad sectors of the minority community, especially visible minorities, would argue that neither the gaps identified in *Equality Now!*, nor the recommendations proposed to bridge these gaps have brought substantial change that would fundamentally enhance their social status. Neither has the way been paved for the desired transition from group interest to national interest, based on current citizenship education agendas. Attempts to foster positive ethnic/race relations through conferences and seminars, and particularly through "grass-root" community organizations and activities, seem to have rekindled a new interest among older ethnic groups in their own cultures. But they could not be said to have propelled race-relations into a more "collective" dialogue related to issues about national unity/identity and citizenship.

Today, multicultural education in Manitoba, for example, with the recent pre-occupation of teachers and administrators with matters concerning new initiatives for education, has not fully addressed issues of an inclusive school curriculum in terms of assurances, on one hand, and expectations, on the other. For the most part, curriculum is still grounded in residual notions of bilingualism and biculturalism. The Ministry of Education and Training's most current documents — designed for "education renewal"— have elicited both positive and negative comments. Some have noted the scant attention paid to multicultural/diversity education alongside a broad promotion of technology, for example. Others, however, have viewed commitments to issues of diversity, anti-bias education, gender-fairness, and Aboriginal perspectives as forward-looking.[16] The merit of the latter cannot be disputed. However, explicit policy references to teacher training as an imperative to "multiculturalizing" schools and their curricula has not been vigorously translated into practice. Though some progress has been made, teacher training for diversity has not had top priority in any co-ordinated and sustained way. The school is the microcosm of society which looks to education for the nurturing of responsible citizens especially in diverse societies where cultural literacy has become a vital component. And teachers have a vital role to play in helping young people to accommodate and respect difference. But cutbacks to the educational enterprise also have far-reaching effects beyond the boundaries of schools for if schools cannot provide legitimate ways for young people to practise "good citizenship," they are likely to find undesirable ways to vent their feelings.

History shows that it is the issue of difference/colour, which many perceive as "new" and visible elements within the population, that would trigger the latest type of racism which has generated a plethora of reactions against educational, social, and other responses to the diversity of Canadian society. It comes as no surprise that, with very shallow anchorage in shifting emphases on multicultural/citizenship initiatives and in the wake of a diminishing defence, there has been a backlash against multiculturalism generally. Minority groups, especially visible minorities, become easy targets for blame in cases of economic depression, employment crises, conflict of language/cultural rights, school and play-ground conflicts, concerns regarding integration, lack of national unity, and so forth. Kymlicka makes the point that "it is difficult to avoid the conclusion that much of the backlash against 'multiculturalism' arises from a racist or xenophobic fear of these new immigrant groups."[17]

Critics may argue that Canada is a multicultural nation that historically and constitutionally promotes cultural diversity rather than homogeneity of cultures, conceptualized in the notion of "collective citizenry." But what this argument does, in fact, is to raise questions about how the multiplicity of minority cultures (and sub-cultures) are positioned, and how these cultures perceive themselves and their interests within the historical British-French duality. McLeod's perspective perhaps offers some clarification of positions when he notes that "[e]quality of status was not intended to mean that all ethnic groups would have equal impact. Historically, English and French Canadians have had a great influence on Canadian society and cultural life. That they will continue to do so, is not a major issue. ..."[18]

This context of historical development is crucial to the Canadian situation, but it is not without problems. Those who have found it easy to assimilate have often shared their status. And while the national discourse around multiculturalism has revived status claims and rights for Aboriginal peoples, it is the so-called "visible minorities" who have become associated with the social, cultural, and educational responses to multiculturalism. In addition, the collective voice of these "other" ethnic groups has often been presented as not problematic. These "other" ethnic groups make relatively few demands for the preservation of their culture when compared to the French or the Aboriginals. Important as these demands are, they do not pose a threat to national unity, and so are likely to receive less attention.

It is within the context of the above-mentioned official assurances and hopes for equality, as well as from a more pragmatic perspective (through first-hand experience), that I examine effective possibilities for inclusive citizenship education and citizenship status for visible minorities, especially in the light of the current and renewed emphasis on citizenship and citizenship education.

A "Visible Minority" Perspective
on Multicultural and Citizenship Education

Education has always played a central role in the evolution of multicultural strategies in the context of cultural pluralism. The debate about the kind of education necessary for advancing a viable multicultural society has been passionate and the issues contested. A primary issue relates to the need for thoroughgoing reform in the education process. There appears to be consensus on the need for revising traditional assumptions, philosophies, and, therefore, content, administrative structures, and emphases. The argument in the communities of the "visible minorities" is that extant approaches to the articulation and management of education policy have been constraining, not facilitating, the progress of multiculturalism. Specifically, they regard issues of access and equity, of participation and relevance, and of scope and levels of funding as some of the irritants that must be addressed. Like other voices in mainstream society, they are pressing for the re-invention of citizenship and citizenship education in Canada. But first there must be a deconstruction of myths of divisiveness with the more rigorous promotion of the merits of multiculturalism, supported by a swift and sustained defense of it.[19] It has been well documented that expectations of, and demands from, the "new" multicultural population regarding schooling, social services, political representation, and so on, followed the same aspirations and patterns of "earlier" populations except for one difference: Whose aspirations? Whose demands?[20] This new brand of citizenship education, unlike a multicultural education *for all*, would need to offer a framework that is capable of bridging the gap between "*we*" and "*they*," for, currently, there can be no assumption that negative social attitudes toward the concept of multiculturalism will not influence decisions surrounding deeper issues about citizenship.

Historically, the concept of citizenship in Canadian public policy has also been socially and politically contested. Often citizenship has been conceived in essentially legalistic and personal terms. As such, it has focused rather mechanically on rights and responsibilities and on the exercise of personal capacity and commitment to some vision of a civic ethos. The hallmarks appear to be civic competence and civic responsibility. Another view associates citizenship with "common rights" that suggest equal community access to mainstream culture and, by implication, a common identity shared by the political community regardless of group membership. Sometimes the duality of meaning or emphasis may be construed, especially among the visible minorities, as deliberate strategies to engender debates and confusion, to facilitate official manipulation, and to win breathing space for the prevailing doctrines of multiculturalism. Yet there are points of convergence in these concepts of "personal" and "common" rights of citizenship.

Both concepts functionally require much "informed thinking" and a disposition toward "social action"[21] within the community. It is self-evident that these requirements impose on communities the need to respect and accommodate ethnocultural differences as well as a willingness to engage in public discourse about all the issues, contentious or otherwise, that affect multiculturalism. These requirements themselves imply commitment to creating opportunities for all to participate in public life. Needless to say, a relevant kind of citizenship education is germane to meeting these minimum socio-political standards of citizenship.

From the ethnocultural minority perspective, however, a confluence of forces continues to militate against the smooth emergence of a settled regime of citizenship education in Canada. One basic factor is the resistance of traditional educational culture to change. The educational establishment has been equally slow in adapting to socio-technical demands of globalization and post-industrial society. In an effort to compensate, it has minimized the role of diversity and citizenship education as a necessary balance. Our thesis, however, is that a relevant regime of citizenship education would require fundamental changes in the assumptions, administrative arrangements, and curriculum of education as we know it in Canada today. At least four building blocks are necessary as the starting point for the construction of such a regime, given the context already outlined and certain paradoxes to be outlined later.

The first building block is the identification of sources of unity. It is self-evident that the fundamental challenge in fabricating citizenship education relates to identifying these sources in the multicultural state and then consolidating them, using education as one vehicle. To be sure, the central difficulty is to mobilize and sustain consensus on what the sources of unity are, and to find ways and means to weaken the impulse to politicize ethnic differences. Relatedly, there is the difficulty of isolating the premises on which to design and deliver citizenship education that can accommodate the multiplicity of diversities now defining Canadian multiculturalism. Further, given the lop-sided development of the social sections making up this diversity, it would be especially difficult to secure the even spread of the cement that will make multiculturalism work.[22]

Second, citizenship requires a special species of multi-disciplinary education, transcending the focus on constitutionalism and civics. Its disciplinary tentacles must also embrace and facilitate opportunities for learning to deal with life problems, including social adjustment, teamwork, conflict resolution, and the like, and to cope with tensions and bottlenecks inherent in diversity. Additionally, it must aid the rapid development and reproduction of the usual and new social and technical skills that now drive the political economy of post-industrial societies. It must provide for young people, including visible minorities, a model of global citizenship that encourages interdependence as opposed to a culture of dependency at the personal, national, and international levels. In the article "Students of Color Abroad: Marginalized or Empowered?," Chambers stresses the importance of American students studying abroad as a new phenomenon that will "profoundly affect our understanding and respect for diverse cultures as well as our understanding of the human spirit."[23] He further cites Carew's views that, although some countries may treat "students of color" within the context of the global negative image of minorities in the United States, they also can experience personal and interpersonal changes. "Ideally, these experiences can bring future opportunities that further the progress toward cultural and economic parity among races [in the United States]. Global inter-changes that actively involve [U.S.] citizens across social, racial, and cultural strata will allow all of the 'players' to approach the global playing field on relatively equal footing."[24]

Furthermore, and equally relevant to the Canadian situation, the article raises questions about personal and national identities. One question is, if minority students are perceived by the host citizens as more American than their ethnic distinction, how would this "Americanization" reconcile with students' perceptions of themselves, as minorities, in the United States?[25] In the U.S., as in Canada, the answer points to sound citizenship education aimed at ameliorating these ambiguities inherent in pluralistic societies. Thus, the architecture of relevant citizenship education should embody an international component, emphasizing Canada's place in the world and tracking and learning from comparative experience how others address generic issues such as human rights, social dialogue, and gender justice. Like the other issues mentioned above, the content, assumptions, and extant delivery mechanisms of citizenship education seem to give rise to certain paradoxes.

Third, experience in other jurisdictions characterized by cultural pluralism suggests that citizenship education tends to achieve reasonable levels of success when built on foundations of the voice and inclusion of, and avoidance of "degraded exits" by, ethnocultural minorities in processes of design and delivery.

Fourth, meaningful citizenship education undermines its own rationale when it is predominantly or only school-centered and when it "underconcentrates" on educating adults, as it tends to do. It is perhaps also best taught within the ethnocultural communities that must be properly resourced.

Multiculturalism and Citizenship: Some Paradoxes

Multiculturalism could become self-defeating unless the basic paradoxes are addressed at both the conceptual and policy levels. The whole range of paradoxes need not be cited to validate this claim since they carry similar messages for policy and theory. One expression of paradox resides in the "overconcentration," at least in the 1970s and 1980s, on the anatomy and taxonomy of "multiculturalism" and corresponding de-emphasis on citizenship education, narrowly defined until the 1980s. The correction of that imbalance and the meaningful reform of the civics curriculum have not taken place. In discussing the displacement of citizenship education in the modern school curriculum, Ken Osborne makes the following observations:

> Today, ... citizenship seems to have vanished from the educational agenda. Since about the mid-1980's schools have directed their energies largely to economic ends. ... Schools are now expected to prepare students for the labor market of the future, which, we are told, will require workers to be flexible, adaptable, able to think on their feet, and to move from job to job.[26]

In a similar vein, Adam Kozar, a retired teacher in Vancouver, couched his criticism of the absence of citizenship education in the following statement-question: "The Ministry has poured hundreds of millions of dollars into technology training; where is citizenship training?" He goes on to make the point that, as a social studies teacher, his first mandate was to teach people how to relate to, and care for, one another.[27]

Moreover, the exercise of provincial autonomy over educational matters has effectively subverted the emergence of a coherent package for citizenship education that is consistent with the national vision and rate of progress envisioned at the center for the advancement of the multicultural project. This is not to say that attempts have not been made to coordinate efforts, but it is necessary to emphasize that, with education being a provincial jurisdiction, it is difficult, if not impossible, to develop a "coherent package" within the realities of provincial diversity. Education, too, must have a broader mandate which transcends the limitations of physical borders.

To cite another set of paradoxes, the articulation of "group differentiated rights" may have encouraged an inward focus on differences to an extent that is not known to central policy makers. The promotion of "group rights" can stand in inherent conflict with individual rights and needs, particularly in instances involving the distribution of development-oriented benefits. Consider, too, how easy it has been for the essentially legalistic understanding of citizenship to neglect the broader socio-cultural aspects of membership. D.K. Gordon has, for example, argued that the designation "visible minority" in Canadian public policy language is nothing more than rationalization for the ideology of bigotry, and that it has been divisive of community, idealizes *white* objects and symbols, and, therefore, self-defeats the goals of genuine multiculturalism.[28]

Gordon's concern is not without significance to this discussion for a Black sub-culture could very well develop from social trends to differentiate groups even among the "visible minorities" and to accord differential treatment according to the degree of "visual blackness." Hence, the term is problematic for it creates barriers to harmonious race relations. Studies have confirmed that "Blacks in Canada face obstacles that other non-white groups do not," and that the term "visible minorities" could mask that fact if it is perceived as referring to non-white groups.[29] Here is a situation that could have wide implications for the integration of some "visible minorities" into Canadian society.

Another paradox that should be noted concerns the lack of progress in addressing the educational problems affecting visible minority adults and children, despite the popularization of multicultural education during the 1970s and the 1980s. New immigrants have had their own reasons for resentment — mainly centering on issues of language, but frequently related to the economic prospects for immigrant adults and their children. On the one hand, immigrant adults have suffered from the absence of any kind of official structure for evaluating foreign educational credentials. Denigration of their credentials and experiences has resulted also in the creation of a very educated under-class among the adult population. On the other hand, for school-aged immigrant children, appropriate placement, where knowledge of English has been the criterion of the day, has proved problematic because it has resulted in the over-representation of visible minority children in non-academic streams. These streams have predominantly included students from the Caribbean (mostly Jamaicans) for whom the language of instruction would be Standard English, although most students would speak a "dialect" variation of the classroom language. The lack of distinction between English as a Second Language (ESL) or English as a Second Dialect (ESD) and Limited English Proficient (LEP) students has become an issue of grave concern — academic as well as social — for both teachers and students.

In addition, the exclusive curriculum contributed nothing to harmonious classroom relations. Where attempts were made at inclusiveness, without the sensitivity of introducing new and often controversial materials, teachers often left the minority children's frail self-confidence further eroded or undermined. In addition to these classroom scenarios, teacher attitudes and personal biases are sometimes acted out, and both classrooms and playgrounds remain sites of conflicts from which many students have been known to take "degraded exits," with the potential of becoming less than productive citizens in the larger society. Thus, there is a moral imperative for school systems to provide for the development of the human capacities of children of immigrant and other minority communities. The moral principle of equality mandates not only that they should be given instruction equivalent to what is provided other children whose cultural background facilitates learning in the normal pace, but also that they be offered further instruction that will enable them to learn what their counterparts are learning. Clearly to allow them to lag in terms of learning at least at the minimum level allowable for each grade is to do injustice to them.[30]

Finally, again despite the wide acceptance of the policy of multiculturalism in the 1970s and the 1980s, it is paradoxical that racism and a lack of equity remains a huge problem in Canada. In 1984, the report *Equality Now!* stated:

Most visible minorities are not participating fully in Canadian society. Opportunities are being denied because visible minorities are frequently believed to be from a different culture, and it is believed they will not "fit" the structures of public and private institutions in Canada. One need only look at the employment practices of police departments, fire departments, government services, universities, the media, and private companies to see that visible minorities are consciously or unconsciously denied full participation in almost all Canadian institutions. Visible minorities are, in fact, the invisible members of our society. Canada will be the ultimate loser if we do not take advantage of the skills and abilities which visible minority Canadians have to offer.[31]

Almost two decades later, visible minorities continue to raise this concern, together with the not unjustified claim that this manifests racism in Canada. In her book *The Invisible Empire*, Margaret Cannon has no reservations in depicting the various dimensions of racism which she has seen in her travels throughout the country. Her research records an eclectic array of viewpoints, from real to grossly exaggerated. An example of her reference to public perceptions of visible minorities in Canada follows:

In private conversations, immigration is blamed for worsening unemployment, high welfare costs, increasing crimes, and problems in the schools. There are too many of "them" coming in, overwhelming the resources of Canada.

... "They" are accused of being too demanding, of wanting
to hang on to their old country ways. They are fractious
tiles in the Canadian Mosaic, refusing to fit in. They want
to wear turbans in the RCMP, to have Black history classes
in the schools. ... With all those images before us Canadians
still think of their society as multicultural, one where there
is equality of opportunity and equal justice for all. But what
justice?[32]

Concluding Observations

Despite the paradoxes, there may still be hope. According to Kymlicka,
race relations have become an increasingly important goal for the federal
multiculturalism policy.[33] Also, the newly restructured federal
multicultural program now focuses on three main goals. First is *identity*,
for fostering a society in which people of all backgrounds feel a sense of
belonging and attachment to Canada. Second is *civic participation,* for
developing citizens who are actively involved in shaping the future of
their various communities and their country. Third is *social justice,* for
building a nation that ensures fair and equitable treatment and that
respects and accommodates people of all origins.[34] This restructuring of
goals not only demonstrates the government's commitments to
multiculturalism, but also its understanding of the dynamics of initiatives
in effectively serving the needs of its citizens. This understanding needs
to be reflected in policy matters. In speaking of anti-Black racism in
Canada, and with specific reference to Caribbean Blacks in Toronto,
Kymlicka concludes that "we are at a turning point of race relations in
Canada. With meaningful reforms, Caribbean Blacks could overcome
the barriers of racism and follow the historical pattern of immigrant
integration."[35]

In a very provocative article, Gutmann uses some everyday incidents
that cross national, cultural, and religious boundaries to remind readers
of the inherent tensions and paradoxes of diversity. She also dwells on
one lasting underpinning of effective multiculturalism when she notes:

> Democratic education should try to teach all students not
> only about their shared citizenship but also about their
> shared humanity with all individuals regardless of their
> citizenship. ... [O]nly when children are educated for a
> deliberative citizenship that is informed by multiculturalism
> and committed to treating all individuals as equals,
> regardless of their nationality, can we begin to reconcile
> civic education with cultural diversity.[36]

Gutmann's point regarding a humanitarian approach to the education of children within a model for "deliberative citizenship that is informed by multiculturalism" is consistent with our views on "multiculturalism and citizenship," as expressed in this paper. The underlying humanitarian principles and values reflected in policy, both legal and social, are essentially a model for citizenship education conceptualized and constitutionalized within a multiculturalism framework. There is no doubt that legislation is an invaluable dimension/component in the process of growth toward the concept of citizenship within Canadian diversity — a great challenge in itself. But it is self-evident that legislation alone cannot resolve or ameliorate differences of beliefs and values, practices and tensions that prevail alongside political action toward "equality rights" for all citizens.

There are fundamental issues/attitudes that cannot be addressed at the superficial levels at which they are often perceived. They include the broad, inclusive parameters of public policy vis-à-vis inherent conflict in equality initiatives for *all* — social justice, individual/human rights, and affirmative action issues, for example — and a "majority" that often perceives equality measures as a threat to its traditional position of power and advantage and, therefore, interprets "equality" measures in a negative sense as "reverse discrimination." Similarly, there are often demands from minority groups, basically for "rights" perceived as reasonable — the transplantation of cultural practices and the demands for the acknowledgement of these practices (cultural relativism)— without careful analysis relevant to the possibilities for conflict; yet, a denial of their demands is interpreted as an act of cultural discrimination.

The way forward is, obviously, to forge bonds of understanding through mutual respect and trust. We clearly embrace the concept of participatory citizenship as community involvement at various levels — school, community, local, regional, national, and global — as well as a multidimensional approach to multicultural education as a continuous process for growth in which to nurture a shared identity and a shared vision for the collective good.[37] Furthermore, we would argue for a model of multicultural citizenship based not only on shared cultures but, more importantly, on our shared humanity. In stating our position, we are equally mindful of the challenges. In a society where language clearly draws a distinction between individuals and groups, the success (or lack of it) in this process of growth depends largely on the extent to which the majority is willing, not merely to accommodate minorities (in terms of an acceptance which maintains the status quo), but to share space within its position of power and advantage with all minority ethnic groups including "visible minorities."

Without minimizing the merits of multiculturalism, the author has attempted throughout the paper to emphasize that there are systemic roadblocks that continue to militate against the full participation of "visible minorities." The ultimate goal for multicultural education is "good" citizenship. The concept of Canadian multiculturalism can be used advantageously to lay a sound foundation for a model of citizenship education for all members of society. This means the establishment of a framework for inclusive participatory citizenship education, a framework which minimizes the potential for the cultivation of different "classes" of citizens.

ACKNOWLEDGEMENT

The author would like to thank Dr. Romulo Magsino for his suggestions on the earlier draft of the paper.

NOTES

1. Will Kymlicka, *Multicultural Citizenship: A Liberal Theory of Minority Rights* (New York: Oxford University Press, 1995). See p. 198, n. 9 for protection of minority groups against discrimination; p. 8 for a discussion of the potentials of multiculturalism in the integration of ethnic groups in Canada; chapter 2 for broader arguments for understanding integration; and p. 183 for immigrants' motivation to integrate into society.

2. Regarding integration as a natural process toward citizenship, see Will Kymlicka, *Finding Our Way: Rethinking Ethnocultural Relations in Canada* (Toronto: Oxford University Press, 1998), specifically 78-89.

3. John J. Cogan and Ray Derricott, eds., *Citizenship for the 21st Century: An International Perspective on Education* (London: Kogan Page, 1998), 1-20, 155-167. See also Rosa Bruno-Joffré and Lois Greiger, eds. *Papers on Contemporary Issues in Education Policy and Administration in Canada: A Foundations Perspective*, Monographs in Education 23 (Winnipeg: Faculty of Education, University of Manitoba, 1996).

4. World Bank, *Governance and Development* (Washington: World Bank, 1992).

5. Kymlicka, *Multicultural Citizenship*, 173-192.

6. Multiculturalism Directorate, *Multiculturalism and the Government of Canada* ([Ottawa]: Multiculturalism Canada, 1984); Multiculturalism and Citizenship Canada, *The Canadian Multiculturalism Act: A Guide for Canadians* (Ottawa: Multiculturalism and Citizenship Canada, 1990).

7. *Toward Achieving Cultural Harmony* (Ottawa: Government of Canada, n.d.). The document outlines language rights for the two founding races, but also discusses minority languages.

8. Multiculturalism Directorate, *Multiculturalism and the Government of Canada*, 8.

9. See *The Canadian Multiculturalism Act: A Guide for Canadians*, 13, for more details on the legal implications.

10. Multiculturalism Directorate, *Multiculturalism and the Government* of Canada, 9-10.

11. House of Commons, Special Committee on Participation of Visible Minorities in Canadian Society, *Equality Now!: Report of the Special Committee on Visible Minorities in Canadian Society* (Ottawa: Supply and Services Canada, 1984). Also includes recommendations pertaining to all aspects of equal opportunity.

12. Multiculturalism Directorate, *Multiculturalism and the Government of Canada*, 10.

13. Ibid.

14. Ibid. Author's emphasis.

15. Province of Manitoba, *Manitoba's Policy for a Multicultural Society: Building Pride, Equality and Partnership* ([Winnipeg: Manitoba Statutory Publications], 1990); and Manitoba Education and Training, *Multicultural Education: A Policy for the 1990s* (Winnipeg: Manitoba Education and Training, 1989).

16. Antonio J. Tavares, "'New Directions': An Opportunity," *Manitoba Multicultural Association Newsletter* (winter 1998): 1-2.

17. Kymlicka, *Multicultural Citizenship*, 179.

18. K. McLeod, "Multiculturalism and Multicultural Education: Policy and Practice," in *Multiculturalism in Canada: Social and Educational Perspectives*, ed. Ronald J. Samuda, John W. Berry, and Michel Laferrière (Toronto: Allyn and Bacon, 1984), 31.

19. Neil Bissoondath, *Selling Illusions: The Cult of Multiculturalism in Canada* (Toronto: Penguin Books, 1994).

20. Ben Levin, "Moving Away from the Common School?" *Papers on Contemporary Issues in Education Policy and Administration in Canada*, 33-34; and Rosa Bruno-Jofré, "Schooling and the Struggles to Develop a Common Polity, 1919-1971," ibid., 90-93. See also Kymlicka, *Multicultural Citizenship*, 176-195; and Kymlicka, *Finding Our Way*, 8-9, 60-71.

21. Kymlicka, *Multicultural Citizenship*.

22. Ibid.

23. International Consortium of the National Council of Teachers of English, *Inflections* 3, no.1 (1995): 4.

24. Tony Chambers, in his "Students of Color Abroad: Marginalized or Empowered?" *Inflections* [International Consortium of the National Council of Teachers of English] 3, no. 1 (1995): 4, analyzes Joy Gleason

Carew's "For Students of Color, Study Abroad Can Be Inspiring and Liberating," *Inflections* 2, no. 2 (1994). While he applauds Carew's views, he points out the "reality" that "the predominant global image of U.S. minority groups is negative. Nonwhites in the United States are often perceived as violent, uneducated, and poor." Furthermore, "people of color, at home and abroad, are quite often perceived or treated differently than their white peers."

25. Chambers, "Students of Color Abroad," 5.

26. Ken Osborne, "Citizenship Education and Canadian Schools" (paper presented at the conference Citizenship within the Next Millennium, Winnipeg, 30 October 1998), 38.

27. Greater Vancouver Citizenship Council, *Citizenship: Challenging Our Youth, Challenging Our Educators* (Vancouver: Greater Vancouver Citizenship Council, 1999), 6.

28. D.K. Gordon, "Bigotry Visible in 'Visible Minority,'" *Toronto Star*, 23 February 1993, sec. A, p. 15.

29. See Kymlicka, *Finding Our Way*, 72-89; for a reference to Stephen Lewis' controversial 1992 *Report on Race Relations in Ontario*, see Kymlicka's *Multicultural Citizenship*, 80.

30. Romulo F. Magsino, "Toward a Framework for Educational Policy-Making in the Multicultural Society," in *Papers on Contemporary Issues in Education Policy and Administration in Canada*, 126.

31. *Equality Now!*, 7.

32. Margaret Cannon, *The Invisible Empire: Racism in Canada* (Toronto: Random House of Canada, 1995), 51-52.

33. For Kymlicka's review of the status of race relations in Canada and where Blacks are positioned, see *Finding Our Way*, 72-89.

34. [Online]; available from <http://canada.cio-bic.gc.ca/facts/multi-e.html>; Internet; accessed 26 October 2000.

35. Kymlicka, *Finding Our Way*, 83. In chapter 5, he discusses issues of whiteness/blackness that could change perceptions of the term "visible minority" to refer to Blacks only, and how this, along with negative images, could possibly lead to the creation of a Black sub-culture in Canada.

36. Amy Gutmann, "Challenges of Multiculturalism in Democratic Education," in *Public Education in a Multicultural Society*, ed. Robert Fullinwider (New York: Cambridge University Press, 1996), 174, 176.

37. Cogan and Derricott, eds. *Citizenship for the 21st Century*, 11-21.

8 A White Paper on Aboriginal Education in Universities

BEVERLEY BAILEY

A B S T R A C T / R É S U M É

In this paper, I recount the circumstances which have caused me to question deeply my own complicity in Eurocentric education, which is really all we have to offer our Aboriginal students. Coming from my position as a white, female, middle-aged university professor with a history of school teaching and school counselling, I outline the concerns I have with both schools and faculties of education, fearing personal complicity in cultural genocide. In particular, I am concerned with three things: one, how we frame and name our own racism — to come to feel comfortable talking about our own biases and prejudicial thoughts, actions, and attitudes–as a necessary first step to action; two, how we disadvantage Aboriginal students in our universities, for whom success may require some form of personal "amputation," and three, how we, as teacher educators, can begin to model, through our own culturally sensitive actions and through our teaching, ways of becoming culturally sensitive classroom teachers. While I do not provide answers to the thorny question of "what to do," I do hold out hope that working in arrangements of mutual respect with those of another culture can lead us to idiosyncratic and powerful models of change.

Dans cet article je raconte les circonstances qui m'ont causé de questionner d'une façon profonde ma propre complicité dans l'éducation eurocentrique, qui est vraiment tout ce que nous avons à offrir à nos étudiants autochtones. A partir de ma position comme un professeur d'une université et d'une personne qui est blanche, féminine et entre deux âges, avec une histoire d'enseignement et d'orientation scolaires, j'expose dans les grandes lignes les inquiétudes que j'ai avec autant les écoles que les facultés d'éducation, ayant peur de complicité personnelle dans la génocide culturelle. En particulier, trois choses me préoccupent. La première chose est comment on encadre et nomme notre propre racisme — arriver à sentir à l'aise en discutant de nos propres préjugés et nos pensées, nos actions et nos attitudes préjudiciables — comme un premier pas nécessaire pour l'action. La deuxième chose est comment on défavorise les étudiants autochtones dans nos universités pour qui le succès peut exiger quelque forme d'amputation personelle. La troisième chose est comment nous, en tant qu'éducateurs des enseignants, peuvent commencer à modeler au moyen de nos propres actions culturellement sensibles, et au moyen de notre enseignment, des manières de devenir des professeurs culturellement sensibles dans la salle de classe. Tandis que je ne fournis pas de réponses à la question épineuse de "quoi faire," je conserve toujours l'espoir que le fait de travailler dans des arrangements de respect mutuel avec ceux d'une autre culture puisse nous mener à des modèles particuliers et puissants du changement.

Introduction

I am a white, middle-aged, female university professor. I have been an educator for more than thirty years — mostly in schools working with "underprivileged" students. As a teacher I had ongoing concerns about how we frame children and label the pictures so constructed. I have found that here in the university we also have ways of framing those of our students who are "different." We less often deal with those who do not learn in the way we deem appropriate or with those whose poverty hampers learning. Here we *deal* with those from different cultures and struggle with the ways in which they do not fit our mold. Particularly in my small prairie university, we face the challenges offered us by our Aboriginal students. My hope is that we learn to listen, my fear is that we will continue to force those who are different into the "one size fits all" mould which marks a successful university graduate.

In our teacher education faculty, access programs to Northern, Native, and Hutterite populations have been in place for some years. Most of our classes on campus have some Aboriginal students. In my graduate courses, there are usually Aboriginal students. I have been privileged to work with Aboriginal people in access programs and in undergraduate and graduate classes. At this time I am searching for the best way to move my students to the degree they desire without expecting them to turn inside out to meet our culturally biased expectations.

In 1989 *Where the Spirit Lives*, a Canadian film about residential schools, was released. As I am struggling with writing this article, the movie is playing on late night television and I watch it again. In one scene, the Anglican priest who runs the school is helping a new and idealistic teacher to "settle in." She is to remember that the children come from a "dead society," a society which is a millstone around their necks. It is her duty to help them remove the millstone, to enable them to enter into mainstream white society. The movie is set in Alberta in 1937.

In 1999 I am not sure how much we have changed. We expect our students from very different cultures to fit into our "one size fits all" institution. We have a list of largely unwritten expectations: you will all speak English; you will all write research papers and exams; you will be on time and always present; you will learn what we decide you need to know in a series of unrelated courses. This feels harsh as I write, but upon rereading it I cannot see how to change this reality.

Some of my fellow professors would say that such is necessary if we want our Native students to succeed in the world as it is today. This is an argument that assumes that success in white man's terms is "the" way to be. It is also an argument that assumes we are educating others to take an equal place in our society; yet reality, either historically or currently, does not show that such is the result of our schooling practices, or a reality at all. Residential school children were minimally prepared for life in the white world, taking low-paying jobs or not able to get work at all.[1] Our access programs, in place for twenty-five years, are supplying Native teachers for reserve schools, not mainstream white schools. Further, we are training Natives how to teach in our western cultural tradition of education. With the best will in the world to be helpful and supportive and thoughtful, we are still practising cultural genocide. Perhaps, as Hampton points out, that is inevitable given educators who have no personal or professional notion of multicultural competence, who have unresolved issues of racism and no sense of their own ethnocentrism.[2]

I am used to seeing a blinkered approach to teaching "others" in white institutions of education; we are what we are, sure we are right and that everyone wants to be as we are. I am distressed, though, when I visit schools which are controlled by Aboriginal people and find a white-clone school, disadvantaging its students in much the same way that white schools do: structures, content, process, and even staff are white. I am not sure that it could be otherwise, given the reality that we are preparing our Aboriginal teachers for the school teaching task in our ethnocentric institution with little or no regard for difference. Cultural genocide appears to be alive and well in our schools and in our faculties of education.

In this paper I outline the ways in which I, as a university professor and teacher educator, am a part of a process which is, in Hampton's words, "actively hostile to Native culture."[3] I also begin an exploration of how we could be doing things differently.

Before I get into the core of this paper I wish to make four things clear. First is the matter of naming. I had a friend on the West Coast who felt strongly that he was an Indian, as it was this term that everyone understood. I have a friend here who is insulted when he is called an

Indian. I have been involved in countless discussions on what to call our "Indians." For the purposes of this paper I have chosen to use the term Aboriginal to mean those of our students who are of Native ancestry.

Second, I am aware of the fact that not all Aboriginal people are the same. I recognise that, through a process of time, oppression, and acculturation, the Aboriginal culture has lost much of its pre-contact integrity and purpose. Therefore, the children who come to our schools come from a wide variety of backgrounds — northern and urban, Christian, traditional, Metis, and Inuit, and all possible blendings and permutations growing out of their unique history. To a large extent this does not matter for the purpose of understanding how to make education for Aboriginal people more culturally sensitive. Most communities are struggling with processes of reclaiming past understanding and identities. I realise that Aboriginal people are not returning to a past era, but are, rather, reaffirming their knowing by using the old with the new, using both traditional and western modes of physical and mental healing. As Brown, points out:

> In their relationships to this troubled America, Indian groups are seen to be situated across a wide spectrum of positions. On the one hand are the few traditional and conservative groups which, against enormous pressures, have miraculously remained very close to the essence of their ancient and still viable life-ways; and on the other hand are those groups which have been completely assimilated within the larger American society. Yet today, virtually all Indian groups who retain any degree of self-identity are now also reevaluating, and giving positive valuation to the fundamental premises of their own traditional cultures. They are also reexamining, through a wide range of means and expressions, their relationships to a larger society which today tends to represent diminishing attractions.[4]

Third, I am aware that this is a collection about multicultural education. Because of the place I find myself in today, the stories and experiences told here are about Aboriginal peoples on the prairies of Canada. However, in my many years in education I have taught children and adults from a wide range of racial, ethnic, and cultural backgrounds. There is a common thread which runs through and connects these different groups. Maybe the connector, particularly for tribal groups, is a shared history of animism, coming from a culture which until recently (and even today) saw everything as possessing a spirit, living always in the presence of some form of Higher Power. Such groups also share a fundamental belief in family and in the rituals and ceremonies of their people. The sensitivity we develop for one group of people will lay a solid groundwork for our interactions with all peoples who choose or who were born into a different way of viewing and interacting with the world.

Fourth, I use the word "culture" in its broadest form. I do believe that the bulk of what I ponder, while pinned to my experiences with Aboriginal students, applies to all who suffer because they are not white, middle-class, male, heterosexual, able-bodied — for whatever reason not clearly members of the designated mainstream.

On that foundation I will build an argument for examining our institutions based on the following concerns:

> • how we frame and name our own racism — to come to feel comfortable talking about our own biases and prejudicial thoughts, actions, and attitudes, as a necessary first step to action;
> • how we disadvantage Aboriginal students in our universities, for whom success may require some form of personal amputation;
> • how we, as teacher educators, can begin to model through our own culturally sensitive actions, and through our teaching, ways of becoming culturally sensitive classroom teachers.

Naming the Beast

In a third year class, we were working on issues of multicultural education. Asked to be candid, one brave student said with some confusion that Indians were "drunks" and that behaviour was what was keeping them "back." An Aboriginal woman in the class stood up and held the class spellbound, some in tears, for forty-five minutes. She spoke of soul loss, the impact of residential schooling, her own family life, the relatives she venerated and why. She also spoke of the ways in which her university work was oppressing her culture and her spirit. In my course end evaluations that class was written of as of particular significance.

How do I understand the power of that class? I can only think that the beast was named in open forum and as result of that naming open talk could happen. Two students showed great bravery, tackling head on some of the issues which keep us apart. A white student took the risk of saying, with all due respect, what her perceptions really were. As a result, "real" talk took place. It is not easy to create spaces where such talk can happen. As Graveline points out, "Helping people unveil their own racism is a difficult and emotional task."[5]

Gustafson has helped me to find the words to frame the "beast," the conundrum that keeps us silent. He writes a book that is

> a response to a fear of the earth itself that is manifested in so many ways in so many places in our times and that has produced so much human anguish. It [the book] is designed for the western mindset that sees the earth, one's own earthly body and anything representing the earth as a dark trail best left to be avoided.[6]

Gustafson is concerned that in losing our connection to our own indigenous roots we are instinctively resistant to accepting the ways of those whose connections to their own indigenous roots are alive and well. In Jungian terms, we often fear that which we most desire.

Another face of the "beast" may be the facade of the educated. I remember hearing Malcolm X say that he preferred the Southern White to the Northern White because he knew, as a Black man, where he stood with the Southerners, whereas the Northerners knew how to hide their racism behind politically correct fronts. I vividly remembered that statement when an Aboriginal friend of mine was in a group of people and one of them made a statement based on negative stereotyping. She knew exactly how to respond to this person and to deal with the overt racism. Much harder for her to deal with is the covert racism of the university institution which appears to be "okay" with various forms of institutional racism but would never tolerate racial slurs. The one student in my class who was courageous enough to say what she really thought was the person who triggered a meaningful learning experience. Yet, as so-called educated persons, we have been taught the power of language, and we know not to use certain phrases and words.

If we share what we really think, it is usually in the safety of our own trusted circle, by definition within a group of like-minded and like-knowledged people. We thus do not learn; rather, we have our own prejudices reinforced. It takes courage to say what you really think when you are not sure if you will hurt others and when you are not sure what you will hear in response. As members of the privileged race, we all have notions which we are reluctant to give up. Surrendering such notions may mean that we, as individuals and as members of the white race, have to change. Graveline talks of her work with a group of university students, helping them to name the process, hoping to alter consciousness and articulate the feelings generated as a result of that naming — a process which she finds powerful learning for all the students in her classroom regardless of ethnicity. While Graveline takes on the challenge of transformational work with students in the controlled environment of a university classroom, another challenge becomes, How do we live our lives in a way that we name the beast, finding respectful ways to help others understand the impact of their words and actions in ways that bring about new thinking?[7]

The woman who was so insulted by the racial slur had a private talk with the man who offended her. What touched her was that the other men who had been there came to see her the next day and asked what they should have done and said at the time. They did not wish to be associated with the name-calling, but at the same time were not pleased with their lack of action. Now there is a group of men who do know a respectful but clear way to let people know that their racism will not be tolerated because the beast was brought out and dealt with.

I had a group of Aboriginal students in the field doing Practica in counselling. A young man was placed in a classroom working only with Aboriginal boys, in itself a form of racism. When he went to the staffroom and refused the offer of coffee, he was told, "Too bad, there isn't any beer." A young woman, who was job-shadowing a probation officer, was waiting on a bench outside the courtrooms. Three times she was "collected" by a police officer who assumed that she was there for her court appearance. I cannot assume that the coffee lady was not trying to be humorous or that the police officers were not rushed and harried. What I do know is that these young people were hurt and offended and did not know how to handle the situation in such a way that they did not, once again, become the victim. Because we do not openly name the beast, we can go along assuming that all is well.

One Name for the Beast

I am a result of the education deemed suitable by the culture I live in. Therefore, I am literate, easily understood by others, find great pleasure in reading the great works of our past and present, have always had a decent job, and currently find myself with a doctorate, a university appointment — and an article to write. It is easy for me to say that if others wish to be successful it is important that they learn to do things the way I did — and do — them. Our access programs are predicated on that assumption.

However, in the process of carrying out the mandate of preparing our Aboriginal students for a successful life based on our standards, I am afraid that we are practising a gentle, benign, and inevitable process of cultural genocide. I believe that there are several ways in which we expect our students from different cultures to become like us in order to be what we consider to be successful. Here I outline those expectations that I have found to be an uncomfortable fit for the Aboriginal students in my classes.

Lates and Absences

Today I did the second class of a course composed totally of Aboriginal students. Finally, fifteen minutes after class started, all the students were there including several whom I had not seen before. I did not ask why they were late or had been absent. From past experience I feel quite convinced that I would have heard of babysitters who were late, buses that did not show up, funerals in the north, a job that had to be finished, a relative who needed to be taken somewhere, a kid's teacher who needed to be told something. Many of my students lead highly complicated lives, getting somewhere "on time" can be a very hard thing to do. Of first importance is the person, the child, the extended family, and those of the community who are in need. As Stiegelbauer points out, not only are the cultural priorities different, but such an approach may be strengthening and may be a strong foundation from which to approach a somewhat hostile world.[8] By insisting that our requirements be met, we may be weakening some of the essential health giving ingredients of the cultural group.

More than the problem with "fitting it all in" and sorting out priorities, there may be a very basic, different sense of time. Cultures that lived a short time ago without watches and artificial time constraints may have a hard time sensing the need for being in a certain place at a certain time just because someone said so. Their understanding of time, even if only vestiges of that understanding remain in the current period, may be very different. According to Courtney, in indigenous cultures time was spatial rather than linear:

> In great contrast (to linear time), all hunting societies understand time by collapsing it within the performance of their ritual-myths. The Australian aboriginal, in his great ceremonies, recreates "the Dreamtime" when the world was first created. Likewise the Amerindians of the Northwest Coast and the Southwest deserts recreate their myths in their annual dance-dramas. What happens to time within such performances. The performance takes place in the *now*, the present, yet by recreating the myth, it forces the past into present; and by ensuring fecundity for the following year, it brings the future back to present. Past and future are thereby viewed as the present: all time, there, exist *now*.[9]

My "successful" students do learn how to respect linear time and my requirements for being present and on time. I always feel badly that I, constrained by the expectations of the university, can only in small ways create spaces where they can set the way of being.

The Way We Teach

Getting places on time becomes important because we have developed a certain structure in universities, a structure that has existed for so long that we are unable to see other ways of providing education. The basis of a university education in North America is to take a series of courses, all of which have to be gotten to on time. Typically our courses fit into a program. However, each course is taught in isolation from the other courses; professors tend not to get together for lengthy discussions on the what and why and how of teaching. This in itself is another concern for our Aboriginal students. As Courtney found, being forced to learn within a non-indigenous worldview, where one context does not relate to the other causes, at best, bewilderment and, at worst, resentment.[10] Not only are we delivering education in a discordant fashion, we are asking people to learn what we think they need to know, in a context divorced from the world in which they will have to work. Even in a professional school such as a faculty of education, which is working to prepare teachers for schools, there are few programs where the fit between what is required in the schools and what is taught in the faculty is functionally close. While this is a reality for all our students, for the Aboriginal students, whose own cultural history is so different, our method of educating the next generation is particularly dysfunctional. Historically, shamanic societies did not use schools. Courtney makes it clear that education in such society was a lifelong process, based on an oral tradition, focussing on the sharing of skills and knowledge.[11]

Socrates used to sit under a tree and wait until enough people came together to listen to his talk and join in debates. I learned to knit, one of the more useful skills I have, from watching my Mother. I learned more from the self-directed and mentored task of writing my thesis than I did in the courses I was required to take. I realised that as a grade seven teacher I was giving my students more autonomy over their learning than I was giving my university students or, given the structure or the institution, than I can give them. Now I am expecting students to be on time and present for a course which says little or nothing to their current reality, which may or may not have anything to give them which helps them in the teaching situations they are likely to enter, which ignores both the past and present realities of their culture, which teaches rather than allows for the uprising of learning. As I write I feel very itchy.

Imposing Culture

My itchiness comes because I am imposing my system of doing things and my notion of what *should* be imposed on a particular group of people, and I fear I have little to say which speaks to their reality. For Hampton, his traditions define and preserve his people, providing continuity with the past, giving a solid foundation to the work of the present.[12] I do little which recognises and honours that way of seeing.

Our Aboriginal students place themselves in our institutions. They do recognise the need for "moving forward." They come to us for what we have to teach and give them. However, it is important for me, as a white educator, to recognise two things. One is that any people must be able to ground themselves in their own knowledge of self, and much of that knowledge has to do with a people's unique history and embedded way of learning — that education grows out of a culture and is part of it. The second is that oppressed peoples have little choice: education is legislated by a white government. Wolcott suggests that white teachers of Native students would do less harm if they recognised their status as cultural enemies of their students.[13] If I wish to become at the very least not the enemy, there are certain things I need to understand.

The first learning for me is that the purpose of education for Natives is "to serve the people. Its purpose is not individual advancement or status."[14] Lowery points out that Pueblos are taught from childhood to make sure they contribute, are useful, help one another, pay attention to the Earth, and pray.[15] Integrating this philosophy with life in academic institutions is not easy.

The Aboriginal view of education is in marked contrast to the "me-first" attitude which is found in most universities, where so much of our work is directed to what we can put on our curriculum vitae for purposes of promotion and tenure. That is not really our choice as individuals. It is the reality of our situations in institutions grounded in Eurocentrism. But Lowery makes the point that for those from a more community minded and spiritually grounded culture, integrating their way of life into our academic institution is difficult.[16] Thus I am faced with a clear clash of cultural values. On the one hand, are the requirements of the institution for which I work. These requirements do not value group work. They are predicated on each individual forging her/his lonely way through the accreditation process. On the other hand, is a group of people which values connections, one with the other, in a quest for community wholeness, and which "demands relationships of personal respect."[17]

We bring our Aboriginal students into our universities and find pride in the fact that we are creating a safe place for them to "better" themselves. We are supportive and helpful as we shoehorn them into our way of doing things.

Using Other's Words

All of my graduate students struggle with the thesis writing task, a struggle which I remember clearly. It took a while for me to understand that the exertion of my Aboriginal students was quite different from that of my white students. One of the students not only completed her thesis but received offers to have it published. I assumed that she would find the thesis writing process to have been, in the long run, a useful and fulfilling experience. In fact, she had found the process to have been one which did not honour her oral tradition. For her, an apparently assimilated person living a successful life in a white community, the process of writing a thesis had been disrespectful.

Take the student who is a traditional teacher and leader in his/her community. (S)he has been taught in his/her tradition the value of the oral learnings. (S)he has also been taught not to use the words of others without their express permission — stories and teachings are given, not taken. Now, we have had the discussion about public property: authors who publish their works are giving explicit permission to others to use their words. (S)he understands, but (s)he is not comfortable. I struggle with how comfortable I would be supervising a thesis which was non-referenced, yet I can begin to make her/his argument.

An Aboriginal friend asked me, "What is the purpose of a thesis?" Her question was not easy for me to answer. A thesis is one of the requirements of all students who take a graduate degree. A thesis is something you do which proves that you can research and write. A good master's thesis is important for acceptance into a doctoral program. When you become a doctor you can work in a university and research and write. The question of who reads our work and of how much value it is to the larger community is more often left unexplored and unanswered.[18]

In contrast, my friend pointed out to me that all the work she did was to be of value to the community. We agreed that a thesis could do two things: satisfy the requirements of the institution and give something to the community. However, I am left pondering the dilemma of my traditional teacher student who is made uncomfortable with the referencing needs of a thesis, who wants to write a piece of work which is of value to the community and to write it in a way which makes that value clear and sure. The Spirits are always with him/her, they know when (s)he is doing something which is motivated essentially by self-interest and which goes against the grain.

The thesis is the final step in the graduate program. But all through the university process our students are expected to write research papers, to read and use the words of others, to squeeze their writing into our accepted "styles," to cut their cloth to fit our pattern:

> You can follow a paper down and understand what they are saying, but you don't understand why they don't understand what you're saying, because, to you, your logic is there, but it's not recognised as being logical. ... We were talking a lot about what is logical to us and what is logical to the instructors here, or what is obvious to us and what is not obvious, I guess. It ... made me start thinking about how we think and how we relate this in our papers. There is a big gap there and I don't know how to close it. I'm trying very hard.[19]

These are the words of a successful Aboriginal student at Harvard. Apparently my dilemmas are universal. I am wondering why nothing has been done to actively solve the problem. Universities may be resistant to change, but surely they are not impervious.

A Course of Action?

As I was writing this paper and had shut down the computer for the night, I was listening to the CBC radio show *Ideas*. They were rebroadcasting an earlier series called "The Education Debates," and I was hearing Paul Goodman lecture. I listened to him explain how we somehow have come to think that the only way to educate is the way we are doing it — not only is there no better way, there is no *other* way.

This narrow understanding of education had always been a concern for me in my school teaching days because such a limited definition meant that we were creating deviance in children (hyperactivity, learning disabilities, behaviour disorders, emotional trauma). Through our narrow concept of what is normal and acceptable and through our feeling that what we are doing in schools is the only way to do things, we have school structures which can be highly problematic for children from other than white, middle-class cultures. Eber Hampton suggests that we should not even *be* in the business of educating Aboriginal students, that we are not able to do a competent job, that we are hampered by a largely unconscious pathology:

> 1) a perverse ignorance of the facts of racism and oppression;
> 2) delusions of superiority, motivated by fear of inadequacy;
> 3) a vicious spiral of self-justifying action, as the blame is shifted to the victims who must be "helped," that is,

controlled for their own good; and 4) denial that the oppressor profits from the oppression materially, as well as by casting themselves as superior, powerful, and altruistic persons.[20]

As a result of our blindness:

> Indian children face a daily struggle against attacks on their identity, their intelligence, their way of life, their essential worth. They must continually struggle to find self-worth, dignity, and freedom in being who they are.[21]

Whether or not we agree with Hampton, I do believe that we have to attend to his concerns, both in schools and in universities. Now, on the whole, Aboriginal students in university classes have mastered our system. They know how — or want to know how — to look alert, to take notes, to produce the sort of papers and projects we want, and to pass the tests we give them. Yet, as I have already pointed out, our university students are just as much at a disadvantage as our school children. They, too, are working in an institution that ignores the facts of racism and oppression, that believes it knows what is best for them, that finds ways to justify the acts of cultural genocide it is perpetrating, and that positions itself as the best path to the one good life.

Hampton wants us to realise that education as currently done is cultural genocide.[22] Wolcott asks us, as teachers from another culture, to be clear that we are, in fact, the enemy of that culture.[23] How do we become the teachers who are not practising cultural genocide, who are not the enemy? And how much can we do in an institution which is inherently racist but is also notoriously resistant to change? In order to make changes in how we interact with our students from different cultures, we have to do some careful self-examination and self-work. Change is never easy, whether it is change of ourselves or change of the institutions in which we work. But, as Paul Goodman said on the radio, there is really no reason why we do things as we do, it is just the way we have done it in our own memories. We can make changes — in our institutions and in ourselves.

Making a Beginning

David Hunt says, that if we want to create change, we have to start with ourselves. In order to understand others, we have to clearly understand ourselves.[24] Through work on ourselves we can have a grounded approach to the work we do with each other and in our places of learning. Working for self-knowledge is the place to begin.

We are aware, and have been for some time, of the importance of moving beyond making totem poles out of cereal boxes. We are aware that it is often inappropriate to expect eye contact. However, it takes time and work to begin to understand why so often one's direct questions go unanswered or why one's thesis students are struggling so hard with the thesis task. I have so often caused offence through my ignorance and, after some time of working to learn, I am still stumbling, uncertain, grateful for the tolerance I am given and the laughter I cause. It is the nuances which are hard to grasp, the ways in which I act in thoughtlessness because I do not know enough to know when to be thoughtful.

I can come to know, through reading, talking, experiencing, many aspects of a different culture. I can begin to understand the different terms, the different views of the world. Through opening myself to the experience of becoming truly knowledgeable about another culture, I come to have new knowledge and increased respect. I can no longer function from a place of superficial knowledge and ignorance. Such work is a good start. However, I can also go further.

Tedlock and Tedlock quote a Seneca medicine man:

> Beeman Logan tells us, we have come to underestimate our own potential as human beings:
>
>> You don't *respect* yourselves
>> You don't believe anything unless you can read it in a *book*
>> You have to learn to use your *eyes*
>> You have to learn to see with your eyes *shut* ...[25]

We can consciously work to unearth our own prejudices, biases, and racist notions. In so doing we would begin to find parts of ourselves which have kept us from truly respecting ourselves. We can begin to grow. We can come to have faith in the ancient knowledge of our Aboriginal students and trust in its worth to our lives today. We can learn from them and with them. We can discover how to unearth knowledge in new and exciting ways, finding our balance with our eyes shut.

Understanding the Core Beliefs of Others

In a graduate class the students were presenting, one woman had us all sit in a circle. She explained that Smudging was a burning of medicine plants, the smoke of which helped us to cleanse. With our permission, she had us all Smudge. She then explained what a Sharing Circle was and, once again with our permission, started the Talking Stone on its circuit of the Circle. There was a deep sense of peace and meaningful work about our time together that evening. In fact, it changed the tone of the class for the remainder of the sessions. We had a sense of working together toward a common goal. Each person was a part of the class, and each found her/his own way to contribute. Our last class was a feast and a celebration of work well done.

The idea of spirituality informing our work in universities is increasingly a topic of scholarly work.[26] Often the notion of spirituality remains unclear, each writer using her or his own sense of what it means; all too frequently the terms "religious" and "spiritual" become mixed. In many other cultures, and certainly in the traditional Aboriginal culture, the sense of a Higher Power has a significant impact on how people see their world and their actions within it.

In my classes I have had respected Elders, Teachers, and Storytellers. If the space is opened up for them, they will bring their considerable gifts to the class and enlighten and deepen our work. Because their work is always grounded in their own spirituality, it has a different dimension to it — it loses any sense of competition, egos are softened, words are heard, learning is deepened. In our Eurocentric culture we have lost the sense of "walking with God," which still is very much a part of the reality of many other peoples. When we "walk with God," all our actions affect the world we live in. They become important. Doing something, anything, must have reason and thought behind it, for its consequences are far-reaching. Can we make spaces for those who "walk with God" in our classrooms? Are we prepared for the consequences? Because until we can make the space and deal with the consequences, I am not sure we have the right to determine the educational path of "others."

Coming Together through Our Stories

A student who is also a Pipe Carrier and Story Teller presents to a graduate class in counselling. Through story he shows us the value of humour to psychic healing. In oblique ways he brings us to understand not to take ourselves too seriously, but also to quite seriously get to work to solve the problems that get in the way of our full growth. The teaching was humorous, clear, and not easily forgotten.

When I share my stories with my students, I become a little more vulnerable, a little more human and approachable. I can no longer easily maintain a facade of superiority, of knowing more, of being inherently of more worth — whether I position my superiority as coming from my race or my education. Stories become a leveller. I hear stories which humble me and leave me the learner in the classroom. All of my students have something to teach me if I open up the space for the stories to be told.

The sharing of stories brings together the two cultures, as we find common ground through our human experiences. As Storm says, stories are "magical Teachers. ... They are Flowers of Truth whose petals can be unfolded by the Seeker without end."[27]

Changing the Institution

I clearly understand from my own research and from reading the work of others that, while changing ourselves is never easy, changing institutions is a monumental task. However, on the principle of nothing tried, nothing done, I would like to make some suggestions for ways in which our universities could become more culturally sensitive.

First, I want to look at the issue of students who are late and students who are absent. What would happen if we decided that not only was it okay for students to be late and absent, but that it was often necessary for them to be so? How then could we structure ourselves in such a way that it didn't matter either to their progress or to our sense that we were doing a good job of teaching? At Arctic College, which operates throughout Nunavut, courses are offered in three-week chunks. The reasoning is that if the students have to be away for two weeks or so, then they have only lost a three-week course and not a whole semester. It also means that students need not enrol if they know that they will be involved in ceremony or hunting.

Second, there appears to be a problem with the course structure itself. A constant through the literature is the concern that the courses of studies are separate, the work of one not closely connected with the work of others. Furthermore, courses are not always easily seen as useful in the lives that our students go on to live. In a culture which traditionally was educated by and through lived experiences, much of what we do in Western education is not seen as — and indeed may not be — purposeful. In some universities classes are not held at all. Lectures are given and supervisors are assigned. Students work in their own area of study in a quite independent fashion. They do the work they need to to do to find the answers and learning they need, and they do it at times which best suit their personal circumstances.

Third, I do believe, as do others such as Eisner and Kilbourn, that we can take a serious look at our requirements for major papers and theses.[28] Maybe a novel can be a thesis, as Eisner suggests. And, as my student suggests, maybe the words of Story Tellers can be used to create a thesis.

While I have given examples of other ways of doing things, I am not suggesting that we adopt what others have done in response to their particular situations. I am suggesting that we begin in earnest the search for other ways of doing things, ways that are more culturally sensitive. Such work could include the kind of concrete examples suggested above. However, we really have no idea the direction such work would take; combining the best of both cultures could lead to some amazing innovations in our educational institutions.

The idiosyncratic direction that any one institution takes would be based on the needs of the particular institution working within the context of its community. We are researchers and thoughtful academics; creative solutions can be found to troubling problems. We have many constituents, white and Aboriginal, who would be willing to help us in our quest.

Conclusion

I am reluctant to do more than outline the problem and point the direction for some possible areas we could begin to look at, from changing our own attitudes to working to change, at some level, the requirements of an institution. I do hope that I have clearly outlined my own discomfort with a process of working with other cultures in ways that expect them to be just like us, in the process of becoming just like us. I also hope that I have made clear my expectation that we develop educational environments for our culturally different students which both respects them and prepares them for the reality of the world in which they will have to live and succeed.

As a school counsellor, one of my tasks was to determine what learning environment would work best for particular problems. The children and I developed many strategies for them to use to help them complete the school task. These strategies included individual work programs, independent choice of both content and process of learning, and use of idiosyncratic aids for concentration. When I went back into classroom teaching, I took many of these strategies with me and found that I was using them with my whole class. Thus, all my students benefited from working in ways that best advanced their own particular learning needs, be they "learning challenged" or "gifted."

I have no doubt that the work we would do as university educators to create success on our culturally different students, without expecting cultural transformation, would be work that many of our students would find of personal value. In general terms, it may be time to seriously look at the structures of our universities.[29] In specific terms, grounding our work in change on the needs of a particular population may be of significant benefit to all. Certainly the thought of doing such meaningful work is both exciting and liberating.

NOTES

1. Both Agnes Grant, *No End of Grief: Indian Residential Schools in Canada* (Winnipeg: Pemmican Press, 1996) and John S. Milloy, *A National Crime: The Canadian Government and the Residential School System, 1879 to 1986* (Winnipeg: University of Manitoba Press, 1999) speak with some passion about the residential school system for Aboriginal children in Canada.

2. Eber Hampton, "Towards a Redefining of Indian Education," in *First Nations Education in Canada: The Circle Unfolds*, ed. Marie Battiste and Jean Barman (Vancouver: University of British Columbia Press, 1995), 5-46.

3. Ibid.

4. *The Sacred Pipe: Black Elk's Account of the Seven Rites of the Oglala Sioux*, as told by Joseph E. Brown and Elk Black (Norman, OK: University of Oklahoma Press, 1953), xvi.

5. Jean Frye Graveline, *Circle Works: Transforming Eurocentric Consciousness* (Halifax: Fernwood Publishing, 1998), 220.

6. F. Gustafson, *Dancing between Two Worlds: Jung and the Native American Spirit* (New York: Paulist Press, 1997), 6.

7. Graveline, *Circle Works*.

8. Suzanne Stiegelbauer, "The Individual is the Community: The Community is the World; Native Elders Talk about What Young People Need to Know" (paper presented at the meeting of the American Educational Research Association, San Francisco, April 1992).

9. Richard Courtney, "Islands of Remorse: Amerindian Education in the Contemporary World," *Curriculum Inquiry* 16, no.1 (1986): 43-65.

10. Ibid.

11. Ibid.

12. Hampton, "Towards a Redefining of Indian Education."

13. Harry Wolcott, "The Teacher as an Enemy," in *Education and Cultural Process: Anthropological Approaches*, ed. George Dearborn Spindler, 2d ed. (Prospect Heights, IL: Waveland Press, 1987), 136-150.

14. Hampton, "Towards a Redefining of Indian Education," 21.

15. Christine T. Lowery, "Hearing the Messages: Integrating Pueblo Philosophy into Academic Life," *Journal of American Indian Education* 36, no. 2 (1997): 1-8.

16. Ibid.

17. Hampton, "Towards a Redefining of Indian Education," 31.

18. With the notable exception of a debate on the lack of impact that our work as educational researchers has had on schools and policy makers begun in the *Educational Researcher* by Robert Donmoyer. Donmoyer, as editor, challenged educational researchers to think about why our research does not appear to have much impact on school practices. The debate was heated and considerable and ran through much of the 1997 and 1998 issues.

19. Hampton, "Towards a Redefining of Indian Education," 27-28.

20. Ibid., 34-35.

21. Ibid., 35.

22. Ibid.

23. Wolcott, "The Teacher as an Enemy."

24. David E. Hunt, *Beginning with Ourselves in Practice, Theory, and Human Affairs* (Cambridge: Brookline Books, 1987).

25. Dennis Tedlock and Barbara Tedlock, eds, *Teachings from the American Earth: Indian Religion and Philosophy*, 1ˢᵗ ed. (New York: Liveright, 1975), xxi.

26. Hampton, Courtney, Graveline, and Stiegelbauer, all of whom have been previously cited, stress the essential component that spirituality is in the life of the Aboriginal. Other writers also are working with spirituality as an important aspect of education, from either Western or traditional Aboriginal perspectives: Beverley Bailey and Roy Mason, "The Sacred Tree of Knowledge" (paper presented at WestCAST, Brandon University, February 1999); D. Huebner, "Education and Spirituality," *An Interdisciplinary Journal of Curriculum Studies* 11, no. 2 (1995): 13-33; R.E. Ingersoll, "Teaching a Course on Counselling and Spirituality," *Counsellor Education and Supervision* 36 (1997): 224-232; E.W. Kelly, "Counsellor Preparation: The Role of Religion and Spirituality in Counsellor Education: A National Survey," *Counsellor Education and Supervision* 33 (1994): 227-237; D.A. Long, "Trials of the Spirit: The Native Social Movement in Canada," in *Visions of the Heart: Canadian Aboriginal Issues*, ed. David Alan Long and Olive Patricia Dickason (Toronto: Harcourt Brace, 1996); M.L. Mack, "Understanding Spirituality in Counselling Psychology: Considerations for Research, Training, and Practice," *Counselling and Values* 39 (1994): 15-31; Peter Marin, "Spiritual Obedience," *Harper's* (February 1979): 43-58; M.S. Prakash, "Gandhi's Postmodern Education: Ecology, Peace, and Multiculturalism Relinked," *Holistic Education Review* 6, no. 3 (1993): 8-17; J. Rolph, "Can There be Quality in Teacher Education without Spirituality?" *Assessment and Evaluation in Higher Education* 16, no. 1 (1991): 49-55; and Greg Sarris, "Telling Dreams and Keeping Secrets: The Bole Maru as American Indian Religious Resistance," *American Indian Culture and Research Journal* 16, no. 1 (1992): 71-85.

27. Hyemeyohsts Storm, *Seven Arrows* (New York: Ballantine Books, 1972), 20.

28. Elliot W. Eisner, "Forms of Understanding and the Future of Education Research," *Educational Researcher* 22, no. 7 (1993): 5-11; and Brent Kilbourn, "Fictional Theses," *Educational Researcher* 28, no. 9 (1999): 27-32.

29. The following have all devoted time to the general issue of change in universities: Beverley Bailey, "The New Professor as Change Agent," in *The Heart of the Matter*, ed. Ardra Cole, Rosemary Elijah, and Gary Knowles (San Francisco: Gaddo Press, 1998), 273-288; Warren Bennis, *Why Leaders Can't Lead: The Unconscious Conspiracy Continues* (San Francisco: Jossey-Bass, 1989); Ardra Cole and Gary Knowles, "Reform and Being 'True to Oneself': Pedagogy, Professional Practice and the Promotional Process," in *The Heart of the Matter*, 353-376; E. Eubanks, "We're Not in Kansas Anymore: Transforming Conditions and Relationships in an Urban School," in *The Wizard of Odds: Leadership Journeys of Education Deans*, ed. L. Bowen (Washington: AACTE, 1995), 27-36; and G. Fenstermacher, "From Camelot to Chechnya: The Journey of an Education Dean," in *The Wizard of Odds*, 8-26.

9 School and Curriculum Reform: Manitoba Frameworks and Multicultural Teacher Education

JOHN YOUNG AND ROBERT J. GRAHAM

ABSTRACT/RÉSUMÉ

In the 1990s Manitoba, in common with all other provinces in Canada, undertook an extensive program of centrally-driven school and curriculum reform. At the forefront of this reform movement in this province was a series of tightly-linked government publications that ranged from key statements of reform policy to specific curriculum frameworks of outcomes and standards with their corresponding implementation manuals — documents that offered teachers adaptable instances of strategic knowledge, application, and "best practice." The provincial government's commitment to the substance and ideology of these reform initiatives, along with the ambiguous process by which they have been introduced, understood, and taken up by teachers has, we argue, significantly reconfigured the nature of teachers' work and the way that teachers think about their work. It has also reconfigured the terrain over which the explicit and hidden processes of citizenship development take place in schools and, as a central aspect of this, the context within which the struggle for multicultural and anti-racist education takes place. In order to make some of the contours of this terrain more visible, this paper will explore: 1) how the discourse of race, culture, and diversity has been articulated in these public statements of policy and in their implementation within the public school system; and 2) briefly explore the significance of these developments for pre-service teacher candidates. These explorations will be grounded within the specific context of curricular reform in English language arts and in English language arts teacher education.

Dans les années 1990, le Manitoba, en commun avec toutes les autres provinces du Canada, s'est chargé d'un programme considérable de réforme des écoles et des programmes d'études dirigée de façon centralisée. Au premier plan de ce mouvement de réforme dans cette province est une série de publications gouvernementales bien unies qui s'étendent de déclarations clé de la politique de réforme aux cadres spécifiques de programmes d'études qui portent sur les résultats et les standards avec leurs manuels correspondants d'exécution — des documents qui offrent aux professeurs des instances adaptables de connaissances stratégiques, l'application et "la meilleure pratique." L'engagement du gouvernement provincial à la substance et à l'idéologie de ces initiatives de réforme, en plus du processus ambigu par lequel elles ont été présentées, comprises et adoptées par les professeurs, nous soutenons, a modifié d'une façon significative la nature du travail des professeurs et la manière dont les professeurs pensent à leur travail. L'engagement a aussi modifié le terrrain sur lequel les processus explicites et cachés du développement de la citoyenneté ont lieu dans les écoles, et comme un aspect central de ces processus, le contexte dans lequel la lutte pour l'éducation multiculturelle et antiraciste a lieu. Pour rendre quelques-uns de ces contours de ce terrain plus visibles, cet article explorera: 1) comment les discours sur la race, la culture et la diversité ont été exprimées dans ces déclarations publiques de la politique et dans leur exécution dans le système scolaire public; et 2) explorera brièvement la signification de ces développements pour les candidats en voie d'être enseignants. Ces explorations seront fondées à l'intérieur du contexte spécifique de la réforme des programmes d'études dans la langue anglaise et dans l'éducation pour les professeurs des arts dans la langue anglaise.

Introduction

In the 1990s Manitoba, in common with all the other provinces in Canada, undertook an extensive program of centrally-driven school and curriculum reform. At the forefront of this reform movement in this province was a series of tightly-linked government publications that ranged from key statements of reform policy to specific curriculum frameworks of outcomes and standards with their corresponding implementation manuals — documents that offered teachers adaptable instances of strategic knowledge, application, and "best practice."[1]

The provincial government's commitment to the substance and ideology of these reform initiatives, along with the ambiguous process by which they have been introduced, understood, and taken up by teachers has, we argue, significantly reconfigured the nature of teachers' work and the way that teachers think about their work. It has also reconfigured the terrain over which the explicit and hidden processes of citizenship development take place in schools and, as a central aspect of this, the context within which the struggle for multicultural and anti-racist education takes place. In order to make some of the contours of this terrain more visible, this paper will explore: 1) how the discourse of race, culture, and diversity has been articulated in these public statements of policy and in their implementation within the public school system; and 2) briefly explore the significance of these developments for pre-service teacher candidates. We have elected to focus on the experiences of pre-service teachers because, as individuals in the formative stages of professional socialization, they inevitably find themselves located within the ideological cross-currents and tensions of these reform initiatives. Furthermore, we believe that the potential impact of how candidate teachers attempt to resolve these tensions will have an enduring impact on the capacity of the teaching profession to respond effectively to issues of equity as a central ideal of the Canadian state and its citizenry. These explorations will be grounded within the specific context of curricular reform in English language arts and in English language arts teacher education.

Fundamentally, we want to argue that the tensions experienced by the teacher candidates reflect what we believe are the contradictions inherent in the policy documents themselves and the truncated and underdeveloped concepts of race and culture that are subsumed under a functionalist preoccupation with accountability and the raising of standards. Furthermore, it is our contention that the "managerial" and "technical" orientation that dominates the implementation of these school and curriculum reforms is inconsistent with a version of multicultural education for which the significance of race and culture to school experience is viewed as complex, contextual, and which requires the active engagement of teachers in its daily construction.[2] To the extent that faculties of education can provide students with oppositional lenses with which to inspect the shifting demands and expectations placed upon them as teachers in a public education system, they offer the opportunity to deepen a dialogue and commitment to the ideals of equity, social justice, and citizenship.

Our paper is an extension of two ongoing research projects. The first is a three-year action research initiative undertaken by the two authors as part of the larger "Immigration and the Metropolis" project. This action research focussed on the construction of pre-service teachers' professional identities as multicultural English language arts teachers, as well as inquired into the instructor's own identity as a pre-service teacher and curriculum developer.[3] The second project, undertaken for the Canadian Council for Multicultural and Intercultural Education (CCMIE), examined practising teachers' views of, and engagement with, multicultural professional development activities across Canada over the last five years.[4] In the course of this research, both projects have served to crystallize for us the significant and powerful ways in which school and curricular reform has permeated the consciousness and affected the practice of pre-service and veteran teachers alike.

School and Curriculum Reform in Manitoba

The term "reform" can be used in a variety of ways. In the context of "School Reform" in the 1990s — in Canada and elsewhere — the term has come to take on a central importance in the discourse around public education. For the purposes of this paper we use it to mean a more or less coherent program of educational change that is government-directed, based on an explicitly political analysis (that is, one driven primarily by the political apparatus of government rather than by educators or bureaucrats), and justified on the basis of the need for a substantial break with current practice.[5]

Used in this way, the main package of education reforms in Manitoba in the 1990s was introduced in July, 1994 by the Education Minister of the day, Clayton Manness, and was called *Renewing Education: New Directions*. Three documents, issued within a year of each other — *Renewing Education: New Directions, A Blueprint for Action; Renewing Education: New Directions, The Action Plan*; and *Renewing Education: New Directions, A Foundation for Excellence*— laid out six education priority areas for the government:

- *Essential Learning*: the definition of basic learning embodied in a prescribed curriculum with a reduced number of course options for high school (senior years) students;
- *Educational Standards and Evaluation*: a new and mandatory program of province-wide standards tests at grades 3, 6, 9 (Senior 1) and 12 (Senior 4);
- *School Effectiveness*: a requirement that each school develop a school development plan;
- *Parental and Community Involvement*: the creation of Advisory Councils for School Leadership to provide more parent and community input into school decision-making and increase the opportunities for parents to choose between schools;
- *Distance Education and Technology*: the greater use of distance education and technology in Manitoba schools; and
- *Teacher Education*: a review of teacher education in the province.

Of these six priority areas it is the first two that have been afforded the most sustained attention and which provide the main focus of this paper.

The Language of Diversity in the *New Directions* Documents

The Blueprint and The Action Plan

A striking feature of the Manitoba reform documents is the lack of ideological justifications for the substantial changes that are called for. Nevertheless, the central theme of these documents is that the school system generally is not adequately meeting the challenge of graduating students ready to take on the requirements of citizenship in the twenty-first century, in particular, the academic competencies deemed necessary for the province's and for the nation's economic well-being. Without a discussion of *which* students are underachieving and with no clear statement on the significance of issues such as race, culture, class, and gender to school achievement or to the competing visions of what qualities might in fact be deemed appropriate for successful citizenship, these shortcomings of the public school system were seen as stemming primarily from: a lack of uniformly applied definition of basic education/essential learning; a lack of rigour and relevance within the existing curriculum; and a lack of accountability within the system for student achievement.

The response of *New Directions* was built around the definition of essential learning from Kindergarten to Grade 12/Senior 4, with a priority placed upon putting in place a revised curriculum based upon grade- and subject-specific outcomes for compulsory core subject areas — language arts, mathematics, science, and social science. Crucial to this definition of essential learning was the development of complementary educational standards that describe the expected level of student performance in relation to grade- and subject-specific outcomes, with standards tests being administered at the end of Grade 3, 6, 9 (Senior 1), and 12 (Senior 4). According to *The Action Plan*, these test were meant to form a part of all students' final mark at each stage with the exception of grade 3, and to be reported to parents and made public on a school-by-school basis.

The language of *The Action Plan* is a language of "success for all" and of raising academic performance through a more tightly structured and more demanding curriculum. It is, we would argue, a language of "abstract universalism and deracialized individualism"[6] that discounts the significance that students' (and parents' and teachers') gendered, racialized, and classed experiences have on their views of the world, school, and learning, and their conceptions of curriculum relevance. Stated clearly at the front of the policy document, *The Action Plan* declares that, "[e]ducational renewal in Manitoba seeks to ensure that effective educational strategies are used consistently and appropriately across the system, and that all students have the opportunity to achieve success at school."[7] On page thirty-seven of a thirty-eight page report, *The Action Plan* acknowledges that "teachers must be able to respond to student diversity. Manitoba is diverse in terms of culture, family structure, values and interests."[8] Yet in the previous thirty-six pages the word "culture" appears twice, "gender" once, and "socio-economic background" once (in each case with reference to students and never to parents or teachers). The word "race" does not appear in the document, neither does "sexual orientation," and there is no reference to Aboriginal people anywhere in the report.

The belief that individual effort combined with high expectation is the recipe for school success is clearly articulated with reference to the introduction of standards testing:

> The full range of high and uniform provincial outcomes and standards will apply to the vast majority of students. ... [A]lthough students learn at different rates or may require different levels or types of support, their hard work, along with the expertise and support of administrators, parents, teachers and community members will enable the vast majority of students to demonstrate the knowledge and skills they are expected to learn.[9]

While the whole reform agenda is premised on the assumption that schools in Manitoba are not meeting the needs of students and that the system is in need of "revitalization and renewal,"[10] *The Action Plan* does not explore *whom* schools are serving less well, and issues of equity or social justice rarely find their way into the report. Implicit in this approach is that a good school and a good curriculum is the same for all students and that raising standards will enhance the opportunities for all students. This latter assumption does not entertain the possibility that one can produce "polarizing improvements" rather than "equalizing improvements"[11]— and that an overall rise in school or system standards may either narrow or increase differences in achievement along the lines of race, class, and gender.

An analysis of schooling that assumes schools are neutral or benevolent institutions with respect to race, class, and gender not only flies in the face of a critical research literature, but is essentially ahistorical and apolitical. To think that success for all students can be achieved with some technical restructuring and the goodwill and professional services of teachers denies the reality that schools and teachers are inextricably implicated in the production of inequality.[12] Buried within an extensive smorgasbord of some sixteen required skills for teachers that emphasise subject area knowledge, pedagogic skills, entrepreneurial skills, skills to help students develop fundamental values and ethics, and the measurement of student achievement, is "the ability to respond to student diversity."[13] Nowhere is there an elaboration of what sorts of responses are required, whether these might form part of a political and oppositional agenda, or whether the existing structures of the school system and teachers' own social locations might work against this. Illustrative of this analysis of schooling is the following response from a question-and-answer section at the end of *The Action Plan*:

> Q: How can we be sure that all parents are heard [on advisory councils for school leadership]?
>
> A: It is up to parents and community members to ensure that candidates who are nominated and elected represent their points of view. Advisory councils for school leadership are required to communicate regularly to parents and community members and should be held responsible for fair representation.[14]

A Foundation for Excellence

A Foundation for Excellence, released by the government in June, 1995, builds from the *Blueprint* and *The Action Plan* to outline a process of curriculum development that would inform the construction of the *Framework of Outcomes and Standards*, documents central to the *New Directions* reform program. Still embedded within the broader rhetoric of "success for all" and "respect for human diversity," the *Foundation for Excellence* cites equity —"ensuring fairness and the best possible learning opportunities for Manitobans, regardless of background or geographic location"[15]— as the second of eight guiding principles. Equity and inclusion get taken up in the document in two important places: through *representation* in the curriculum development process and through curriculum *infusion* in curriculum design.

As part of the *Western Canadian Protocol: Collaboration in Basic Education*, curriculum development in the areas of mathematics, language arts (English and French), science, and social studies is designed to follow a process of curriculum development teams, review panels, field validation, authorized provincial use, and continual updating.[16] Central in this process are curriculum writing teams made up of a departmental project manager, a professional writer, and a team of exemplary classroom teachers "who work extensively in the subject area/course under development, who are knowledgeable about curriculum planning and design, pedagogy, and assessment and evaluation, and who can work well in a group, discuss and synthesize within strict time limitations."[17] With regard to membership, the document concludes, "each curriculum development team has appropriate representation (e.g., geographic, gender, Aboriginal)." [18] A similar orientation to representation is described in the field validation stage where the document states that "[p]ilot teachers are selected based upon departmental selection criteria (e.g., subject area knowledge and expertise, gender, geography, and semestered and non-semestered schools) designed to ensure balanced representation." [19] However, the extent to which such a loosely-defined gesture toward inclusion and "balanced representation" can, in fact, lead to the production of curricular documents grounded in principles of inclusion would seem from the outset fraught with conceptual and practical problems.

In a clear statement of an infusion model of curriculum development, *A Foundation for Excellence* outlines ten elements to be incorporated into all curriculum documents: foundation skill areas (literacy and communication; problem-solving; human relations; and technology); resource based learning; differentiated instruction; curriculum integration; Aboriginal perspectives; gender fairness; appropriate age portrayals; human diversity; anti-racist/anti-bias education; and sustainable development. The document states that Aboriginal perspectives

> will be integrated into curricula to enable students to learn the history of Manitoba and Canada before European settlement and to give the perspective of Aboriginal people since that time. Each subject area will address the perspectives and accomplishments of Aboriginal people as appropriate. The goal of integrating Aboriginal perspectives into curricula is to ensure that all students have the opportunity to understand and respect themselves, their cultural heritage, and the cultural heritage of others. [20]

The document goes on:

> To address the challenges of gender fairness, and to develop student understanding in all subject areas in a balanced way, teaching, learning, and assessment must be equally accessible, relevant, interesting, appropriate, and challenging to male and female students. This will ensure that all students will have opportunities to succeed regardless of gender. Curriculum documents, learning resources and classroom practice should reflect a commitment to gender fairness and inclusion. [21]

Commenting on human diversity, the document states:

Manitoba is a mosaic of people with a diversity of cultures, languages, religions and other characteristics. These aspects of human diversity should be recognized, accepted and celebrated to create learning environments that: prepare all students for participation in society; provide students with opportunities for cultural and linguistic development and encourage inter-cultural understanding and harmony.[22]

Finally, with regard to anti-racist, anti-bias education, the document adds:

Effective schools strive to create and maintain inclusive school programs and environments that welcome diversity and challenge bias and discrimination. An anti-bias and anti-racism educational approach is a critical element in the development of curriculum documents and school environments so that students can experience learning in a safe environment and can develop the required knowledge and skills.[23]

That these statements find their way into this generative document on curriculum reform for the province must be acknowledged and may be seen as signalling significance to the issue of diversity in schooling. However, since there is no accompanying analysis that would serve to suggest their implications for practice, and since these statements are embedded among a plethora of other priorities that curriculum planners and teachers are expected to pay attention to, their impact is likely to be, at best, tenuous and diffuse. Given this limitation, it is the framework's documents, standards tests, and curriculum implementation documents that are likely to substantially operationalize *New Directions* and to direct teacher practice. Consequently, these documents take on an additional and crucial importance.

The English Language Arts Curriculum Frameworks S1-S4

With the introduction in 1996 of the English language arts Senior 1 *Curriculum Framework of Outcomes and Standards*,[24] Manitoba Education and Training initiated the ambitious project of producing documents delineating not only the outcomes and standards required by students in Senior 1-4, but also of producing four additional implementation documents that would provide a wealth of strategic knowledge and "best teaching practices" for teachers to follow. The stated purpose of the *Framework* document was to describe "the general and specific student learning outcomes by grade" and to show how these outcomes "integrate the four foundation skill areas of literacy and communication, problem solving, human relations, and technology."[25] These general student learning outcomes "identify the knowledge, skills, and attitudes that students are expected to learn in English language arts,"[26] while the specific outcomes identify the "component knowledge, skills, and attitudes that contribute to the general learning outcomes."[27] Further, the document was explicit in making visible its beliefs about language learning and the central importance of helping students "to develop and apply strategies for anticipating, comprehending, composing, and responding to a variety of texts and situations."[28] The *Frameworks* is equally clear that "[c]ompetence in a variety of observable and measurable skills, strategies, and interactive processes fosters student learning"[29] and, in particular, the "[s]tudents' development of metacognition — the awareness and knowledge of their own mental processes — enables them to monitor, regulate, and direct these processes to achieve particular learning goals."[30]

This emphasis on cognitive and metacognitive processes, with balanced instruction in the skills and strategies designed to help students maximize their control over, and facility with, the English language, seemed to signal a victory of sorts in the historical struggle within the ranks of English teachers for a language-centred over a literature-centred view of the English curriculum.[31] The concomitant image of the language arts teacher that emerges from the *Framework* document is the language teacher as *rhetorician*, a person deeply immersed in her understanding of how words (and images) work in the world and unwilling to grant the language of literature any pre-eminent or privileged ontological status. This image certainly contrasts with the view of the English teacher contained in the *cultural heritage* model under which the teacher's major preoccupation was to put students in contact with "great literature," mostly with the literary masterpieces of the Western tradition.[32] In addition, by making no mention of any literary works that every student *must* read, the *Framework* document pins its hopes firmly on the decision-making capacities of the individual teacher to ensure that the range of texts studied represents a cross-section of works that not only employ the English language in exemplary ways, but that also to a large extent captures the interest of the diverse student population in the province's many multi-racial, multi-ethnic, and multicultural classrooms. These changes of emphasis and image, reinforced in teachers' minds by the existence of standards tests and the challenge of preparing students from a variety of different cultural and linguistic backgrounds to write these tests, has served to increase the emotional temperature surrounding the debate on the politics of literacy teaching and learning in the province.[33]

The consequences of this debate for student teachers, confronted as they are by the task of adopting and adapting the generalities of the *Framework* into the specifics of classroom practice (or as one candidate teacher Stephanie wrote: "The language arts teacher must take the blueprint and make it a reality in her classroom") has been to put to the test the nature, depth, and extent of their understanding and commitment to anti-racist/multicultural teaching and of trying to create an identity for themselves as they negotiate a number of competing orientations to curriculum.[34] As individuals caught in the crosscurrents of this debate, each student teacher will respond and react differently to the particular ways that this struggle makes itself manifest in the schools in which they complete their student teaching practica. However, we believe that their responses will show in powerful ways the effect these various policy documents might have on the potential future of multicultural teaching and on issues of equity and social justice.

When Policy Meets Practice: The Experience of Student Teachers

While these policy documents, backed by the power of the provincial government, seek to establish a framework for public schooling in the province, there is inevitably some distance between the articulation of policy and the specifics of classroom practice. This is particularly true when the policy changes are as large-scale and as controversial as those envisaged in Manitoba's school reform agenda. That these changes have been introduced very rapidly and in a period of financial constraint only adds to the controversy. As indicated previously, the main focus of our study is not directly related to the practices of experienced teachers; rather, it is on the lived experience of a group of teacher candidates on the threshold of entering their teaching careers. The voices of the student teachers that we include here will dramatize a number of ways in which school reform has impacted upon the politics of literacy education in the province, teacher identities, the nature of teachers' work, and the potential fate of multicultural and anti-racist education and teacher education. From our analyses of student response journals and from extensive interview data (some of which is quoted later in this paper), we currently hold that the initial impact of these policy documents has been: 1) to deflect teachers' attention away from anti-racist education and an anti-racist analysis of the role of the teacher; 2) to legitimate an essentially technical orientation to teaching that universalizes both students and teacher; and 3) to shift the responsibility for anti-racist education to individual teachers with little by way of support or resources.

We believe that a combination of circumstances has served to deflect teachers' attention away from anti-racist education. First, there has been an emphasis on essential learning and a curriculum development process that has focussed on mathematics and on language arts before, and at the expense of, social studies, and has served to narrow the curriculum and the most readily available space for teachers to be comfortable engaging with anti-racist education. Second, without doubt the introduction of standards tests with their strong element of teacher accountability has captured teachers' time and attention. The impact of this to date has been to stifle anti-racist education. And third, the demands of implementing these government priorities without additional funds have contributed to the draining of anti-racist expertise from the public school system.

For example, as she reflects on the current status and possible fate of multicultural/anti-racist education, Caroline writes:

> I believe that multicultural education could possibly fade as a valid teaching practice, and that it will be viewed as increasing the already heavy workload of teachers, due to the simple fact that no one administration or legislation has taken the responsibility to define and guide its implementation; and that many teachers, disillusioned with the manner in which to teach this topic, must take the matter into their own hands and decide how they will implement this in their classroom.

This lack of clarity in the concept and in the policy can create feelings of ambivalence and even cynicism within the teaching profession toward multicultural education in that, lacking a systemic commitment to its principles and to creating a dialogue around its implementation, a candidate teacher like Caroline can express the tensions she has felt and observed as follows:

> There is a view (among some teachers) that due to the changing demographics of our country and our cities, multicultural education is a necessity in our schools. However, within this group there is a division among teachers who see multicultural education simply as a fad that will fade away in a few years, but for now is a required specialty in order to get a job and others who feel frustrated at the lack of professional development in this field. ... Multicultural education as an individual project allows teachers not to engage.

Similarly, the exigencies experienced by candidate teachers around issues of survival in the classroom, as well as by the importance to them of performing well in the eyes of co-operating teachers and faculty advisors, can deflect attention away from integrating multicultural/anti-racist principles and practices into their teaching, opting instead for what is safe and comfortable.

With this in mind, in addition to raising questions about candidate teachers' own identities and sense of "being prepared," Patricia writes:

> The problem I foresee is that my own experience does not lend itself to using a multicultural curriculum. ... [I know] we need to bring in other elements of cultural identity, class, gender, nationality, ability, and race ... [but] right now I cannot properly address these issues ... . Presently, I am more concerned with classroom management, lesson and unit planning, getting good evaluations from my co-operating teachers and faculty advisors, and maintaining a home and a marriage. Once I settle into my "groove," I think I will be able to focus on myself as a multicultural teacher and hone my skills.

For those of us who see anti-racist education as essentially oppositional within the current school arrangements, the concept of settling "into a groove"– i.e., of negotiating a comfort level and an identity for oneself from a range of professionally approved images of teachers and teaching-learning to teach with, rather than "against the grain"[35]— before turning to multicultural education, becomes highly problematic.

The overall intention of the *Framework* documents for English language arts is, as we have seen, to advance an essentially cognitive orientation to language teaching and learning, an orientation that recognizes but does not fully engage with the significance of the racial and cultural identities of both student and teacher. For, as Sarah writes,

> In September, I saw curriculum mostly as a "development of cognitive Processes;" this is no longer accurate. I tend now to side more with the "social Reconstructionist" view of curriculum. This is an ongoing debate within myself. ... I realize through my last teaching block that I took a somewhat lazy approach to multicultural literature. I took what Fishman[36] calls the "Disney/Coca-Cola" approach that "denies that people, including children, see with their eyes."

As we have seen, within these English language arts frameworks, as within the policy documents themselves, an appreciation of diversity is focussed primarily on a dual concern with "getting on together"— community harmony and conflict management — and of broadening the canon of curriculum content. This abstract and decontextualized picture of teaching and learning ignores vital issues of power within schools and the complex interplay of race, class, gender, and identity that constitutes the daily life of classrooms. However, it would be incorrect to assert that the *New Directions* documents do not acknowledge the significance of diversity to education in Manitoba. They clearly do not preclude teachers from engaging issues of race, culture, and schooling. For example, Sabiha exhibits a complex and layered version of diversity and its relation to identity (her students and her own) when she writes:

> A student in my class may be of Korean ethnicity but that is not all I need to know of him or her. ... That particular student may also be an upper-class female with a mild hearing disability and those experiences will also shape how she interprets, internalizes, and expresses her opinions about material. The fact that she is Korean does not automatically mean that she will learn, think, and feel the same way as other Koreans do. ... Being somewhat removed from the cultural norm myself, I can perhaps feel all the more strongly for education to be all the more multicultural. ... I also obviously (by my religious dress) was associated with "the other."

But for Sabiha, located as she is as a woman from a non-Western religious background, a multicultural/anti-racist approach to the curriculum may still remain an individual project of the few minority teachers on staff, or of those teachers who, like Sarah, tend to take a social reconstructionist view of curriculum[37] for personal and political reasons. However, in the absence of greater racial and ethnic representation within the teaching force, issues of equity and social justice have taken on a less prominent role in the emerging professional commitments, understandings, and practices of many of these beginning teachers.

Conclusion

The dust has not yet settled on school reform in Manitoba. Key curriculum frameworks such as those for social studies remain to be developed and the implementation of others is still at a relatively early stage. Similarly, a provincial Aboriginal/Aboriginal Education strategy that will cut across *New Directions* is still being developed. This situation alone should caution against any effort to make definitive statements about the long-term impact of the province's *New Directions* initiatives on the equity agenda of public schools and of anti-racist education.

Nevertheless, it is within this "dusty" and ambiguous context that pre-service teachers currently find themselves and within which faculty of education instructors must work with students in preparation for, and orientation to, the profession. Neither instructor nor student, we argue, can legitimately (pragmatically) ignore the requirements of provincially-mandated curricula or the various ways they are being taken up by practising teachers – this is the world within which faculty of education graduates will build their careers and develop their professional identities. Our argument in this paper has been that the *New Directions* documents and the ways in which they have been implemented do not provide for a coherent and well-developed articulation of an anti-racist approach to education in the province. Nor have they created a context within which teachers (and particularly pre-service teachers) are encouraged to see this approach as a defining feature of their work and as a basis on which their success and professional competence will be judged. On the contrary, the potential exists to reinforce an overly technical view of teachers' work, a view which ultimately mitigates the creation of such an agenda.

If faculties of education are to live up to the expectations of their status as a professional school within a university setting, they have a vital role to play. This role, we would argue, is neither to transmit uncritically the requirements of the proposed *New Directions* reforms nor to ignore them as politically or ideologically unpalatable. Rather, it is to provide students with a variety of oppositional lenses with which to examine the shifting demands and expectations made of them as public school teachers and to promote a deeper dialogue about, and commitment to, the ideals of equity and social justice, which have long been close to the heart of (at least) the rhetoric of Canadian public schooling. It is with these ideas in mind that we conclude with a student's voice in order to endorse both the content and spirit behind Sarah's hard-won realization of her own developing identity and commitments as a multicultural teacher.

> In September, I saw curriculum mostly as the "development of cognitive processes." This is no longer accurate. I now tend to side more with the "social reconstructionist" view of curriculum. ... Students are in school not to learn about other cultures; they are there to be part of a larger multicultural and democratic society. I must go back and find out what gets these kids to care, what matters to them, and how I can reach them as a stranger. This is something that the Faculty of Education cannot teach me — nor would I want it to. I need to learn this lesson on my own, for myself and for my students. I didn't sign up to get a neat

little package of tools at the end of my four years. I didn't
expect a high school instruction book or a "Teaching ESL
for Dummies" manual. I knew that it would be hard work,
and I knew that there would be lots of learning after
graduation, and I don't think the Faculty tried to trick us
into thinking anything different. There are some lessons
that cannot be taught, and for me, how to be a good English
language arts teacher is one that I will have to learn on my
own.

ACKNOWLEDGEMENTS

The authors gratefully acknowledge the assistance of a
research grant from the Prairie Centre of Excellence at the
University of Alberta, part of its "Culture, Teaching, and
Identities" Project, and a University of Manitoba/Social
Sciences and Humanities Research Council (UM/SSHRC)
research grant from the University of Manitoba.

NOTES

1. Manitoba Education and Training, *Multicultural Education: A Policy for the 1990s* (Winnipeg: Manitoba Education and Training, 1992); and Manitoba Education and Training's *Renewing Education: New Directions; A Blueprint for Action* (1994); *Renewing Education: New Directions; The Action Plan* (1995); and *Renewing Education: New Directions; A Foundation for Excellence* (1995).

2. Patrick Solomon and Cynthia Levine-Rasky, *Accommodation and Resistance: Educators' Response to Multicultural and Anti-Racist Education* (North York: Faculty of Education, York University, 1994).

3. Robert J. Graham and Jon Young, "Curriculum, Identity, and Experience in Multicultural Teacher Education," *Alberta Journal of Educational Research* 44, no. 4 (1998): 397-407.

4. Canadian Council for Multicultural and Intercultural Education, *Multicultural/Intercultural/Anti-Racist Education and In-Service Teacher Education: A Review of Literature* (Ottawa: CCMIE, 1997); *Multicultural/Intercultural/Anti-Racist Education and In-Service Teacher Education:*

A Review of Western Canadian Teachers (1998); and *Multicultural/ Intercultural/Anti-Racist Education and In-Service Teacher Education: A National Survey* (1999).

5. Ben Levin and Jon Young, "The Origins of Educational Reform: A Comparative Perspective" (paper presented at the annual meeting of the Canadian Society for the Study of Education, St. John's, NF 1997), ERIC, ED 424 641.

6. Richard Hatcher, "Social Justice and the Politics of School Effectiveness and School Improvement," *Race, Ethnicity, and Education* 1, no. 2 (1998): 280.

7. Manitoba Education and Training, *Action Plan*, 3.

8. Ibid., 37.

9. Ibid., 13.

10. Ibid., 4.

11. Hatcher, "Social Justice," 269.

12. R.W. Connell, *Schools and Social Justice* (Philadelphia: Temple University Press, 1993).

13. Manitoba Education and Training, *Action Plan*, 37.

14. Ibid., 54.

15. Manitoba Education and Training, *A Foundation for Excellence*, 3.

16. Ibid., 10.

17. Ibid., 10-11.

18. Ibid., 11.

19. Ibid., 2.

20. Ibid.,18-19.

21. Ibid., 19-20.

22. Ibid., 20.

23. Ibid.

24. Manitoba Education and Training, *Senior 1 English Language Arts: Manitoba Curriculum Framework of Outcomes and Senior 1 Standards* (Winnipeg: Manitoba Education and Training, 1996).

25. Manitoba Education and Training, *Action Plan*, 1.

26. Ibid.

27. Ibid.

28. Ibid., 3.

29. Ibid., 4.

30. Ibid.

31. Arthur N. Applebee, *Tradition and Reform in the Teaching of English: A History* (Urbana, IL: National Council of Teachers of English, 1974); James Britton, *Language and Learning* (Harmandsworth, UK: Penguin, 1972); and Robert J. Graham, *Reading and Writing the Self: Autobiography in Education and the Curriculum* (New York: Teachers College Press, 1991).

32. Robert Protherough and Jane Atkinson, "Shaping the Image of an English Teacher," in *Teaching English*, ed. Susan Brindley (London, New York: Routledge, 1994), 5-15.

33. Tannis Miller, "Speak Your Mind!" in *Classmate*, ed. K. Clark and P. Lockman (Winnipeg: Manitoba Association of Teachers of English, 1999), 16.

34. Elliott W. Eisner, *The Educational Imagination: On the Design and Evaluation of School Programs* (New York: Macmillan, 1985).

35. Roger T. Simon, *Teaching against the Grain: Texts for a Pedagogy of Possibility* (Greenwood: Bergin and Garvey, 1992).

36. Andrea Fishman, "Finding Ways In: Redefining Multicultural Literature," *English Journal* 84 (1997): 73-79.

37. Eisner, *Educational Imagination*.

10 From Heritage to International Languages: Globalism and Western Canadian Trends in Heritage Language Education

ANTONIO (TONY) J. TAVARES

ABSTRACT/RÉSUMÉ

Throughout the late 1970s and 1980s, educational systems in Canada responded to diversity in their populations by expanding heritage language programming in public schools. The support for heritage languages was directly related to federal and provincial multiculturalism policies. Heritage language education was seen as an essential part of the Canadian cultural mosaic. It also reflected a response to pressures from various cultural groups, especially Ukrainian Canadians, for inclusion and recognition. Government support for maintaining their languages was often a question, from their perspective, of equality and the right to full participation in a multicultural Canadian society. The inclusion of heritage language programs in mainstream educational institutions was one means of asserting their multicultural rights. By 1980, English-Ukrainian bilingual programs had been established in Alberta, Saskatchewan, and Manitoba. These three provinces have recently agreed to participate in a series of projects through the Western Canadian Protocol for Collaboration in Basic Education aimed at developing common curriculum frameworks for international languages. The shift in terminology from heritage to international languages reflects the impact of globalism on education systems in Canada, as well as significant shifts in multicultural policies and perspectives.

Vers la fin des années 1970 et pendant toutes les années 1980, les systèmes éducatifs au Canada ont répondu à la diversité de leurs populations en étendant la programmation des langues patrimoniales dans les écoles publiques. L'appui pour les langues patrimoniales était directement lié aux politiques fédérales et provinciales sur le multiculturalisme. On regardait l'éducation sur les langues patrimoniales comme une partie essentielle de la mosaïque culturelle canadienne.

L'appui réflétait aussi une réponse aux pressions de plusieurs groupes culturels, en particulier les Ukrainiens-Canadiens, pour l'inclusion et la reconnaissance. Il s'agissait, de leur point de vue, de l'égalité et du droit de la pleine participation dans la société canadienne multiculturelle; leur revendication pour l'appui gouvernemental pour la conservation de leur langue s'ensuivait. Dès 1980, des programmes bilingues anglais-ukrainiens avaient été établis en Alberta, en Saskatchewan, et au Manitoba. Ces trois provinces se sont récemment mises d'accord pour participer à une série de projets par le truchement du Protocole de collaboration concernant l'éducation de base dans l'Ouest canadien, visé à développer des cadres de programmes d'études communs pour les langues internationales. Le changement de terminologie de langues patrimoniales aux langues internationales réflète l'impact du globalisme sur les systèmes éducatifs au Canada ainsi que des changements significatifs de politiques et perspectives multiculturelles.

Introduction

Throughout the late 1970s and 1980s, educational systems in Western Canada (specifically in Alberta, Saskatchewan, and Manitoba) responded to diversity in their populations by expanding "heritage" language programming in public schools.[1] The support for heritage language programs in the educational system and in community-based or supplementary school programs in the West, as in Ontario, was directly related to the increased provincial attention to multiculturalism and, in some cases, the formal adoption of multicultural policies. In Quebec, similar trends resulted in increased attention being given by governments of all political stripes, albeit for different reasons, to pluralism and "intercultural" education, resulting in the emergence of similar heritage-focused language programs, *Programmes d'ensignment de langues d'origine*. Heritage language education was seen as an essential part of the Canadian cultural mosaic, at least from the perspective of the various cultural/linguistic groups. Federal and provincial ministries responsible for culture and/or multiculturalism commonly offered financial support for heritage language programming.

At this point, the growth in language programming did not flow from an increased sense of global interdependence and internationalism. It was a direct response to pressures from various cultural groups, especially Ukrainian Canadians, for inclusion and recognition. Government support for maintaining their languages and cultures through "bilingual" and other forms of heritage language programs was equated with equality and the right to full participation in a multicultural Canadian society.[2] By 1979, English-Ukrainian bilingual programs had been established in Alberta, Saskatchewan, and Manitoba.

In 1993, these three provinces agreed to participate in a series of projects through the auspices of the Western Canadian Protocol for Collaboration in Basic Education (WCP) aimed at developing common curriculum frameworks[3] for "international languages."[4] In this case, the term "international languages" refers to what were previously called "heritage languages" and, technically, any other modern or second language other than English or French.[5] The change in terminology from "heritage" to "international" reflects both the impact of globalism on education systems in Canada and provincial policies, as well as multicultural education policies and perspectives.

The Emergence of Heritage Languages

As has been documented in the literature on multiculturalism in Canada, the 1960s were a period of significant social and political upheaval. The assimilationist policies and monocultural perspectives in Canada were being challenged by Quebec and French Canadian activists throughout Canada. The demands of the French for greater recognition of their language and culture, the sharing of power, and autonomy shook English Canada. At the same time, Canada's growth as a modern democratic nation that respected human rights and the changing ethnic mix of its population were calling into question dominant perspectives on cultural and linguistic diversity — perspectives such as those articulated by J.S. Woodsworth in *Strangers within Our Gates*.[6] While open to immigration, Woodsworth argued in his book for the assimilation of immigrants and minority cultural groups in Canada. Diversity was disruptive and was something to be feared . Therefore, in his view the mandate of the social and educational systems and agencies in Canada was to facilitate the assimilation of immigrant and minority groups and inculcate "Canadian" values, culture, and language. Woodsworth's views reflected the popular attitudes of the dominant Anglo-Celtic community of the time and attested to the strength and wide-spread acceptance of the assimilationist and monocultural approach which shaped public education systems in Manitoba and English Canada until fairly recently.

The report of the Bilingualism and Biculturalism Commission in 1968 acknowledged the fact that Canada was a multicultural nation and that cultural diversity in Canada needed to be recognized. This was a point that Ukrainian Canadians in Western Canada, among others, made abundantly clear during the commission hearings. They expressed strongly their views about their contributions to Canada's development and the need for their rights as citizens to be acknowledged and valued.[7] The report led to the introduction of the Liberal federal government's

1971 policy of multiculturalism within a bilingual framework. Whether or not the policy was intended to "buy" support or to reduce opposition to the Official Languages Act of 1969 is, to some degree, irrelevant, for Trudeau's policy had a significant and lasting impact on Canadian public policy.

The policy stated that the promotion of equality and the preservation of the multicultural nature of Canada were primary objectives. This included support for activities intended to preserve and maintain the linguistic and cultural heritage of various ethnocultural communities. This, in turn, launched the federal government's entry into the world of heritage languages, that is, it promoted "the development and expression of heritage cultures and languages as an integral part of Canadian artistic, cultural and academic life."[8]

The federal multiculturalism policy influenced provincial governments to adopt parallel multicultural policies in some fashion, thus opening up opportunities for various cultural groups in Ontario, Western Canada, and even Quebec for the expansion of heritage language programs. In Western Canada, with its many large ethnocultural groups, there came a demand for "bilingual" heritage language programs. In Manitoba, there was a historical link between French "bilingual" programs and heritage languages. From 1897 to 1916 the Laurier-Greenway Accord not only allowed for French-English public schools, but opened the door for bilingual Ukrainian, Polish, and German schools. With the re-introduction of French bilingual schools in Manitoba in 1969 and, later, French immersion programs, the Ukrainian Canadian community lobbied for changes in legislation allowing for the use of languages other than French or English as languages of instruction in public schools. While Saskatchewan and Alberta did not have the same historical link between heritage language programs and French language instruction in public schools, the expansion of French language programming in both provinces provided an impetus for new demands for the enhancement of heritage languages programming. Alberta was the first province to introduce an English-Ukrainian bilingual program in 1978. Other bilingual programs were introduced at the local level by the Edmonton public school system and several other school boards. Manitoba passed amendments allowing for bilingual instruction in other languages in 1979, and English-Ukrainian bilingual programming was introduced as a pilot in the 1979-1980 school year. This was followed in subsequent years by German and Hebrew bilingual programs.

In the 1980s in Western Canada, more recent ethnocultural groups were emerging as significant demographic and political factors. Thus, in Winnipeg and Edmonton from the mid-1980s to the early 1990s, there was a significant growth in the number of heritage languages offered. For example, in Manitoba between 1984 and 1990, new curricula for Portuguese, Filipino, and Mandarin were developed and implemented primarily in Winnipeg School Division No. 1. These were in addition to the "older" languages such as Icelandic, German, Hebrew, Spanish, and Ukrainian already offered as "language of study" programs in various public schools. In Saskatchewan, a system was devised whereby students could receive high school credits for heritage languages taught by community groups or organizations that followed guidelines developed by Saskatchewan Education.

During this period, the term "heritage languages" came to be preferred by ethnocultural communities and multicultural education activists. It tended to reinforce the idea that languages other than English or French were not "foreign" languages, as they were spoken by many Canadians and were part of their Canadian heritage. The maintenance of these languages was presented as a rational extension of the efforts to recognize and celebrate Canada's multicultural heritage and was in keeping with multicultural policies espoused by various levels of governments.

Heritage Language Education and Multicultural Policies

It is beyond the scope of this paper to fully document and analyze the development of multicultural policies at the federal and provincial levels. However, it is important to note that "multiculturalism" had been embraced in some form by most political parties throughout Canada by the 1980s. A testimony to this fact at the federal level was the adoption of Canada's Multiculturalism Act in 1988 by the Conservatives under Brian Mulroney.[9] Esses and Gardner note that one of the objectives of the Act was to "preserve and enhance the use of languages other than English or French, while strengthening the status and use of the official languages of Canada."[10]

Federal policies played an important role in shaping and stimulating the development of similar provincial policies and legislation. By 1990, Manitoba, Saskatchewan, and Alberta had developed their own provincial multicultural policies or acts. Manitoba formally passed its Multiculturalism Act in 1990. Saskatchewan, one of the first provinces to introduce such an act in 1974, introduced a revised version in 1997.[11] Alberta passed its first Alberta Multiculturalism Act in 1984, and in 1996 revised and integrated its human rights and multiculturalism legislation by passing a new act, The Human Rights, Multiculturalism, and Citizenship Act.[12] British Columbia was slower in passing official legislation to complement its multicultural policies. However, it, too, passed its Multiculturalism Act in 1996.[13] While provincial policies and legislation vary to some degree, they all include some form of recognition of heritage languages and a commitment to preserving and enhancing their use. The1994 Saskatchewan *Multicultural Education and Heritage Language Policies* document attests to this linkage between federal and provincial policies and support for heritage languages: "Inherent in federal and provincial legislation and policies is a recognition that heritage languages are fundamental to the multicultural nature of our province and our country. Heritage language instruction in Saskatchewan has been funded both federally and provincially."[14]

Thus, at both the federal and provincial levels, heritage language education has been a part of the development and implementation of multicultural policies and has been reflected in multicultural education approaches and initiatives that flow from these policies.

The Western Canadian Protocol

The Western Canadian Protocol for Collaboration in Basic Education (WCP), K - 12, reflects an emerging trend toward a greater emphasis on consistency and complementarity across Canada in terms of curriculum and educational programming. It may also reflect the increasing concern of Canada's ministers of education with globalization and international economic developments that have resulted in the belief that Canada's educational systems needed to be modified in view of global concerns. Participation in international comparative studies of student achievement indicators raised concerns about Canada's effectiveness in mathematics and science education. Among other initiatives, the concern with education "standards" resulted in the Council of Ministers of Education introducing the School Achievement Indicators Program (SAIP) with mathematics being the first subject of interprovincial comparison.[15] Not surprisingly, in light of these concerns, mathematics (K-8) was the first WCP curriculum development project to be initiated and completed in 1995.[16] With respect to science, there was sufficient agreement across Canada to initiate the development of a Pan-Canadian Framework for Science, K - 12, which was completed in 1998.

The WCP agreement extended to a number of other subject areas. The agreement included, as areas of potential cooperation, languages other than English or French, as well as Aboriginal (Native) education. This opened the door to the development of new collaborative initiatives to support heritage language programming.

In Western Canada, there had been an ongoing pattern of collaboration between Alberta, Saskatchewan, and Manitoba with respect to Ukrainian language education since the late 1970s. An interprovincial advisory committee composed of representatives of the ministries of education and the Ukrainian Canadian Congress was established in 1978 to guide the development of the *Mova i rozmova* [Language and conversation] series of learning resources. Collaboration in Ukrainian language education among the three provinces continued into the early 1990s on a number of projects. For example, Manitoba provided financial and other support for a project initiated in Alberta to develop the *Nova* Ukrainian language arts series of resources.

However, by the late 1980s and early 1990s, curriculum development had slowed down quite significantly in Alberta and Manitoba as a result of two factors: the maturity of the programs and the impact on education budgets resulting from the efforts of governments to trim budgets.

Thus, the WCP presented an opportunity to "re-energize" curriculum development in heritage language education and to do so in a more cost effective manner. In 1996, Alberta proposed that Saskatchewan and Manitoba join it, and possibly British Columbia, in developing a proposal under the auspices of WCP for a project in heritage language education. British Columbia had recently introduced a new languages policy requiring all students in that province to study a second language (French or another language) between grades five and eight. As British Columbia was in the midst of implementing the policy and developing a series of "provincial" curricula for different languages under some rather restrictive time constraints, it chose to opt out of the WCP initiative, as did the Yukon and Northwest Territories. At approximately the same time, a project was initiated with the participation of all the WCP partners to develop a common curriculum framework for Aboriginal language and culture programs.[17] As a result, the three provinces agreed to collaborate in two curriculum development projects. These were *The Common Curriculum Framework for Bilingual Programming in International Languages, Kindergarten to Grade 12* and "The Common Curriculum Framework for International Languages, Kindergarten to Grade 12."[18]

The Emergence of International Languages:
The Impact of Globalization

In the discussions leading up to the WCP agreement in this area and the launching of the two projects, Alberta proposed that the term "international languages" be used instead of "heritage languages." Alberta Education (now Alberta Learning) had adopted the term to refer to languages other than English, French, or Aboriginal (Native) languages. This was reflected in the creation of an International and Native Languages Unit within the Curriculum Standards Branch and the use of the terminology in department documents and communication.[19] Second, the term reflected Alberta's increasing interest in languages as part of its "international strategies," as affirmed in the document *A Framework for Alberta's International Strategies* and reflected in the action plan that flowed from the strategy.[20] The action plan sought to increase substantially the number of students enrolled in international and second language programming. Third, it reflected a more accurate and emerging focus of contemporary second languages curricula across all provinces, i.e., there should be less emphasis on cultural maintenance and more emphasis on the application of languages for career opportunities and economic development in a multilingual global society.

The Alberta position underscored the emergence of significant developments in all three provinces and, to some extent, throughout Canada. In the early 1990s, interest in Asian languages, such as Japanese, Mandarin, and, to a lesser extent, Korean, had resulted from a growing awareness of the impact of globalization and the significance of Asia in the new global economy. Japanese language programs were introduced in Manitoba and Alberta.[21] Mandarin was introduced in a Saskatchewan school division. The significance of these programs is that they were not introduced as "heritage" programs targeted at Canadian students of Japanese or Chinese origin, but were primarily directed at students with no heritage connection to either language or culture but with an interest in Asia-Pacific studies. In fact, the Asia-Pacific Foundation of Canada, a joint business and government funded agency, promoted the introduction of Japanese language curricula throughout Canada, as did the Japan Foundation. For example, the Asia-Pacific Foundation funded the development of the Alberta Japanese language and culture 10-20-30 program of studies.[22] The following excerpt from the document demonstrates the concern with Japanese as a language of global commerce and of international economic significance:

> Increased trade and growing investment by Japan in Alberta mean that Japanese language and cultural knowledge have taken on new importance. ... As Japan's global role widens to include business, science, politics and social development, individuals need cultural and linguistic knowledge about Japan. ... Today, individuals, companies, provinces and nations must compete as they export science and technology. To do this, linguistic and cultural knowledge are necessary.[23]

The involvement of the Asia Pacific Foundation of Canada in promoting Japanese and other Asian languages points to another emerging trend, i.e., corporations and business organizations beginning to actively support and promote "international" language education. Interestingly, there was not the same level of interest from this sector during the push for heritage language education.

Spanish language programming also began to flourish across Canada during the 1990s. With increasing ties to Mexico and other Spanish-speaking countries in Central and South America, Spanish became an increasingly popular international language. In Manitoba from 1990 to 1999, the number of senior years (high) schools offering Spanish grew by over 400 percent (from five to twenty-three). The former Premier of Manitoba, Gary Filmon, an advocate of international trade and of Spanish language education, had his efforts at learning Spanish frequently highlighted in the local media. In Alberta, a similar interest in Spanish was evident. A survey of second-language program enrollment in Alberta undertaken in the fall of 1999 revealed that Spanish was the most frequently requested language for new language programs, and it had the highest enrollment of languages other than French (French Immersion and French as a Second Language programs).[24]

The same survey acknowledged the impact of globalization on education in the section that deals with school district recommendations about the need for greater promotion and marketing of language programs. The report stated that "[t]his was seen as essential to make all Albertans aware of second-language research, and the impact of globalization and career opportunities in second languages."[25]

The dismantling of the former USSR and the "opening up" of Eastern Europe to the West were also relevant to the WCP international languages projects. The three Western provinces have a significant population of Ukrainian origin, and all three provinces have signed memorandums of agreement for educational, cultural, and economic development with the government of Ukraine in recent years.[26] The large Ukrainian Canadian communities in each of the provinces are seen as an important link in establishing stronger economic ties with Ukraine and opening up opportunities for international trade. Thus, the Ukrainian language is seen as being of increasing international and economic significance.

In summary, the 1990s were a period of a significant shift in the rationale for and the focus of heritage and second-language education in Canada. Increasingly, the rationale for heritage language education or learning another language was based on international communication, career application, and participation in the global workplace and marketplace. In Canada, globalization and international competitiveness were highlighted as key factors in promoting the study of languages. A similar trend was evident in the United States: "In our increasingly global society knowledge of other languages and cultures is crucial for students and professionals who work, or plan to work, in a wide range of fields, whether in the United States or abroad."[27] The adoption of the term "international languages" by the WCP and in other jurisdictions is just one example of the impact of globalization on our education systems.

Global Citizenship and International Languages Curricula

The impact of globalization and an increasing awareness of the "global village" on the two WCP curriculum framework projects was not limited to the choice of terminology for the title of the two documents. They are also quite evident in the focus on "global citizenship" that emerges in both documents as an essential component of international language education.

In the WCP *Common Curriculum Framework for Bilingual Programming in International Languages*, one of the eight "general learning outcomes" statements, specifically focuses on culture: "Students will explore, understand and appreciate culture for personal growth and satisfaction, and for participating in and contributing to an interdependent and multicultural global society."[28]

In the document, culture is defined as an integral element of language learning, and the statement clearly reflects a greater emphasis on language learning as a means for full participation in the emerging global economy. This emphasis contrasts quite significantly with the rationale and perspective on the value of language learning that historically formed the basis for "heritage" language education. For example, the *Manitoba English-Ukrainian Bilingual Program Grades 1-6* curriculum document provides the following rationale: "On the community and national levels, the preservation of heritage and traditions of different ethnolinguistic communities enriches and adds variety to Canadian culture, produces an informed Canadian citizenry and fosters local, regional and national spirit."[29]

This specific document recognizes diversity in the global context, but as a secondary or even tertiary concern. The real focus is on application of language skills for local community development and participation, as stated in the goal statement in the document.

1. Through the Ukrainian language arts program students will acquire:

    a. a new code for thinking and communication;
    b. a deeper appreciation of Ukrainian people and their values, customs, and culture;
    c. a broader perception of the Canadian and global multicultural mosaic;

d. skills that will enable them to be full participants in Canada's Ukrainian communities.[30]

English-German bilingual education documents from approximately the same period tend to show a greater inclination toward an international focus: "The rationale for teaching German is based on the fact that German is both an international and heritage language."[31] In part, this may be due to Canada's significant economic links with Germany and that nation's important role in the European Economic Community. However, the "immediate and practical objectives" that are listed for the program do not suggest an indication of a strong international focus; nor do they point to an emphasis on the preparation of students for an emerging global society and economy. Rather, the "immediate and practical objectives" indicate a much more local and cultural focus:

- to help students learn about the German-Canadian community in Manitoba and Canada;

- to give students opportunities to enrich their understanding of the culture of those countries where German is the mother tongue;

- to promote general and cultural knowledge and appreciation.[32]

A deeper analysis of the culture outcomes in the WCP bilingual framework reveals other important influences and important changes in perspective. The "Culture" general outcome statement is organized into four subsections; Self-Identity, Specific-Language/Culture, Building Community, and Global Citizenship. The Self-Identity outcomes focus on the student's positive self-identity as an individual and the valuing of bilingualism and multiculturalism for lifelong learning. The Specific Language/Culture outcomes focus on:

- students developing a knowledge of the traditional/historical and contemporary nature of the specific ethnocultural group

- how these forces have shaped its development

- exploring the impact of diversity within the group, both at the Canadian and international level

- the significance of diversity on contemporary society.[33]

The Building Community outcomes reflect an attention to developing social responsibility and intercultural skills that recognize difference and commonalities among all peoples. The Global Citizenship outcomes relate to responsible global decision-making and conflict resolution, as well as the application of bilingual, intercultural, and multicultural knowledge and skills for interpersonal communication and for career purposes and participation in the "global workplace."

These outcome statements not only demonstrate, as argued earlier, the impact of globalism and the emerging global economy, but reflect an attempt to integrate much more forcibly a strong multicultural approach to second-language and bilingual education.[34] The idea of a strong global ethnic identity and the concept of global citizenship are often a feature of a multicultural perspective. These ideas are reflected in the writings of such authors as James Banks, who sees "globalism and global competency" as an advanced stage of ethnic identity,[35] and James Lynch, who argues for a new paradigm for citizenship that is multicultural and global in nature.[36] Socially-responsible action and decision-making that is multicultural and global in nature resonates in the anti-racism perspective of George J. Sefa Dei[37] and the "social reconstructionist" approach of Christine E. Sleeter and Carl A. Grant.[38] All argue that an understanding of issues of diversity and power at the local level must be understood within a broad political and economic perspective.

However, it must be said that "globalization," that is, the rapid integration of economies and the impact of multinationals on local policy and social and political structures, is often seen in the anti-racism and multicultural education literature as a barrier to achieving equity and a fairer redistribution of power. Dei points out that "[c]urrent national and global economic restructuring has serious implications for Canadian schooling, particularly for racial minority women and economically disadvantaged youths."[39] Nevertheless, the ideal of youth who act locally but think globally is a goal shared by many equity-seeking and progressive groups.

Multicultural education policies have also put an emphasis on making all curricula more inclusive and multicultural in perspective. For example, both Manitoba and Saskatchewan have multicultural education policies that have led to a commitment to make multicultural education an integral part of all curricula.[40]

The attention to the diversity within the specific culture/language group and making sense of the group's contemporary social and political condition demonstrates an attempt to achieve a meaningful and less stereotypical approach to exploring culture. Many traditional multicultural instructional approaches overly emphasized traditional or exotic cultural practices and paid insufficient attention to important aspects of contemporary culture and the social condition of the group in a Canadian context.

The concept of "global citizenship" plays an even greater role in the second and most recent WCP international languages curriculum document. In the December 1999 draft of "The Common Curriculum Framework for International Languages, Kindergarten to Grade 12," international language learning is conceptualized as being composed of four interrelated components which are the basis for the four "general outcome statements" that form the curriculum framework — Applications, Language Competence, Strategies, and Global Citizenship.[41] The general outcome statement and cluster headings for Global Citizenship, as presented in the framework, are:

> Students will acquire the knowledge, skills, and attitudes to be effective global citizens:
>
> • historical and contemporary elements of the culture
> • affirming diversity
> • personal and career opportunities.[42]

Global citizenship in this framework deals with the development of intercultural competence needed for students to become effective global citizens. "The concept of global citizenship encompasses citizenship at all levels, from the local school and community to Canada and the world."[43]

We can see that many of the influences in this document were present in the bilingual framework document. Again, balancing the historical and contemporary knowledge of the specific cultural/linguistic group and exploring the diversity within the specific culture are key elements. There is a strong "multicultural" focus in affirming diversity as students are encouraged to become aware of and value their own cultures and languages, as well as to value cultural and linguistic diversity. Finally, there is a strong emphasis on exploring the "applications of language and knowledge of culture learning in the global workplace and marketplace."[44]

Perhaps the most significant difference between the two documents is that the second framework does not seem to directly include an exploration of the idea of responsible decision-making and action that is reflected in the bilingual framework. In part, this may be due to the fact that "basic" international language programs are only one of the subjects that students study, and they are allocated a relatively small portion of instructional time. Therefore, there is a more limited expectation of what students may reasonably explore within the international languages classroom.

Global Citizenship: A Multicultural Perspective

The two WCP documents seem to be influenced by an emerging trend to link or merge multicultural education and citizenship education. To some degree this should not be surprising as multicultural education and anti-racism education approaches have often included a strong emphasis on social action. Students are encouraged to develop the skills and predisposition to make personal choices and take actions which demonstrate a commitment to equity and achieving systemic change, a goal that is reflected in the work of Banks, Sleeter and Grant, and Dei. Second, the exploration of diversity implies some discussion of the social and political dimensions of how diversity is reflected in specific nations and in the international context.

What is significant and attests to the impact of globalism and globalization is the increased emphasis on the idea of global citizenship as a key aspect and focus of multicultural education, which is linked to other "progressive" approaches such as environmental education. For example, the Association for Supervision and Curriculum Development (ASCD) published *Global Understandings: A Framework for Teaching and Learning* that clearly demonstrates how the concepts of multicultural education and citizenship are merging.[45] *Global Understandings* incorporates a social action approach that encourages responsible decision-making and action: "To become truly global citizens, participants in global education must develop skills that put these thoughts to action. Students must learn, care about, choose, and act on the messages to ensure that desirable outcomes are achieved."[46] The framework then sets out a series of outcomes that focus on learning, caring, choosing, and acting with respect to the key concepts of students as human beings; their home is planet earth, they are citizens of a multicultural society, and they live in an interrelated world. This resource is intended to serve as a model for the development of multidisciplinary units that integrate these "global understandings" into all curricula.

Educators are not the only ones making connections between multiculturalism and the ideas of responsible citizenship, We see these influences in the federal government's redesigned multiculturalism program.[47] The "new" approach, which is built on the three pillars of respect, equality, and diversity, states that identity, civic participation, and social justice are fundamental goals.

Conclusion

The development of the two WCP curriculum frameworks for international languages with their focus on "global citizenship" and cultural diversity reveals both the impacts of globalization, globalism, and multiculturalism on curriculum development and education in Canada. However, it also points to the tension that exists in society and is reflected in the education system as to how to make sense of the emerging world order. However, there are fears that the emerging global economy and political systems dominated by transnational corporations and the drive to ever-increasing profits will have a negative impact on social conditions around the world.

At the same time, globalism and global education are seen as being progressive. Both WCP documents seem to acknowledge an emerging concern with developing an informed and socially responsible citizenry that is able to understand and act on important social and international issues and that recognizes and values diversity at the local, national, and global level.

Thus, there appear to be two competing and contradictory objectives that have been melded together, indicating a poor conceptual base or unresolved conflict. Alternatively, this may be a very "Canadian" attempt to balance both the positive and negative aspects of globalism and the emerging global economy and society.

NOTES

1. What to call languages other than English in Canada has been a matter of some debate and flux since "foreign" languages became popular in Canadian high schools following the Second World War. The term "classical languages" was used to denote Latin and Greek and, to a large extent, remains in vogue today. However, the terms used to denote other languages have been the focus of much political and semantic debate and, to some degree, fashion. French was commonly offered as a "foreign" language in English Canada in the 1950s, along with Spanish and German. In the 1960s, in concert with the growth of Quebec nationalism and concern about the state of French in Quebec, coupled with the introduction of an array of contemporary European languages, the term "modern languages" became broadly accepted. With the emergence of bilingual education in the 1970s and 1980s in North America and the efforts of various ethnic groups in Canada to have their languages taught in public schools, the term "heritage languages" ("langues d'origine" in Quebec) became increasingly popular throughout Canada and, to a lesser extent, the United States. As the word "heritage" implies something passed down from one's predecessors or that results from one's natural situation or birth, this term was deemed to be more appropriate in referring to community languages spoken by various ethnocultural groups in Canada. The term "second languages" is sometimes used in an international context or as a more inclusive term as it simply denotes a language that is not the student's home or first language. By the late 1990s, with an increased awareness of the emerging global economy and the importance of multilingual communication, "international" languages began to be the term of choice in Canada and, to some degree, in the United States. Some American states have opted for the term "world languages." The issue of

terminology is made more complex since these terms are often used interchangeably, and the adoption of terminology has not been linear or consistent.

2. The use of the term "bilingual" in Canada has also been somewhat problematic. The term is usually applied when two languages are used for instructional purposes for a substantial part of the school day (ideally each language is allocated approximately fifty percent of the instructional time). The intent is to achieve balanced bilingual speakers.

   Following the federal government's Official Languages Act of 1969 and the introduction of the policy of "bilingualism," there emerged a movement, partially stimulated by federal financial incentives, by provincial policies, and as a result of court challenges, to provide greater opportunities for learning French outside Quebec. Bilingual, publicly funded French-English programming was introduced in Manitoba in 1969, and similar developments took place in other provinces. By 1971, changes in programming and policy resulted in the current "French Immersion" model. In this model, the majority of instructional time is allocated to French. While the aim is still to achieve balanced bilingual speakers, students are "immersed" in French in kindergarten to Grade 4. *Anglais* (English) is a compulsory subject from grade five onwards. *Français* programs emerged as the Franco-Manitoban community asserted its historic and "minority" official language rights as guaranteed in the 1982 Canadian Charter of Rights and Freedoms and in other legislation. The *Français* programs are similar to French Immersion but are intended to serve Manitobans for whom French is the first or home language. With the exception of a few schools that have increased time allocated to English, the students receive the majority of their instruction in French with *Anglais* being a mandatory subject. In a sense these two models are "bilingual" in their goals but not in their instructional methods. Other provinces and territories have developed similar models of French programs. The terms used to refer to various French program models differ, especially for French as a first language model.

   The introduction of "bilingual heritage" language programming in Manitoba in 1979, following the introduction of similar programs in Alberta and Saskatchewan, further complicated matters. (These three provinces are still unique in Canada in having legislation that allows for instruction in languages other than English or French in a bilingual model and in providing support for curriculum development and implementation.) The legislation that allows for these programs provides that the "heritage" language be used for instructional purposes for no more than fifty per cent of the school day.

Thus, the term "bilingual programs" in Western Canada is usually applied to heritage language programming and not French Immersion or *Français* programming models. However, this is not necessarily the case in other provinces where the only bilingual programs are French-English models.

3. Common in two senses. First, it is common to the three participating provinces as each participated with the intent to implement the resulting curriculum frameworks. Second, the frameworks are intended to be a general, non-language specific or common curriculum framework that will be the basis for developing language specific curricula.

4. The Western Canadian Protocol for Collaboration in Basic Education (WCP) memorandum of agreement does not use the term "international languages." However, the adoption of this term for the two curriculum frameworks that emerged from the WCP initiative is testimony to the shift in terminology and provincial policies that has occurred since the WCP agreement was signed in 1993.

5. This, too, reflects the very political and contextual nature of terminology. English and French are "international" languages in the international arena. However, as official languages of Canada and of instruction in the Canadian educational systems, they do not fall under the category of international languages.

6. J.S. Woodsworth, *Strangers within Our Gates: Or Coming Canadians* (1909; reprint, Toronto: University of Toronto Press, 1972).

7. Victoria M. Esses and R.C. Gardner, "Multiculturalism in Canada: Context and Current Status," in *Ethnic Relations in a Multicultural Society*, ed. Victoria M. Esses and R.C. Gardner, special issue of *Canadian Journal of Behavioural Science* 28, no. 3 (1996) [journal online]; available from <http://www.cpa.ca/cjbsnew/1996/vol28-3.html>; Internet; accessed 26 October 2000.

8. National Crime Prevention Council of Canada, "The Multiculturalism Policy," *People from Ethnocultural and Visible Minority Communities* no. 135 [database online], available from <http://www.crime-prevention.org/ncpc/council/database/invent/minor_e.htm>;Internet: accessed 29 October 2000.

The support for heritage languages was a somewhat problematic aspect of the federal government's programs as some deemed it to conflict with the goals of bilingualism that the federal government espoused. By the early 1990s, support for heritage language schools and programming was eliminated. Some support continued for heritage languages under the Heritage Languages and Cultures Program, under the auspices of the Department of Canadian Heritage, Multiculturalism and Citizenship Canada. More recently this has disappeared as a focus of the Department's programs.

9. Esses and Gardner, "Multiculturalism in Canada."

10. Ibid.

11. Government of Saskatchewan, "New Multiculturalism Act One Step Closer to Reality" (Regina: Government of Saskatchewan, Media Services, News Release Archives no. 164, Municipal Government 97-164, 10 April 1997) [news release online]; available from <http://www.gov.sk.ca/newsrel/1997/04/10-164.html>; Internet; accessed 29 October 2000.

12. Government of Alberta, *Human Rights, Citizenship and Multiculturalism Act*, ch. H-11.7 (Edmonton: Queen's Printer Bookstore, Legislative Assembly of Alberta, Statutes and Regulations, 1996) [legislation online]; available from <http://www.gov.ab.ca/qp/ascii/acts/H11P7.TXT; Internet; accessed 29 October 2000.

13. British Columbia Heritage Language Association (BCHLA), "Multiculturalism BC" (Government Departments and Branches, Teachers Centre) [resource online]; available from <http://www.bchla.org/teachers/gbd3.html>; Internet; accessed 29 October 2000.

14. Saskatchewan Education, Training and Employment, *Multicultural Education and Heritage Language Education Policies* (Regina: Saskatchewan Education, Training, and Employment, 1994).

15. Council of Ministers of Education, Canada, "School Achievement Indicators Program (SAIP)" [online]; available from <http://www.cmec.ca/saip/indexe.stm>; Internet; accessed 29 October 2000.

16. Western Canadian Protocol for Collaboration in Basic Education, "Common Curriculum Framework" [online]; available from <http://www.wcp.ca>; Internet; accessed 29 October 2000.

17. Ibid.

18. Further citations will read WCP, *Bilingual Framework* and WCP, "International Languages Framework."

19. Alberta Learning, [online]; available from <http://ednet.edc.gov.ab.ca>; Internet; accessed 29 October 2000.

20. Government of Alberta, *A Framework for Alberta's International Strategies* (Edmonton: Government of Alberta, February 2000).

21. Japanese was introduced in 1992 as part of the Asia-Pacific studies programming at Dakota and Vincent Massey Collegiates in Winnipeg.

22. Alberta Education, *Japanese Language and Culture 10-20-30 (Senior High)* (Edmonton: Alberta Education, 1995).

23. Alberta, "Japanese Language (Senior High)," 2-3.

24. Alberta Learning, *Enhancing Language Learning: A Survey of Second Language Program Enrolments* (Edmonton: Alberta Learning, 2000).

25. Ibid., 13.

26. Manitoba signed its accord in 1997.

27. Lucinda E. Branaman, "Foreign Languages and Job Opportunities in K-12 Foreign Language Education," *ERIC Review* 6, no. 1 (1998), 67-69.

28. WCP, *Bilingual Framework*, 7.

29. Manitoba Education, *English-Ukrainian Bilingual Program: Grades 1-6* (Winnipeg: Manitoba Education, 1988), 2.

30. Ibid., 3.

31. Manitoba Education and Training, *English-German Bilingual Program: Overview K-6* (Winnipeg: Manitoba Education and Training, 1990), 1.

32. Ibid.

33. WCP, "Bilingual Framework."

34. The terms globalism and globalization have a variety of meanings in the literature and sometimes are used interchangeably. Indeed, after a panel on globalization at the World Sociology Congress held in Montreal in 1998, a web site <http://www2.hawaii.edu/'fredr/glocon.htm> was created by Fred. W. Riggs to explore the variety of meanings that are attributed to the term. For the purposes of this paper, "globalization" will be used to refer to economic globalization resulting in integrated economies that are

dominated by multinational or transnational corporations. As an ideological position, it reflects the view that unfettered expansion of the global marketplace is a good thing. Globalism, for the purposes of this paper, denotes an awareness of the wider world, the recognition of global interdependence at various levels, and includes political, environmental, economic, cultural, and communicative dimensions. It also implies the need to find common solutions to major challenges facing all nations and peoples. As an ideological position it implies a sense of being a world citizen and a concern with making the world a more equitable and sustainable place.

35. See, e.g., James A. Banks, *Teaching Strategies for Ethnic Studies*, 6th ed. (Boston.: Allyn and Bacon Publishers, 1997), chap. 3.

36. James Lynch, *Education for Citizenship in a Multicultural Society* (London: Cassell Publishers, 1992).

37. George J. Sefa Dei, *Anti-Racism Education: Theory and Practice* (Halifax: Fernwood Publishers, 1996).

38. Christine E. Sleeter and Carl A. Grant, *Making Choices for Multicultural Education: Five Approaches to Race, Class, and Gender*, 3d ed. (Upper Saddle River, NJ: Merrill Publishing, 1999).

39. Dei, *Anti-Racism Education*, 35.

40. Manitoba's commitment in this respect was reaffirmed in Manitoba Education and Training, *Renewing Education: New Directions; A Foundation for Excellence* (Winnipeg: Manitoba Education and Training, 1995). The document specifies the "integratables" that are to be the lenses through which all curricula are to be developed. Anti-racism and human diversity are two significant elements that are to be integrated into all curricula.

41. WCP, "International Languages."

42. Ibid., 6.

43. Ibid., 60.

44. Ibid., 73.

45. Charlotte Anderson, Susan K. Nicklas, and Agnes R. Crawford, *Global Understandings: A Framework for Teaching and Learning* (Alexandria, VA: Association for Supervision and Curriculum Development, 1994).

46. Ibid., 6.

47. Canadian Heritage, Multiculturalism Program, *Multiculturalism: Program Guidelines* (Ottawa: Canadian Heritage, 1997).

11 The *TimeLinks Image Archive*: A Case Study in Using Photographic Images in Teaching about Ethnic Relations

HELEN BOCHONKO AND CHRIS DOOLEY

ABSTRACT/RÉSUMÉ

The *TimeLinks Image Archive* (http://timelinks.merlin.mb.ca) contains more than two thousand visual representations of life in Manitoba in the second decade of the twentieth century. It provides an unparalleled opportunity for students to engage this decade through the interpretation of visual documents. These documents provide a lens through which students can explore several themes relating to life in the early decades of the century, including the emergence on the prairies of a patchwork of culturally and linguistically different communities that were forced to interact with and accommodate one another. One of the perils inherent in the *Image Archive* also presents one of the greatest opportunities for historical document interpretation. The vast majority of the images are representations created by and for members of the Anglo-Canadian majority culture, a culture which was wrestling in the early decades of the century with the loss of its numerical dominance and cultural hegemony. By decoding the cultural messages in the images, students can gain insights not only into the details of everyday life, but also the values, perceptions, and constructs that governed the interactions, and sometimes conflict, between this majority culture and non-Anglo communities.

L'Archive d'images TimeLinks (http://timelinks.merlin.mb.ca) contient plus de deux milles représentations visuelles de la vie au Manitoba pendant la deuxième décennie du vingtième siècle. Il fournit une occasion sans précédent pour les étudiants de s'embarquer dans cette décennie au moyen de l'interprétation de documents visuels. Ces documents fournissent une lentille par laquelle les étudiants peuvent explorer plusieurs thèmes qui portent sur la vie des premières décennies du siècle, y compris l'apparition sur les plaines d'une mosaïque de communautés culturellement et linguistiquement différentes qui ont été obligées d'interagir et de s'accommoder les unes aux autres. Un des dangers inhérents dans *l'Archive d'images* présente aussi une des grandes occasions pour l'interprétation des documents historiques. La grande majorité des images sont des représentations créés par les membres de la culture majoritaire anglo-canadienne et destinées pour eux. C'était une culture qui se débattait dans les premières décennies du siècle avec la perte de sa prédominance numérique et son hégémonie culturelle. En décodant les messages culturels trouvés dans les images, les étudiants peuvent pénétrer non seulement dans les détails de la vie quotidienne, mais aussi dans des valeurs, perceptions et constructions qui gouvernaient les interactions, et quelquefois les conflits, entre cette culture majoritaire et les communautés non-anglophones.

Introduction

The *TimeLinks Image Archive* is part of a larger World Wide Web site called *TimeLinks* (http://timelinks.merlin.mb.ca). This site, a co-creation of River East School Division and the University of Manitoba, is an Internet-based project in prairie history designed primarily to fit the Manitoba senior 1 and 3 (grades IX and XI) curricula for history and Canadian studies. Its primary goal is to enhance students' interest in a period of social history that is not well covered by existing classroom resources by exposing them to the rhythms of everyday life in Manitoba communities in the second decade of the twentieth century, thus encouraging them to explore the intersection of political, economic, and social changes in the lives of ordinary Manitobans.

TimeLinks began as a project of River East Collegiate in early 1996. In its original conception, it was loosely modelled on *Village Prologue,* an Internet site developed in Quebec which offers visitors the opportunity to visit an imaginary village in Lower Canada in 1853. Through a variety of resources including a village "newspaper," student "visitors" to *Village Prologue* become aware of the rhythms of life in a rural agricultural community. They are then given the opportunity to initiate an e-mail correspondence with an array of village residents — fictional townspeople of all trades and occupations, played by teachers, historians, writers, and archivists — who go on-line in the roles of particular characters.[1]

When the *TimeLinks* project was first conceived, it was limited to a variant on electronic penpals for classrooms built on the *Village Prologue* model. Students were to correspond via electronic mail with characters "animated" by their teachers and community volunteers. Though this capacity continues, the site has grown with the inclusion of several large annexes created in a partnership with the History Department and the Faculty of Education Computer Program at the University of Manitoba.

These annexes, which have evolved to become central elements of the site, include a large archive of visual and textual materials.

The development of *TimeLinks* is viewed as significant on several counts. Most importantly, it represents a major step in establishing a Manitoba historical and cultural presence on the Internet in the social sciences and humanities. Considerable attention and resources have been channelled into providing Manitoba schools with access to the Internet without comparable effort being expended to ensure that what students are accessing is culturally relevant and of high quality. *TimeLinks*, as a fully referenced publication, seeks to set a standard for educational materials with a regional cultural content. Similarly, *TimeLinks* recognizes the potential of the Internet for the provision of supplementary teaching resources to social science and humanities classrooms. As such, it plays to the strengths of the Internet medium. The use of computers in classrooms has hitherto largely been in sciences and mathematics classrooms, and the same can be said of the Internet. The strength of the Internet, however, is in the delivery of text and static images, and it may be argued that it is underutilized in the social sciences, humanities, and arts, where text and static images are the most basic tools. The *TimeLinks* project team, therefore, premised its activities on the belief that using the Internet in classrooms should also include reading, writing, and the interpretation of historically and culturally significant documents from our own communities and cultures.

The *TimeLinks Image Archive* is also important because it is among the first North American Internet sites to make significant use of primary visual sources and archival photographs. Thanks in large part to the generosity of the Provincial Archives of Manitoba, the *TimeLinks* project has placed over 2,000 images on the Internet where they are readily accessible to students and the Manitoba public. While these images are primarily photographic, a small number of editorial cartoons, advertisements, pamphlets, and textual documents have also been included. The project in this way ensures that a growing proportion of the rich visual heritage held at the Provincial Archives is made available to a wider public than would have been possible using traditional publishing methods.

The *TimeLinks* site was created to satisfy several curricular goals. As an instrument for the communication of social history, the interactive portion of the site helps students to contemplate historical problems and events from the point of view of the participants. By allowing them to formulate questions on everything from "great events" to aspects of day-to-day life too mundane to be considered in many traditional classrooms, it creates avenues for students to explore the intersection of political, economic, and social changes with the lives of ordinary people. The inclusion of primary documents, chiefly photographic images, further enriches the students' understanding of the period and their ability to understand history as an aggregation of individual experiences.

TimeLinks occupies a place within several prescribed curricula taught in Manitoba. Although the primary linkage is with the senior 3 (grade XI) history curriculum, portions of the site will be of use in classrooms working on the senior 1 (grade IX) Canadian studies curriculum, in the grade VI history curriculum, and for undergraduate university teaching. The content of the site is particularly germane to those units dealing with immigration and related themes ("The Peopling of Canada"), the emergence of a mature agricultural economy and the advent of industrial capitalism in western Canada ("Social and Economic Change in Modern Canada since 1850"), and with the elective units on local and regional history that comprise about thirty percent of the contact time in most classrooms.[2] The authors believe that, in addition to the advantages offered by the medium, *TimeLinks* provides a fitting compliment to the *Our Canada* textbook used in most Manitoba schools.[3]

While its primary use is in the teaching of history, *TimeLinks* also has a place in the cross-curricular exploration of themes related to multiculturalism and citizenship. Situated as it is in the first decades of the twentieth century, *TimeLinks* provides opportunities to explore Manitoba at the time of its first significant infusion of non-Anglo immigrants. While not all images fit these themes, portions of the site offer opportunities to explore the emergence on the prairies of a patchwork of culturally and linguistically different communities that were forced to interact with and accommodate one another. Themes such as assimilation, nativism, the perception of new immigrants by the majority culture, and the struggles and compromises of new immigrants, both to fit in and to retain aspects of their own national or ethnic culture, are all apparent in varying degrees in the photographs in the *Image Archive*. Moreover, aspects of the day-to-day lives of recent immigrants in the pre-war period, aspects which might have been assimilated into the cultural memory of later generations, can often be discerned from an analysis of the photographs.

Finally, the *Image Archive* tells the story not only of the immigrant experience, but of the reaction of an earlier generation of immigrants to a later one. The vast majority of the images are representations created by and for members of the Anglo-Canadian majority culture, which was wrestling in the early decades of the century with the potential loss of its numerical dominance and cultural hegemony. By decoding the cultural messages in these images, students can potentially gain insights into the values, perceptions, and constructs that governed the interactions, and sometimes conflict, between this majority culture and non-Anglo communities.

Content and Context — Manitoba's Third Wave of Immigrants

Gerald Friesen has observed that Canada's Prairie West has experienced five significant infusions of immigrants in the post-contact era.[4] This periodization provides a useful tool for understanding and interpreting the images in *TimeLinks*. The first and longest of these periods can be said to stretch from the point of first contact between Aboriginal and European people up to the period immediately before Confederation. This was a period of English and French settlement along fur trade routes, and it was intimately connected with the emergence of two new cultural groups who were briefly the dominant culture in the region: the English-speaking mixed blood and French-speaking Métis.

The second phase of immigration, lasting from around the time of Confederation to the late 1890s, saw the Aboriginal and Métis cultures eclipsed by a wave of British Canadian immigrants. This period saw the rapid transformation of the Prairie West from a region whose economy was based on subsistence agriculture and the fur trade to one whose economy was based on export-oriented agriculture. These new immigrants created communities which mirrored those they came from in Ontario. Also in this period, hints of the later multi-ethnic society that emerged on the Prairies were in evidence. Pockets of immigrants arrived from Hungary, Iceland, Scandinavia, and from Mennonite and Jewish communities of Eastern Europe, while others, primarily Québécois, arrived from Quebec and New England.

The third phase, and that which most closely corresponds to the period treated in *TimeLinks*, stretches from the late 1890s to the beginning of the First World War.[5] This was a period of unprecedented population growth in Manitoba, and it was concurrent with, and occasioned by, the transformation of the West into a modern capitalist society. Immigrants in this period comprised, in almost equal proportions, British, Canadian, American, and Continental European immigrants, with a smattering of others from Asia and the Indian subcontinent. It was also a period of shifting immigration policies, where successive federal governments attempted both to regulate and to promote immigration so as to ensure that the Dominion's labour needs were met only by "desirable" classes of immigrants.

This immigration pattern was broken by the First World War and immigration decreased in the years immediately following as Canada struggled through an economic slump and was slow to reopen its borders. The fourth phase, which began in the early-1920s, was a brief one, curtailed by the reversal of economic fortunes that led to the Depression after 1929. Immigration patterns in this period mirrored those of the first decade of the century, and they had the consequence of firmly entrenching Manitoba's status as a multi-ethnic community.

The fifth and most recent phase of immigration stretches from the end of the Second World War to the present. This is a period of continued immigration from European communities, especially in the postwar period, but it is also the period in which the first major immigrations from Asia, the Indian subcontinent, Africa, the Caribbean, and the Middle East occurred. This immigration was occasioned in part by decolonization in the 1960s and 1970s and the removal of the legislated and non-legislated barriers to non-white immigration that had been established in earlier periods.

The Choice of a Decade — The Emergence of a Plural Society

It was decided early in the conceptualization of *TimeLinks* that a narrow temporal focus was necessary, both from the point of view of matching ambitions to resources and of providing some thematic consistency in the materials presented. *TimeLinks* is concerned with the decade from 1910 to 1920, although the authors have taken some liberties with this periodization. The *Image Archive,* for example, contains some images from as early as the 1890s and as late as 1930 when they are in support of important themes.[6] The election to situate *TimeLinks* in this decade was quite deliberate. The authors felt that this choice offered several advantages. First, the second decade of the twentieth century was one which contained a number of "marquee" events – the outbreak of war in 1914; the extension of female suffrage in 1916; the Winnipeg General Strike in 1919 – and this presented opportunities for student analysis and research which fitted well with existing curricula. Moreover, this offered a certain comfort level for teachers and facilitated the integration of *TimeLinks* into developed lesson plans. Second, and more important, its situation at the end of the first major wave of non-Anglo immigration created the context for exploring the emergence of what has come to be regarded as Western Canada's multicultural society.

It can be argued that the second decade of the twentieth century was the one in which Manitoba became a truly plural society for the first time. Over eighty percent British at the time of the 1901 census, only sixty-five percent of Manitobans claimed British ancestry in the 1911 census. By that year Manitoba had the highest proportion of foreign-born residents of any province in Canada and the highest percentage of German, Jewish, and Slavic immigrants.[7] While many of these new Canadians settled in relatively homogenous agricultural communities, creating a patchwork of ethnic enclaves across the province, many more found their way to the city of Winnipeg. There, they became the backbone of a new labour force of largely unskilled and semi-skilled workers who, quite literally, built the new prairie metropolis. At the same time, they built durable institutions that would shape and preserve their distinct cultures. Public and private life was dominated by struggles of class, culture, and religion, with the Anglo-Protestant majority responding consistently as a culture under siege, while the minority cultures struggled for acceptance and resisted total assimilation. In situating *TimeLinks* in the second decade of the century, the intention was not only to capture the emergence of this plural society, but also to encompass some of the most visible manifestations of the nativism that it spawned, like the closure of French, German, and Ukrainian public schools in 1916 and the treatment of Austro-Hungarian immigrants under the Alien Enemy Laws during the War. Such discussions are important not only in the context of Canadian history, but in discussions of an evolving Canadian citizenship and the consolidation of corporate identities within immigrant communities. There are also opportunities for comparisons to the experiences of later waves of immigrants.

The *TimeLinks* Images — Diversity versus Representativity

While the choice of decade was made in a very conscious way, the selection of the images themselves followed a less intentional path. It may be argued, however, that the result presents special opportunities for image analysis in the classroom. Selection for the *TimeLinks Image Archive* began in early 1996 when permission was secured from the Provincial Archives of Manitoba to scan images under the control of the Still Images Section for inclusion in an archive that would be published as an annex to the *TimeLinks* Corresponding Character Site.[8] Over the course of the year that followed, the project gained momentum and the *Image Archive* became a discrete publication in its own right.

The origins of the *Image Archive* have specific implications for the way in which the site was later constructed, specifically for the collection method which was based on communities rather then themes. The communities themselves were selected at the early stages neither for their representativity nor their uniqueness, but for the simple reason that a "corresponding character" was to be placed there.[9] As the project matured and as the immediate needs of the corresponding character capacity were satisfied, the project team was afforded the luxury of stepping back and attempting to construct a more considered approach to image selection. However, community, rather than theme, was retained as the principal guide to the selection process. Attempts were made to select communities that were representative of Manitoba's geographic, cultural, and economic diversity. Within this framework, communities were also selected on the basis of their dominant ethno-cultural identity. Turn of the century settlement patterns generally conformed to a patchwork model where most small communities remained essentially ethnically homogenous. This held true not only for the rural areas, but for Winnipeg. While it was not settled as a city of ethnic enclaves *per se,* Winnipeg was a city whose deep divide along social and economic lines had strong geographic manifestations.[10]

It should be noted that while the selection of communities is representative in the sense that most of the larger ethno-cultural identities are depicted, it is by no means representative of the relative distribution of these populations. Manitoba in 1910 was a largely Anglo-Ontarian province with seven in every ten residents claiming British ancestry. The largest segments of the population were not native-born Manitobans, but immigrants either from Great Britain or from English-speaking Central Canada.[11] In the selection of communities, therefore, the dominant Anglo-Canadian majority is under-represented in order to show the emerging pluralism of Manitoba society. In short, the diversity of communities is privileged over the proportional representation of each of these communities in the prairie mosaic.

Challenges in Portraying Ethnic Diversity

Even an approach which privileges diversity, however, often fails to do justice to many minority communities. Some communities, like the Icelanders of the Gimli region, for example, extensively documented their activities, and there are numerous images of this community in private sector collections at the Provincial Archives of Manitoba. The reality, however, is that the vast majority of the images in the collections at the Provincial Archives are the creations of a few photographers who were themselves exponents of the majority culture. While some inexpensive photographic devices, like Kodak cardboard cameras, were available in the period concerned, few "snapshot" images from family collections have been deposited in the Provincial Archives.[12] Accordingly, the vast majority of images available for selection for the *TimeLinks Image Archive* were taken by commercial photographers. The images are, therefore, largely either commissioned works or images that the photographer perceived to have some inherent commercial value. Given that the photographers themselves were almost exclusively of the majority culture, and given that the largest proportion of their client base would have been also, it might be assumed that the portrayals would contain a number of intentional elements which would serve the needs, ambitions, and expectations of the Anglo-Canadian majority.

TimeLinks in the Classroom

It is not the intention of this article to present a methodology for the use of the *TimeLinks Images* in the classroom. It is enough to say that a broad pedagogical literature exists on this subject which cannot be adequately treated in such a brief space. Suffice it to say that the authors of the *TimeLinks Image Archive* think that the images can be used in a variety of ways. These include in-depth examinations of a single image, direct comparisons of images, or analyses of series of images.[13] More important for the present study is an examination of some of the themes related to the emergence of a plural society. What follows is a schema for the exploration of some of these themes.

Photographs as Historical Documents

Essential to the proper use of the collection in the classroom is the understanding that the images contained within it represent neither a random nor an exhaustive rendering of life as it was in early twentieth-century Manitoba. Germane to understanding the images is an understanding that photographs are not passive records; they are the product of human enterprise. They were crafted at a specific time, with intent, and have survived to the present because the creator or some other individual has ascribed value to them. They are, therefore, documents and should be perceived as no more "accurate" renderings of the past than textual records, of which students are taught to be suspicious. For present purposes, three elements of an image should be considered in the course of an image analysis. They might be termed the intentional elements of the image, the unintentional elements, and the cultural themes.

Intentional Elements

Photographs are made, not taken. This is an adage often cited by modern writers about the art of photography, which was even truer in the time when cameras were bulky and expensive and before the advent of high speed films. Early cameras were far more intrusive upon the scene or subject they were in the process of recording than current cameras. Moreover, in a more formal era, protocol was often observed in the presence of the camera that is less strictly observed in the present, viz. clothing, posture, projected demeanor, etc. The photographic images in the *TimeLinks* site cannot, therefore, be properly appreciated without the acknowledgement that nearly all were in some measure contrived. In some, the subject controlled the situation; in others, the photographer. In either instance, understanding of an image can be advanced by exploring some variant on the question, "For what purpose was this photograph created?"

In many instances an acceptable answer to this question is readily formulated. If the subject is material, the purpose is often substantially documentary. Even in this instance, however, the motivation behind the creation of the image merits some exploration. Images of structures, for example, can convey ideas of progress and development, and images of machines, vehicles, artifacts, and other chattels can reinforce and affirm the importance of private property. If the subject is human, the purpose can be similarly discerned. There is no greater affirmation of the importance of the individual than the recording of the portrait, and most portraits should be taken to represent the contract between photographer and client to present "the best possible face"— a representation which communicates a specific image of the individual which might or might not accord with external realities.

Often the most evocative images show the relationship between people and artifacts. An excellent example is the image entitled "Louis Matias, On Leave," which portrays a young man standing in his soldier's uniform before the family tractor.[14] The coincidence of the three elements cannot be seen to be just photographic convention, but must be seen also to reflect values and functions embraced by the Matias family. Similar messages are communicated by the two portraits taken in Ste. Claude by an unknown photographer in 1912. The first, of Jean Maris Lebrun in his hunting furs with his collection of guns, and the second, of Henri Billard astride his motorcycle, communicate the relationship of the subject to the artifact and imply an identity linked to these artifacts.

Even portraits without artifacts or other contextualizing elements can be very telling. The image of the Narovlansky family, posed for a formal family portrait, communicates a message of substance and respectability.[15] To have one's portrait taken is often to enlist the photographer to help to create a durable image of success, prosperity, or importance that can be communicated over distance and time. For immigrant families, this was often an important function, and photographers were enlisted to provide "material proof" to relatives and friends overseas that the recently departed new immigrants were adapting to their new environs. Reassurance and recruitment could, therefore, both be functions of such a photograph. While affirmative in many respects, such photographs can also be defensive. Portraiture was a hallmark of respectability, and by subjecting themselves to the gaze of the camera, families could affirm their respectability and their belonging in their new community — to show themselves to be as good as anyone else.

In the images cited above, the subject, or rather the implied contractual relationship between subject and photographer, is probably primary in determining the content of the photograph. In other instances, the photographer himself (there is not a single recorded instance of a female photographer in *TimeLinks*, which in itself might offer avenues for exploration) exercises a higher level of control. There is a series, for example, of images of the "New Jerusalem" area of Winnipeg's North End taken by Lewis Foote on commission for J.S. Woodsworth for use as illustrations in one of his books. While these images, some of which are taken in the streets, are no doubt accurate representations of the places that they portrayed, it may be presumed that the locations themselves were carefully selected, not necessarily for their representativity, but rather because they satisfied the themes that the author, an advocate of aggressive assimilation and a vocal critic of the emergence of ethnic ghettos, was trying to communicate.[16] Such images must be seen to fit within a category of "photography as social work," which was pioneered by figures such as Lewis Hine in the United States in the early century.[17] Here the student might productively engage the image with questions about the representativity of such images.

Here, too, opportunities for the discussion of photographic technique are presented. Why, for example, did the photographer choose to assemble the entire family together in one room? How is it that the street children were detained for long enough to permit their portrait to be taken? What other stylistic techniques did the photographer employ to communicate or reinforce the message of his picture? Here, opportunities are present to examine the photograph as an intentional creation where the act of taking a photograph is a political decision in which the framer selects and excludes, with the purpose of communicating a suitable version of the present to a distant or future audience.[18]

Unintentional or Incidental Elements

Often the most accessible elements of a photograph, especially for students whose preference is for the concrete, are those which were incidental to the purpose for which the photograph was made. Generally, those take the form of elements of material culture evident in the image which give indications of how people lived in the period in question. Examples of the kinds of incidental elements which might be observed include architecture, costume, technology, and geography. Incidental details often provide some of the best available information about the way in which communities lived day-to-day. Such depictions are especially useful when they are of communities where the documentary record is fragmentary or unreliable, as is the case for many non-Anglo immigrant communities in the period under discussion.

In many instances there is a close relationship between the intentional and the incidental information presented by an image. Such is often the case where a photograph is intended to be largely documentary in scope, as in the picture of a structure or a machine. The intentional elements of the image often relate to the purpose for which it was taken, commonly to provide a specific record ("This is my house, of which I am proud."). The incidental information is that which goes beyond the simple affirmation of the existence of the subject, but which communicates some additional understanding of its structure, origin, or composition ("This is how my house is constructed.").

The examination and comparison of incidental features is often one of the most productive avenues of exploration for students, as it is one of the most accessible and the one which often communicates the greatest sense of how it was that people lived. Such exercises must not be undertaken uncritically or without consideration of the conventions of the medium — not all features initially identified as incidental may be truly so. In the case of costume, for example, it should be remembered that most images were carefully posed according to relatively strict conventions. In the days of large, single-frame view cameras, candid shots, while possible, were difficult to obtain because the equipment was bulky, obtrusive, and slow to set up. An extreme example of the peril of careless examination for aspects of material culture might be seen in the case of Cyril Jessop's "Girl with Eggs."[19] This image, which portrays a girl of seven or eight gathering eggs in the yard, shows her to be dressed in an elaborate white dress entirely inappropriate for the task at hand. Other of Jessop's photos, which were taken on contract to the Ministry of the Interior for use in promoting immigration to Canada in the United States, show farmyards with telephone lines running in and automobiles parked in the yard. While these elements may appear to have been incidental, it is important to recognize that they were very much intentional. The automobile and the telephone were hallmarks of prosperity and not at all common at the time that the images were created. There can be little doubt that their inclusion was intended to be noted by the target readership of the brochure in which they would appear.

Cultural Themes

This category is concerned with what the image tells us about the perceptions by the dominant culture about a non-dominant one. Although not absolute, it is not an altogether unfair generalization to suggest that the great majority of those images which have been included in the *TimeLinks Image Archive* fall into the category of images taken either by or for the Anglo-Canadian elite. This can be attributed to several factors.

The first is the cost of the technology. Although some inexpensive box cameras were available by the latter nineteenth century, photography remained, by and large, an elite medium due to the expensive technology required to take and to develop pictures. Moreover, the images which have survived to be included in the records of the Provincial Archives of Manitoba, the almost exclusive source of images in the *TimeLinks* collection, have been those from large, well documented collections, primarily those of professional or serious amateur photographers, or photographs that were commissioned by businesses, organizations, or by provincial or municipal governments or agencies, and have found their way into the Still Images Section of the Provincial Archives through Private Sector Collections or Government Records.

As has been indicated above, photographs are constructions, not simple depictions, and the history that they show is inseparable from the history that they enact. Photographs must, therefore, be seen in the context of photographers in the course of trying to make sense of their society or to impose a new order upon it. This provides both peril and opportunity for the student in approaching the analysis of the images. There is the peril of seeing the depictions in the photographs as being representative of the realities of everyday life. This peril, however, can be turned to advantage, and it is when both the subject and the photographer are considered that the possibilities for historical exploration and decoding social relationships are best realized.

With this idea in mind, one of the themes of the period, and one that might prove productive in discussions of the emergence of a multicultural society, concerns the depiction of non-Anglo communities by members of the Anglo-Canadian majority culture. As indicated above, the cultural composition of the Prairie West was fundamentally altered twice in the space of three decades. In the first instance, the arrival of a large number of British and Ontarian immigrants after 1880 established a new social order which enforced new economic, political, and cultural norms. In the second, which was characterized by large numbers of non-Anglo immigrants, the Anglo-Canadian majority culture showed a determination to continue to enforce these norms. The consequence was a majority culture which was aggressively assimilationist in its culture and institutions.[20]

Images that might be interpreted to express outright nativism, that is, portrayals of the perceived worst of immigrant society, are rare. Instead, images often seem intended to confront the challenge of "foreigners" through portrayal of institutions and expressions of assimilation. The students of Aberdeen School, for example, are said to represent twenty-one nationalities in Foote's titling of the image, but one would not conclude this by looking at their costume or apparent demeanor.[21] The uniformity of their dress and appearance might be interpreted to signify that they have been successfully "Canadianized," that they have embraced the Anglo-Canadian model of "good citizenship." By this interpretation, there is a certain smugness about this image that advertises the capacity of the culture to assimilate the "foreign element."[22] Similar messages can be taken from the images of the East Kildonan Little Mothers' League, an organization that was established as a means of instilling Anglo-Canadian models of parenting and family management in young women as a tool of assimilation.[23] Such interpretations, however, deprive the subjects of their agency. At the same time, it must be acknowledged that the immigrant children were not passive instruments on whom the assimilating culture worked. In many instances new immigrants were willing participants who made compromises and who embraced norms and outwardly visible practices, like education and costume for their children, for the purpose of gaining greater acceptance in their host communities.

While the perspective of the Anglo-Canadian majority culture is most evident in urban images like those cited above, it is similarly evident in the portrayal of rural immigrants. Industry, for example, seems a dominant theme in the W.J. Sisler Collection, where portrayals of agricultural immigrants, many of whom are Ukrainians, seem to emphasize both the costume and technology of these new immigrants and their application in productive work. In this respect, these images seem to celebrate the immigrant work ethic as if to advertise the suitability of these immigrants to be agriculturalists.[24] Similar ideals of order and industry are often evident in the portrayals of Aboriginal communities. Such images tend to fall into two broad categories. The first might be called anthropological portrayals of traditional life, portrayals which emphasise artifact and costume or which might be seen to exposit the ways in which Aboriginal life differs from that of the European audience for whom the images were made. The images of the five women with their papooses at Maria Portage probably falls into this category.[25] The second is portrayals which seem to celebrate the assimilation of Aboriginal peoples to Anglo-Canadian norms. The image of the classroom at the unnamed Aboriginal school from the William Gordon Collection, for example, portrays four rows of students at their desks, faces forward and neatly dressed in school uniform. There are many elements that this image shares with that of the children of Aberdeen School.[26]

A final course of investigation which might provide insight into the *Image Archive* concerns the photographers themselves. Although a number of images from private collections have been donated to the Provincial Archives, the vast majority are from the collections of commercial photographers. A useful case study in this respect would be that of Lewis B. Foote, whose images make up the largest single collection within the *Image Archive*. Foote was an independent photographer who worked in Winnipeg between 1902 and 1948. As one of the city's few commercial photographers, Foote worked as the chronicler of social club events, as a portrait artist, as the recorder of picnics and parades. Working for the city's boosters, he documented Winnipeg's rising skyline, but he also worked for dissenting Methodist minister and social reformer J.S. Wordsworth (himself a prominent proponent of the assimilation of the immigrant) to document life in the worst of the city's slums. Foote also worked as the primary photographer for the *Manitoba Free Press,* before it had staff photographers, and for the Winnipeg Coroner's Office.[27]

As his biographer has observed, Foote should be seen as anything but a neutral and objective recorder of the world in which he lived.

> His work documents the tremendous social change of the era — the crushing of the strike, the North End slums he took for J.S. Wordsworth's books, the interiors of the CPR shops — but these are usually commissioned works. We see the workers the way the boss would like us to, lined up in rows, often in their Sunday best; only on rare occasions do we see anyone doing any actual work. Foote is the recorder of orthodoxy and Anglo-conformity; if he can be said to have had a predominant subject, that subject would be private property. The voice we hear of so many of his pictures is that of the person writing the cheque for the print. He is, and it is most certainly he, saying: "I am a man of substance, I own this house, this is my wife, and these are my children; this is my factory, these are my workers. I can have my photograph taken. I am respectable, hard working, and God-fearing."[28]

The question that arises from this is whether Foote himself had any overarching ideology or vision, or whether his images simply reflected the wishes of his clients. In the end, the answer is only marginally relevant. His photographs, for himself and for his clients, represent the efforts of the Anglo-Canadian majority culture to order their world, to enact the vision that they had of their city and their province as the "Last Best West" and the "Gateway to the West," a community founded on the ideals of Protestantism and private property, a community which would assimilate the alien to its way of life, and in which the "way of doing things" of the majority culture was uncontested and unassailable.

The example of Lewis Foote provides but one useful lens through which the images in the *TimeLinks Image Archive* can be examined. One of the criticisms that might be levelled at conventional interpretations of the immigration boom of the early twentieth century is its somewhat anachronistic celebration of cultural and ethnic diversity. In reality, it was a period of significant tension where the Anglo-Canadian majority culture felt assailed and responded with both hostility and with aggressively assimilationist policies. While this cannot be discerned with reference to an image archive alone, the critical examination of portrayals of this diversity in the photographic record can provide some insight into the complexity, function, and self-image of Manitoba society in the early twentieth century. This is but one way in which *TimeLinks* provides a hitherto unavailable opportunity for students to engage this period. The images in the collection present students with opportunities to explore multiple themes relating to life in the early decades of the twentieth century, including costume, technology, labour, commerce, domestic and institutional life, and, of course, the emergence on the prairies of a patchwork of culturally and linguistically different communities that were forced to interact with and accommodate one another.

APPENDIX

CATEGORIES IN THE TIMELINKS IMAGE ARCHIVE

Aboriginal Communities – This section includes images of life in Aboriginal communities, including housing, economic activities, and individual and group portraits.

Agriculture and Farm Life – This section includes images of farms, farming technology and machinery, and farmsteads. Indoor domestic scenes are included primarily under Home Life.

Cartoons, Posters and Pamphlets – This section includes images of printed materials, including pamphlets and broadsides, political cartoons, advertisements, and selected pages from newspapers and periodicals.

Economics and Commerce – This section depicts all sorts of economic activity, excluding agriculture and domestic work. Also included are photographs of businesses and commercial establishments.

Education and Schools – Included in this section are photographs of pupils and teachers engaged in school-related activities, indoors and outdoors. There is a large collection depicting school buildings.

Gender and Women's Issues – This section includes images which depict women at work, women's associations and organizations, and portraits of prominent individuals in these organizations.

Health Care and Healing Institutions – This section includes image of nurses, doctors, and public health workers at work both in institutions and in their patients' homes. It also includes architectural images of healing institutions.

Home Life – Images in this section primarily depict domestic situations, people at home, and the interiors of houses. Additional images depicting home life in rural settings can be found in Agriculture and Farm Life, above. Architectural images of houses and outdoor photos of urban neighbourhoods are found primarily in Housing, below.

Houses and Housing – Includes primarily images of the outsides of houses and apartment buildings and of city and town streets. For images of domestic scenes and the interior of houses, see Home Life, above.

Institutions – Images in this section are of public buildings and institutions, public works, and private and charitable institutions. Not included are images which appear in Education and Health Care, above. It includes images of police and firefighters

Leisure Activities and Sports – This section includes photographs of individuals and groups engaged in sporting or recreational activities or attending festive events. It includes many group portraits as well as pictures of parks, clubhouses, and other places of recreation.

Maps – Maps in this section include sketch maps showing Manitoba's growth and economic development and maps of individual communities and municipalities.

Organizations, Associations, and Clubs – This section includes portraits of groups and individuals, formal and informal, associated with organizations in private life. Most individual portraits are included in People and Portraits, below. Groups and organizations associated primarily with public life are included in Politics, below.

People and Portraits – This section contains photographs of individuals and small groups. Many, although not all, are identified. Portraits of larger groups are to be found in Organizations, Associations, and Clubs, above.

Politics and Government – Images in this section depict public life, including politicians, public buildings and artifacts, and images relating to political campaigns and organizations. Political cartoons are in the Cartoons section, above.

Religious Organizations and Institutions – This section includes images depicting the religious life and ritual of Manitoba's communities. It includes pictures of religious institutions and structures as well as images of clergy and missionaries at work.

Transportation and Communications – This section includes photographs relating to transportation, including images of vehicles and draft animals. It also includes images relating to technology and infrastructure, especially in relation to transportation and communications.

Working People and Labour Movements – This section includes images of urban labourers and their organizations. It also includes images of the Winnipeg General Strike.

World War One – This section includes photographs relating to Manitoba's participation in the First World War. It contains images of soldiers and military officers, both from Canada and from Europe. It also contains images of civilian life during the War and several images related to the Boer War.

NOTES

1. For more information, visit the *Village Prologue* information page [online]; <http://www.eduq.risq.net/DRD/P_telem/Village.html>; Internet; accessed 28 October 2000. *Village Prologue* est disponible seulement en français.

2. Manitoba Education and Training, *Canada: A Social and Political History; Grade Eleven Overview* (Winnipeg: Manitoba Education and Training, 1988); and Manitoba Education and Training, *Canada Today: Canadian Studies; Grade Nine Overview* (Winnipeg: Manitoba Education and Training, 1987).

3. Daniel Francis and Sonia Riddoch, *Our Canada: A Social and Political History,* 2d ed., rev. (Scarborough: Pippin Publishing, 1995).

4. In general, Canada's First Peoples are not considered to be immigrants, nor are they generally subsumed under the term "ethnic group." This paper will follow this convention and treat the Aboriginal communities of the Prairie West separately from other cultural groups, in recognition of the different relationship that they enjoyed with the Anglo-Canadian majority culture in the 1910-1920 period, with which this paper is concerned. This periodization is observed in Gerald A. Friesen, "Immigrant Communities 1870-1940: The Struggle for Cultural Survival," in *The Canadian Prairies: A History* (Toronto: University of Toronto Press, 1987), 242-273.

5. Specifically, this period might be argued to begin in 1896, with the arrival of the Laurier Liberal government and its new immigration policies. Laurier's Minister of the Interior, Clifford Sifton, a lawyer

from Brandon, Manitoba, sought to make the development of the West a keystone of Canadian economic policy.

6. There are also two image series that are drawn from the postwar era. One is a series of images from a Winnipeg architectural inventory done in the 1970s showing commercial buildings constructed in the 1910-1920 period. The other is a series of images from Mennonite communities, primarily architectural, done in the 1950s. The latter series is justified by the continuity in aspects of the Mennonite lifestyle and the virtual absence of any appropriate earlier images.

7. Dominion Bureau of Statistics, *Census of Canada*, 1901, 1911. It should be noted that Treaty Indians are not reported in these figures.

8. Special acknowledgement is due here to Elizabeth Blight, section head for Still Images, for her support of this project.

9. This methodology, however, is not reflected in the ultimate indexing of the *Image Archive*, which is thematic. See the Appendix for the thematic titles that have been used in indexing the archive. This index is based in part on Gerald Friesen and Morris Mott, "The Thematic Structure of Manitoba History" (manuscript prepared for Manitoba Ministry of Culture, Heritage, and Citizenship, Historic Resources Branch, ca. 1989).

10. On the spatial and economic development of Winnipeg, see Ivan Sanders, R.R. Rostecki, and Selwyn Carrington, *Early Buildings in Winnipeg*, Parks Canada Manuscript Report No. 389, 1 (Ottawa: Parks Canada, 1975), 1-31. See also Alan F.J. Artibise and Edward H. Dahl, *Winnipeg in Maps/Winnipeg par les cartes, 1816-1972* (Ottawa: National Map Collection, Public Archives of Canada, 1975).

11. It is important in understanding the reaction of members of the charter culture to this immigration that this number had dropped from 82 percent in 1886. *Census of Canada*, 1886, 1911.

12. For a brief discussion of the impact of the Eastman camera on the art of photography, see Thomas Schlereth, *Victorian America: 1876-1915* (New York: Harper Collins, 1991), 197-200.

13. Readers are counselled to look at the various historical and pedagogical literature that treats material history in general and image interpretation in particular.

14. Available from <http://timelinks.merlin.mb.ca/imagere1/ref0325.htm>; Internet; accessed 28 October 2000.

15. Available from <http://timelinks.merlin.mb.ca/imagere1/ref0027.htm>; Internet; accessed 28 October 2000.

16. See, for example, "Interior of Slum Home" [online]; available from <http://timelinks.merlin.mb.ca/imagere1/ref0012.htm>; Internet; accessed 28 October 2000; "The 'Foreign Quarter' of Winnipeg" [online]; available from <http://timelinks.merlin.mb.ca/imagere1/ref0050.htm>; Internet; accessed 28 October 2000.

17. For a historical treatment of the work of Hine, see Alan Trachtenberg, *Reading American Photographs: Images as History. Mathew Brady to Walker Evans* (New York: Noonday Press, 1990), especially chapter 4, "Camera Work/Social Work."

18. These questions are loosely based on a line of inquiry laid out by Ken Osborne in *Using Canada's Visual History in the Classroom* ([Ottawa]: National Museum of Man: National Film Board of Canada, [1990]), 5. See also Trachtenberg, *Reading American Photographs*.

19. Available from <http://timelinks.merlin.mb.ca/imagere1/ref0038.htm>; Internet; accessed 28 October 2000.

20. For discussions of the composition and behaviour of the Winnipeg elite specifically, see Alan Artibise, *Winnipeg: A Social History of Urban Growth, 1874-1915* (Montréal: McGill-Queen's University Press, 1975).

21. The titling of images — the juxtaposition of text and image either by the original creator or by a later curator or editor — might be construed as a fourth avenue in a schema for the interpretation of images.

22. Available from <http://timelinks.merlin.mb.ca/imagere1/ref0334.htm>; Internet; accessed 28 October 2000.

23. Available from <http://timelinks.merlin.mb.ca/imagere2/ref0586.htm>; Internet; accessed 28 October 2000.

24. Available from <http://timelinks.merlin.mb.ca/imagere3/ref1054.htm>; Internet; accessed 28 October 2000. The family depicted seems in many respects the archetype of Sifton's sturdy peasant in a sheepskin coat.

25. Available from <http://timelinks.merlin.mb.ca/imagere1/ref0052.htm>; Internet; accessed 28 October 2000.

26. Available from <http://timelinks.merlin.mb.ca/imagere4/ref1912.htm>; Internet; accessed 28 October 2000.

27. Doug Smith and Michael Olito, *The Best Possible Face: L.B. Foote's Winnipeg* (Winnipeg: Turnstone Press, 1985), 5.

28. Ibid.

12 Educating Citizens for a Pluralistic Society: A Select Bibliography

ROSA BRUNO-JOFRÉ, NATALIA APONIUK,
AND SHEILA ANDRICH, COMPILERS

A. Educational Reform in the Market Economy

Apple, Michael. "Rhetorical Reforms: Markets, Standards, and Inequality." *Current Issues in Comparative Education.* 1, no. 2 (1999) [journal online]; available from <http://www.tc.columbia.edu/cice/vol01nr2/mwaart1.htm>; Internet; accessed 26 October 2000.

Barlow, Maude, and Heather-Jane Robertson. *Class Warfare: The Assault on Canada's Schools.* Toronto: Key Porter Books, 1994.

Calvert, John, and Larry Kuehn. *Pandora's Box: Corporate Power, Free Trade, and Canadian Education.* Toronto: Our Schools/ Our Selves Education Foundation, 1993.

Canada. Council of Ministers of Education. *Development of Education: Report of Canada.* Toronto: Council of Ministers of Education, 1996; available from <http://www.ibe.unesco.org/Inf_Doc/ Dossiers/rcanada.htm>; Internet; accessed 26 October 2000.

——. *First Meeting of Ministers of Education of the Americas: Report of the Canadian Delegation 20-21 July 1998, Brasilia, Brazil*; available from <http://www.cmec.ca/international/ minedamer1.en.pdf>; Internet; accessed 26 October 2000.

International Finance Corporation. *Private Sector, Private Schools.* Washington, DC: International Finance Corporation, 1999.

Kuchapski, Renee. "Accountability and the Social Good: Utilizing Manzer's Liberal Framework in Canada." *Education and Urban Society* 30, no. 4 (1998): 531-545.

Litchfield, Randall. "Solving an Education Crisis." *Canadian Business* 64, no. 2 (1991): 56-64.

Livingston, D.W. *The Education-Jobs Gap: Underemployment or Economic Democracy.* Toronto: Garamond Press, 1998.

McLaren, Peter. "Contesting Capital: Critical Pedagogy and Globalism; A Response to Michael Apple." *Current Issues in Comparative Education* 1, no. 2 (1999) [journal online]; available from <http://www.tc.columbia.edu>; Internet; accessed 26 October 2000.

——. "Revolutionary Pedagogy in Post-Revolutionary Times: Rethinking the Political Economy of Critical Education." *Educational Theory* 48, no. 4 (1998): 431-462.

McLaren, Peter, and Rodolfo Torres. "Racism and Multicultural Education: Rethinking 'Race' and 'Whiteness' in Late Capitalism." In *Critical Multiculturalism: Rethinking Multicultural and Anti-Racist Education*, ed. Stephen May, 42-76. London: Falmer Press, 1999.

Moll, Marita, ed. *Tech High: Globalization and the Future of Canadian Education: A Collection of Critical Perspectives on Social, Cultural, and Political Dilemmas.* Ottawa: Canadian Centre for Policy Alternatives; Halifax: Fernwood Publishing, 1997.

Patrinos, Harry Anthony. "Market Forces in Education." *European Journal of Education* 35, no. 1 (2000) [journal online]; available from <http://www.worldbank.org/edinvest/pubs.html>; Internet; accessed 26 October 2000.

Robertson, Heather-Jane. *No More Teachers, No More Books: The Commercialization of Canada's Schools.* Toronto: McClelland and Stewart, 1998.

Shaker, Erika. "The North American Education Industry and Education Restructuring in Canada." Special issue of *Education, Limited 1*, no. 1 (1998) [journal online]; available from <http://www.policyalternatives.ca/eduproj/index.html>; Internet; accessed 26 October 2000.

Taylor, Alison. "Education for Industrial and 'Postindustrial' Purposes." *Educational Policy* 11, no.1 (1997): 3-40.

Torres, Gerver, and Sarita Mathur. "The Third Wave of Privatization: Privatization of Social Sectors in Developing Countries." Washington: World Bank, 1995 [online]; available from <http://www.worldbank.org/edinvest/thirdwave.htm>; Internet; accessed 26 October 2000.

Wein, Carol Anne, and Curt Dudley-Marling. "Limited Vision: The Ontario Curriculum and Outcomes Based Learning." *Canadian Journal of Education* 23, no. 4 (1998): 405-421.

World Bank Group. *Education Sector Strategy.* Washington: World Bank Group, 1999 [online]; available from <http://www.worldbank.org/html/extpb/educat.html>; Internet; accessed 26 October 2000.

——. *World Bank Support for Implementation of Summit Goals.* Washington: World Bank Group, 1998 [online]; available from <http://www.summit-americas.org/IOReports/Worldbank-report1.htm>; Internet; accessed 26 October 2000.

B. Citizenship and Canadian Identity

Banting, Keith G. "The Past Speaks to the Future: Lessons from the Postwar Social Union." In *Non-Constitutional Renewal*, ed. Harvey Lazar, 39-69. Kingston: Institute of Intergovernmental Relations, Queen's University, 1998.

Baubock, Rainer, and John Rundell, eds. *Blurred Boundaries: Migration, Ethnicity, Citizenship.* Brookfield, VT: Ashgate Publishing, 1998.

Beiner, Ronald, ed. *Theorizing Citizenship.* Albany: State University of New York Press, 1995.

Blais, François, et al., eds. *Libéralismes et nationalismes: philosophie et politique.* Sainte-Foy: Les Presses de l'Université Laval, 1995.

Borrows, John. "Living between Water and Rocks: First Nations, Environmental Planning, and Democracy." *University of Toronto Law Journal* 47 (1997): 417-468.

Brennan, Samantha, Tracy Isaacs, and Michael Milde, eds. *A Question of Values: New Canadian Perspectives in Ethics and Political Philosophy.* Atlanta: Editions Rodopi, 1997.

Bruno-Jofré, Rosa. "Manitoba Schooling in the Canadian Context and the Building of a Polity: 1919-1971." *Canadian and International Education* 28, no. 2 (1999): 99-128.

——. "Citizenship and Schooling in Manitoba, 1918-1945." *Manitoba History* 36 (1998-99): 26-36.

Cairns, Alan C. "Constitutional Reform: The God That Failed." In *Can Canada Survive?: Under What Terms and Conditions?*, ed. David M. Hayne, 47-66. Toronto: University of Toronto Press, 1996.

——. "The Fragmentation of Canadian Citizenship." In *Reconfigurations: Canadian Citizenship and Constitutional Change: Selected Essays*, ed. Douglas E. Williams, 157-185. Toronto: McClelland and Stewart, 1995.

Cairns, Alan C., John C. Courtney, Peter MacKinnon, Hans J. Michelmann, and David E. Smith, eds. *Citizenship, Diversity, and Pluralism: Canadian and Comparative Perspectives*. Montreal: McGill-Queen's University Press, 1999.

Canada. Citizenship and Immigration Canada. *Into the 21st Century: A Strategy for Immigration and Citizenship*. Hull: Minister of Supply and Services Canada, 1994.

——. Royal Commmission on Aboriginal Peoples. *Report of the Royal Commmission on Aboriginal Peoples*. 5 vols. Ottawa: The Commission, 1996.

Carens, Joseph H. "Immigration, Political Community, and the Transformation of Identity: Quebec's Immigration Policies in Critical Perspective." In *Is Quebec Nationalism Just? Perspectives from Anglophone Canada*, ed. Joseph H. Carens, 20-81. Montreal: McGill-Queen's University Press, 1995.

Cassidy, Frank, ed. *Aboriginal Self-Determination*. Lantzville, BC: Oolichan Press, 1991.

Friesen, Gerald. *Citizens and Nation: An Essay on History, Communication, and Canada*. Toronto: University of Toronto Press, 2000.

Gagnon, Alain-G., ed. *Québec: état et societé*. Montreal: Quebéc/ Amérique, 1994.

Gagnon, France, and Michel Pagé. *Conceptual Framework and Analysis*. Vol. 1 of *Conceptual Framework for an Analysis of Citizenship in the Liberal Democracies*. [Ottawa]: Department of Canadian Heritage (Citizens' Participation, Multiculturalism, and Strategic Research and Analysis Directorates), 1999.

Hébert, Yvonne. "Citizenship Education: Towards a Pedagogy of Social Participation and Identity Formation." *Canadian Ethnic Studies/ Études ethnique au Canada* 29, no. 2 (1997): 82-96.

Jenson, Jane. "Fated To Live in Interesting Times: Canada's Changing Citizenship Regimes." *Canadian Journal of Political Science* 30, no.4 (1997): 627-644.

Kaplan, William, ed. *Belonging: The Meaning and Future of Canadian Citizenship.* Montreal: McGill-Queen's University Press, 1993.

Kymlicka, Will. *Finding Our Way: Rethinking Ethnocultural Relations in Canada.* Toronto: Oxford University Press, 1998.

——. *Liberalism, Community, and Culture.* Oxford: Clarendon Press; New York: Oxford University Press, 1989.

——. *Multicultural Citizenship: A Liberal Theory of Minority Rights.* Oxford: Clarendon Press, 1995.

Kymlicka, Will, and Wayne Norman. "Return of the Citizen: A Survey of Recent Work on Citizenship Theory." In *Theorizing Citizenship*, ed. Ronald Beiner, 283-322. Albany: State University of New York Press, 1995.

Langlois, Simons, ed. *Identité et cultures nationales: l'amérique française en mutation.* Sainte-Foy: Les Presses de l'Université Laval, 1995.

Long, Anthony, and Menno Boldt, eds. *Governments in Conflict: Provinces and Indian Nations in Canada.* In association with Leroy Little Bear. Toronto: University of Toronto Press, 1988.

McKay, Ian. "After Canada: On Amnesia and Apocalypse in the Contemporary Crisis." *Acadiensis* 28, no.1 (1998): 76-97.

Richardson, Boyce. *Drumbeat: Anger and Renewal in Indian Country.* Toronto: Summerhill Press, 1989.

Salée, Daniel. "La mondialisation et la construction de l'identité au Québec." In *Les frontières de l'identité*, ed. Mikhaël Elbaz et al., 105-125. Montreal: L'Hexagone, 1989.

Taylor, Charles. "The Politics of Recognition." In Taylor, Charles, et al., *Multiculturalism, Examining the Politics of Recognition*, ed. Amy Gutmann, 25-74. Princeton: Princeton University Press, 1994.

——. "Shared and Divergent Values." In *Reconciling the Solitudes: Essays on Canadian Federalism and Nationalism*, ed. Guy Laforest, 155-186. Montreal: McGill-Queen's University Press, 1993.

Toward the Common Good. Special issue of *Queen's Quarterly* 106, no.1 (1999).

Weaver, Sally M. *Making Canadian Indian Policy: The Hidden Agenda, 1968-1970.* Toronto: University of Toronto Press, 1981.

Webber, Jeremy. "Multiculturalism and the Limits to Toleration." In *Language, Culture and Values in Canada at the Dawn of the 21st Century,* ed. André Lapièrre, Patricia Smart, and Pierre Savard, 269-279 Ottawa: International Council for Canadian Studies and Carleton University Press, 1996.

———. "The Referendum and the Future of Anglophones in Quebec." *Choices* 1, no 9 (1995): 16-25 [journal online]; available from <http://www.irpp.org/choices/archive/vol1no9.htm>; Internet; accessed 26 October 2000.

———. *Reimagining Canada: Language, Culture, Community, and the Canadian Constitution.* Montreal: McGill-Queen's University Press, 1994.

C. Citizenship Education

Barber, Benjamin R. *An Aristocracy of Everyone: The Politics of Education and the Future of America.* New York: Ballantine Books, 1992.

Bringle, Robert G., Richard Games, and Edward A. Malloy, eds. *Colleges and Universities as Citizens.* Boston: Allyn and Bacon, 1999.

Callan, Eamonn. "Beyond Sentimental Civic Education." *American Journal of Education* 102 (1993-1994): 190-221.

———. *Creating Citizens: Political Education and Liberal Democracy.* Oxford Political Theory Series. Oxford: Clarendon Press, 1997.

Codd, John A. "Managerialism, Market Liberalism, and the Move to Self-Managing Schools in New Zealand." In *A Socially Critical View of the Self-Managing School,* ed. John Smyth, 153-170. London: Falmer Press, 1993.

Gassama, Ibrahim J., Robert S. Chang, and Keith Aoki. "Citizenship and Its Discontents: Centering the Immigrant in the Inter/National Imagination." *Oregon Law Review* 76, no. 1 (1997): 207-232.

Giroux, Henry A. "Critical Theory and Rationality in Citizenship Education." *Curriculum Inquiry* 10, no. 4 (1980): 329-336.

——. *Pedagogy and the Politics of Hope: Theory, Culture, and Schooling: A Critical Reader.* Boulder, CO: Westview Press, 1997.

Hare, Richard M. "Opportunity for What? Some Remarks on Current Disputes about Equality in Education." *Oxford Review of Education* 3, no. 3 (1977): 207-216.

Ichilov, Orit, ed. *Citizenship and Citizenship Education in a Changing World.* London: Woburn Press, 1998.

Mclaughlin, Terence, and J. Mark Halstead, "Education for Citizenship." In *Education in Morality*, ed. J. Mark Halstead, 79-102. International Studies in the Philosophy of Education Series. London: Routledge, 1999.

Osborne, Ken. "Education Is the Best National Insurance: Citizenship Education in Canadian Schools, Past and Present." *Canadian and International Education* 25, no. 2 (1996): 31-58.

——. "Citizenship Education and Social Studies." In *Trends and Issues in Canadian Social Studies,* ed. Ian Wright and Alan Sears, 39-67. Vancouver: Pacific Educational Press, 1997.

[Osborne, Ken]. *Teaching for Democratic Citizenship: Ken Osborne.* Toronto: Our Schools/Our Selves Education Foundation, 1991.

Sears, A. "Social Studies as Citizenship Education in English Canada: A Review of Research." *Theory and Research in Social Education* 22, no. 1 (1994): 6-43.

Selman, Gordon R. *Citizenship and the Adult Education Movement in Canada.* Monographs on Comparative and Area Studies in Adult Education. Vancouver: Centre for Continuing Education, University of British Columbia in cooperation with the International Council for Adult Education, 1991.

Tomkins, George S. "Canadian Education and the Development of a National Consciousness: Historical and Contemporary Perspectives." In *Canadian Schools and Canadian Identity,* ed. Alf Chaiton and Neil McDonald, 6-28. Toronto: Gage Educational Publishing, 1977.

White, Patricia. "Education, Democracy, and the Public Interest." In *The Philosophy of Education,* ed. R.S. Peters, 217-238. London: Oxford University Press, 1973.

Young, Jon, ed. *Breaking the Mosaic: Ethnic Identities in Canadian Schooling.* Toronto: Garamond Press, 1987.

D. Multicultural and Anti-Racist Education

Apple, Michael. "The Absent Presence of Race in Educational Reform." *Race, Ethnicity, and Education* 2, no.1 (1999): 9-16.

Dei, George J. Sefa "The Role of Afrocentricity in the Inclusive Curriculum in Canadian Schools." *Canadian Journal of Education* 21, no. 2 (1996): 170-186.

———. *Anti-Racism Education: Theory and Practice.* Halifax: Fernwood Publishing, 1996.

———, et al. *Reconstructing "Dropout": A Critical Ethnography of the Dynamics of Black Students' Disengagement from School.* Toronto: University of Toronto Press, 1997.

Ghosh, Ratna. *Redefining Multicultural Education.* Toronto: Harcourt Brace, 1996.

Greene, Maxine. "The Passions of Pluralism: Multiculturalism and the Expanding Community." *Educational Researcher* 22, no. 1 (1993): 13-18.

James, Carl E. "Contradictory Tensions in the Experiences of African Canadians in a Faculty of Education with an Access Program." *Canadian Journal of Education* 22, no. 2 (1997): 158-174.

———, ed. *Perspectives on Racism and the Human Services Sector: A Case for Change.* Toronto: University of Toronto Press, 1996.

McLaren, Peter, and Roldolpho Torres. "Racism and Multicultural Education: Rethinking 'Race' and 'Whiteness' in Late Capitalism." In *Critical Multiculturalism: Rethinking Multicultural and Anti-Racist Education*, ed. Stephen May, 42-76. London: Falmer Press, 1999.

Moodley, Kogila A. "Multicultural Education in Canada: Historical Development and Current Status." In *Handbook of Research on Multicultural Education*, ed. James A. Banks, 801-820. New York: MacMillan; New York: Simon and Schuster Macmillan; London: Prentice Hall International, 1995.

Osborne, Ken. "Class or Culture: Some Reflections on Multiculturalism." In *Intercultural Education and Community Development: Papers Presented at a Symposium at the Faculty of Education, University of Toronto*, ed. Keith A. Mcleod, 94-98. Toronto: Guidance Centre, Faculty of Education, University of Toronto, 1980.

Raptis, Helen, and C.A. Banks. "Unraveling Multicultural Education's Meanings: An Analysis of Core Assumptions Found in Academic Writings in Canada and the United States, 1981-1997." *Journal of Educational Thought* 32, no. 2 (1998): 169-194.

Rezai-Rashti, Goli. "Multicultural Education, Anti-Racist Education, and Critical Pedagogy: Reflections on Everyday Practice." In *Anti-Racism, Feminism, and Critical Approaches*, ed. Roxana Ng, Pat Staton, and Joyce Scane, 3-20. Critical Studies in Education and Culture Series. Toronto: OISE Press, 1995.

Solomon, R. Patrick. *Black Resistance in High School: Forging a Separatist Culture*. Frontiers in Education Series. New York: State University of New York Press, 1992.

Willett, Cynthia, ed. *Theorizing Multiculturalism: A Guide to the Current Debate*. Malden, MA: Blackwell Publishing, 1998.

Wotherspoon, Terry, ed. *The Political Economy of Canadian Schooling*. Toronto: Methuen Publications, 1987.

E. Democracy, Citizenship, Identity, and Pluralism

Alesina, A., R. Baqir, and W. Easterly. "Public Goods and Ethnic Divisions." NBER Working Paper Series, no. 6009. Cambridge, MA: National Bureau of Economic Research, 1997.

Ashcroft, Bill, Gareth Griffiths, and Helen Tiffin, eds. *The Post-Colonial Studies Reader*. London: Routledge, 1995.

Beck, Ulrich. *The Reinvention of Politics: Rethinking Modernity in the Global Social Order*, trans. Mark Ritter. Malden, MA: Blackwell Publishing, 1996.

Benhabib, Seyla, ed. *Democracy and Difference: Contesting the Boundaries of the Political*. Princeton: Princeton University Press, 1996.

Bull, Hedley. "The Emergence of a Universal International Society." In *The Expansion of International Society,* ed. Hedley Bull and Adam Watson, 117-126. Oxford: Clarendon Press; New York: Oxford University Press, 1984.

Cheah, Pheng, et al. *Cosmopolitics: Thinking and Feeling beyond the Nation*. Cultural Politics Series. Minneapolis: University of Minnesota Press, 1998.

Cohen, Jean L., and Andrew Arato, eds. *Civil Society and Political Theory*. Studies in Contemporary German Social Thought. Cambridge: MIT Press, 1994.

Couture, Jocelyne, Kai Nielson, and Michel Seymour, eds. *Rethinking Nationalism*. Special issue of *Canadian Journal of Philosophy* 22 (1998).

Dahl, Robert A. *A Preface to Economic Democracy*. Berkeley: University of California Press, 1985.

Grillo, Ralph. *Pluralism and the Politics of Difference: State, Culture, and Ethnicity in Comparative Perspective*. Oxford: Oxford University Press, 1999.

Gutmann, Amy. *Democratic Education*. Princeton: Princeton University Press, 1987.

Habermas, Jürgen. "Citizenship and National Identity (1990)." In *Between Facts and Norms: Contributions to a Discourse Theory of Law and Democracy*, ed. Jürgen Habermas, trans. William Rehg, 491-515. Cambridge: MIT Press, 1998.

Hanagan, Michael, and Charles Tilly, eds. *Recasting Citizenship*. Special issue of *Theory and Society* 26, no. 4 (1997).

Hartsock, Nancy. "Rethinking Modernism: Minority vs. Majority Theories." *Cultural Critique* 7 (1987): 187-205.

Hastings, Adrian. *The Construction of Nationhood: Ethnicity, Religion, and Nationalism*. Cambridge: Cambridge University Press, 1997.

Hefner, Robert W., ed. *Democratic Civility: The History and Cross-Cultural Possibility of a Modern Political Ideal*. Somerset, NJ: Transaction Publishers, 1998.

Held, David. *Models of Democracy*. 2d ed. Stanford: Stanford University Press, 1996.

——, ed. *Prospects for Democracy*. Special issue of *Political Studies* 40 (1992).

Ignatieff, Michael. *Blood and Belonging: Journeys into the New Nationalism*. Toronto: Viking, 1993.

Jackson, Robert. *Quasi-States: Sovereignty, International Relations, and the Third World*. Cambridge: Cambridge University Press, 1990.

Jacobson, David. *Rights across Borders: Immigration and the Decline of Citizenship*. Baltimore: Johns Hopkins University Press, 1997.

Kinder, Donald R., and Lynn M. Sanders. *Divided by Color: Racial Prejudices and Democratic Ideals*. American Politics and Political Economy Series. Chicago: University of Chicago Press, 1997.

Koshan, Jennifer. "Sounds of Silence: The Public/Private Dichotomy, Violence and Aboriginal Women." In *Challenging the Public/ Private Divide: Feminism, Law, and Public Policy*, ed. Susan B. Boyd, 87-109. Toronto: University of Toronto Press, 1997.

Laponce, Jean, and William Safran, eds. *Ethnicity and Citizenship: The Canadian Case*. Special issue of *Nationalism and Ethnic Politics* 1, no. 3 (1995).

Lasch, Christopher. *The Revolt of the Elites: And the Betrayal of Democracy*. New York: W.W. Norton, 1995.

Levine, Andrew. *Rethinking Liberal Equality: From a "Utopian" Point of View*. Ithaca, NY: Cornell University Press, 1998.

Lister, Ruth. "Citizenship Engendered." *Journal of Critical Social Policy* 2, no. 2 (1991): 65-71.

March, James G., and Johan P. Olsen. *Democratic Governance*. New York: Free Press, 1995.

McPherson, James M. *Is Blood Thicker than Water?: Crises of Nationalism in the Modern World*. Toronto: Vintage Canada, 1998.

Meehan, Elizabeth M. *Citizenship and the European Community*. London: Sage Publications, 1993.

Miller, David. "Citizenship and Pluralism." *Political Studies* 43, no. 3 (1995): 432-450.

——. "The Ethical Significance of Nationality." *Ethics* 98 (1988): 647-662.

Nairn, Tom. *Faces of Nationalism*. New York: Verso, 1998.

Pateman, Carole. "Introduction." In *Feminist Challenges: Social and Political Theory,* ed. Carole Pateman and Elizabeth Gross, 1-10. Northeastern Series in Feminist Theory. Boston: Northeastern University Press, 1986.

Phillips, Anne. "Comment: Whose Community? Which Individuals?" In *Reinventing the Left,* ed. David Miliband, 123-127. Cambridge: Polity Press, 1994.

Plant, Raymond. "Comment Citizenship and Political Change." In *Reinventing the Left.* ed. David Miliband, 80-85. Cambridge: Polity Press, 1994.

———. *Citizenship, Rights, and Socialism.* London: Fabian Society, 1988.

Postman, Neil. *Building a Bridge to the Eighteenth Century: How the Past Can Improve Our Future.* New York: Alfred A. Knopf, 1999.

Ricento, Thomas, and Barbara Burnaby, eds. *Language and Politics in the United States and Canada: Myths and Realities.* Mahwah, NJ: Lawrence Erlbaum, 1998.

Rokkan, Stein. "Dimensions of State Formation and Nation-Building: A Possible Paradigm for Research on Variations within Europe." In *The Formation of National States in Western Europe,* ed. Charles Tilley, 562-600. Princeton: Princeton University Press, 1975.

Rowley, Charles K., ed. *Classical Liberalism and Civil Society.* John Locke Series. Williston, VT: Edward Elgar, 1998.

Sandel, Michael. *Democracy's Discontent: America in Search of a Public Philosophy.* Cambridge: Belknap Press of Harvard University Press, 1996.

Saul, John Ralston. *The Unconscious Civilization.* Concord, ON: House of Anansi Press, 1995.

Schnapper, Dominique. *Community of Citizens: On the Modern Idea of Nationality,* trans. Severine Rosée. Somerset, NJ: Transaction Publishers, 1998.

Schuck, Peter H. *Citizens, Strangers, and In-Betweens: Essays on Immigration and Citizenship.* New Perspectives on Law, Culture, and Society Series. Boulder, CO: Westview, 1998.

Shklar, Judith N. *American Citizenship: The Quest for Inclusion.* Cambridge: Harvard University Press, 1991.

Smith, Anthony D. *National Identity.* London: Penguin Books, 1991.

Sommers, Margaret R. "Citizenship and the Place of the Public Sphere: Law, Community, and Political Structure in the Transition to Democracy." *American Sociological Review* 58 (1993): 587-620.

Soysal, Yasemin N. *Limits of Citizenship: Migrants and Postnational Membership in Europe*. Chicago: University of Chicago Press, 1994.

Spencer, Metta. *Separatism: Democracy and Disintegration*. Lanham, MD: Rowman and Littlefield Publishers, 1998.

Tam, Henry. *Communitarianism: A New Agenda for Politics and Citizenship*. New York: New York University Press, 1998.

Taylor, Charles. *The Ethics of Authenticity*. Cambridge: Harvard University Press, 1992.

——. *The Malaise of Modernity*. Concord, ON: House of Anansi Press, 1991.

——. "Globalization and the Future of Canada." *Queen's Quarterly* 105, no. 3 (1998): 331-342.

——. *Philosophical Arguments*. Cambridge: Harvard University Press, 1995.

——. *The Sources of the Self: The Making of Modern Identity*. Cambridge: Harvard University Press, 1989.

Taylor-Gooby, Peter. "Postmodernism and Social Policy: A Great Leap Backwards?" *Journal of Social Policy* 23, no. 3 (1994): 385-404.

Williams, Linda Faye. "Race and the Politics of Social Policy." In *The Social Divide: Political Parties and the Future of Activist Government*, ed. Margaret Weit, 417-463. Washington: Brookings Institution Press; New York: Russell Sage Foundation, 1998.

Wilson, William J. *When Work Disappears: The World of the New Urban Poor*. New York: Knopf, 1996.

Young, Iris Marion. *Justice and the Politics of Difference*. Princeton: Princeton University Press, 1990.

——. "Polity and Group Differences: A Critique of the Ideal of Universal Citizenship." In *Theorizing Citizenship*, ed. Ronald Beiner, 175-207. Albany: State University of New York Press, 1995.